THE COMPLETE
NINJA Foodi
COOKBOOK
FOR BEGINNERS

1000 Days The Most Wanted, Simple, and Healthy Recipes For Frying, Pressure Cooking, Slow Cooking, and Much More with Step By Step Instructions

Okey Schiller

Table of Contents

Chapter 4 Fish and Seafood 26

Chapter 5 Pasta 35

Chapter 6 Poultry 41

Chapter 7 Staples, Sauces, Dips, and Dressings

Chapter 8 Stews and Soups

Chapter 9 Vegetables and Sides   71

Chapter 10 Desserts   83

Chapter 11 Snacks and Appetizers   90

Appendix 1 Measurement Conversion Chart   96

INTRODUCTION

Cooking in the kitchen used to be so challenging. You needed an appliance for every task, and while some homes had a roomy enough kitchen, it left people in apartments, dorms, and other tiny homes behind. Nowadays, only some have the luxury of an oversized kitchen, but no need to fear: modern appliances are smaller and can have enough cooking modes to replace an entire kitchen.

The most significant example of this fact is the Ninja Foodi Pressure Cooker & Air Fryer. Despite only mentioning two features in its title, it has 12 features. You can air fry foods, bake them, make yogurt, saute your meats, and much more. I was skeptical when I first bought it; I believed it would be a jack-of-all-trades appliance. It seemed too good to be true living in a small apartment, yet needing to feed a family.

However, when I used the Ninja Foodi, I was a believer. Each feature works well to cook your favorite foods. I managed to cook some restaurant-quality meals despite not being much of a cook beforehand. This Ninja Foodi Pressure Cooker is quite simple to use, and believe me. You don't need much experience to be an excellent cook.

Because of all my cooking, I've learned some new recipes and wanted to share them with you. These recipes are original and my take on some of your favorites. Also, because this appliance has 12 cooking styles, I used them in this book so that you can fully use them out of your device.

All my recipes are easy to pick up and work well for people of all skill levels. Cooking is for everyone, yet the hustle and bustle of life make it so that sometimes, it's challenging to cook.

I love the Ninja Foodi because it's simple to use and cooks fast food. Being a pressure cooker and air fryer, you can make delicious foods in a fraction of the time. Of course, if you want to slow-cook foods, you can do that, too. With it, you'll spend less money eating out and more time eating delicious, home-cooked meals.

So come with me as I introduce you to the fantastic Ninja Foodi Pressure Cooker & Air Fryer world. You will love what it offers, and I also believe you'll love my recipes.

Chapter 1 Let's Get Down to Basics

The Ninja Foodi Pressure Cooker & Air Fryer is all-in-one, boasting 12 features. This is the cooking device if you live in a small home or want to downsize your kitchen. Whether you want a quick meal or you want to slow cook, this appliance will do it all. It truly is a kitchen miracle. However, all these features can feel intimidating, so I'm breaking them down and giving you a good idea of what to expect when you try this appliance.

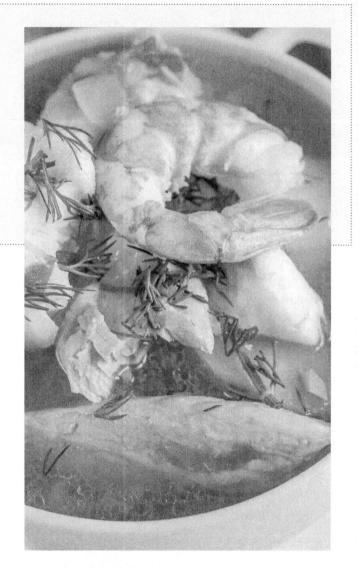

How Does This Work?

The Ninja Foodi Pressure Cooker & Air Fryer uses electricity to cook food and combines pressure cooking with air frying. Pressure cooking involves using steam for cooking foods quickly. Adding water to the pressure cooker can quickly heat your favorite foods, including rice, vegetables, and other dishes.

Also, this device uses air frying. An air fryer heats up like an oven and uses a fan to spread the heat around evenly. Even heating can cook foods faster, preheat faster, and give your food a crispy brown exterior. Air frying is becoming a popular way to cook foods due to its fastness and ability to give you foods similar to deep frying without unwanted calories.

Of course, this appliance has many other components, but these are the basics. So many features going into how it does it all can take us all day. All you need to know is that this appliance can handle almost anything you throw at it, and it does so through 12 settings dedicated to a specific task. In the next section, we will look at the 12 features this device offers and explain some details about them.

12-in-1 Versatility: Breaking Down Everything the Ninja Foodi Offers

With a dozen ways to cook food, you may never use an appliance again. So here's what it offers.

Pressure Cooking

With its pressure cooker, you can make fluffy rice, hearty stews, yummy roasts, and much more. Pressure cooking uses intense heat, meaning you can quickly make some ready-to-eat foods. And it's so simple to do. Let it heat up, cook for whatever minutes are required, release the steam, and enjoy!

Air Fry / Air Crisp

Using convection, you can create crispy foods without covering them in oils, which add unnecessary calories. Instead, you can have crispy fries, chicken strips with a crunch, and even everyday foods with them through air frying. To see what the hype is about.

Steam

This is similar to pressure cooking in that it uses steam to cook your foods but cooks at a lower temperature. It works well for certain foods or if you want to wait to eat your food.

Yogurt

Yogurt is delicious, filling, and high in protein. However, buying it from the store can be expensive. Instead, you can make your yogurt in this cooker, and it's even better. With that said, creating yogurt does take a while, but trust me. It's worth the wait.

Sear/Saute

This method works well if you want to add a bit of oil to sear your foods. It lets you get a perfect brown finish on your meats or helps you make some great sauces. Also, it gets the bottom hot, making it ideal if you only want to cook there.

Bake

Want to bake some fresh bread? You can do so in your Foodi. Better than store-bought! Of course, baking also has other functions. For example, you can make your foods similar to how you do in the oven.

Roast

Roasting uses higher temperatures to cook food, though it uses the same method as baking. Great for foods that require high temperatures or if you want that food faster.

Broil

Broiling only uses top-down heat, letting you cook foods that are already cooked well on one side, or it's used if you wish to brown only a specific side. Great for those delicate foods.

Dehydrate

Do you want to make some dried fruit? You can make some fresh raisins using the dehydrate option, and as usual, it has that authentic taste you will love. Dehydrating foods is also great if you want to preserve them for a long time.

Sous Vide

Sous Vide (under vacuum) is when you put food in a vacuum-sealed bag and cook it under low temperature. Professional cooks use this as a secret technique to get 5-star meals for a fraction of the price.

Keep Warm

If you don't need your food cooked further, but you need it warm (like if you're cooking another food and have finished with this one, the keep warm option will indeed keep it warm.

Now to Look at Parts and Accessories

Because this appliance has 12 features, you better believe it comes with many different parts and accessories. Many involve lids, which you use to cook food under a specific setting. Let's look at some of them right now.

Pressure Lid

This lid keeps your food under pressure when using the pressure cooker or steam mode. When you are pressure cooking, it's sealed on there tight. When finished, you can depressurize it with a flip of the switch. Watch the steam fly!

Crisping Lid

With this lid, you put it on when you're air frying. This lid ensures that your food is evenly cooked and made to perfection. Without it, your food may not turn out as good as expected, so always pop it on whenever you can.

Cooking Pot

This lid works well if you want to cook generally. In other words, if you're baking foods, this lid works well to keep your food cooked the way you want.

Cook and Crisp Basket

This basket is your standard air fryer basket. Put your food in there, shake it up, and then enjoy your air-fried food made to perfection.

Reversible Rack

This rack works well for several cooking needs. You can set it up to touch the bottom or elevate it. Either way is helpful, depending on what you're cooking.

You will need all these accessories; don't throw any of them out! Instead, store them in a place where you can access them quickly and switch them anytime.

How Do I Care for and Clean This?

While you should never immerse your unit in water, you can wipe the unit with a damp cloth when it's unplugged and cooled down.

In addition, you can machine wash the meal pot, crisper tray, and condensation catch. After you wash these parts, let them air dry and use them only when they are completely dried. Rinse and repeat.

Another tip? Be sure you soak any parts if there's food stuck on them. Soak them in warm water and mild detergent. Never use an abrasive cleaner; be sure you don't use scouring pads. Instead, use a brush or nylon pad.

Be sure that you clean after every session. While it can be a hassle, not cleaning it can lead to buildups in food, meaning that your unit can be damaged or not cook as well as it once did.

Also, be sure that you turn it off and unplug it after every use. This way, you conserve the Foodi for as long as possible. If you treat this appliance right, you can have something that will last you a long time.

Chapter 2 Breakfasts

Ham and Egg Casserole

Prep time: 2 minutes | Cook time: 20 minutes | Serves 2 to 4

6 beaten eggs
½ cup plain Greek yogurt
1 cup Cheddar cheese, shredded
1 cup ham, diced
¼ cup chives, chopped
½ teaspoon black pepper
1 cup water

1. In a medium bowl, whisk together eggs and yogurt until combined. 2. Add the cheese, ham, chives, and pepper. Stir well. 3. Add the reversible rack and water to Ninja Foodi pressure cooker. 4. Pour the mixture into the heatproof bowl or cup. 5. Place the bowl on the rack. 6. Assemble pressure lid, making sure the pressure release valve is in the Seal position. Select Pressure and set to high (HI). Set time to 20 minutes. Press Start. 7. Quick release pressure by moving the pressure release valve to the Vent position. 8. Serve warm.

Dried Fruit Compote

Prep time: 5 minutes | Cook time: 4 minutes | Serves 4 to 6

1 pound (454 g) mixed dried fruit
1 cup water
1 cup unsweetened apple juice
½ cup packed light brown sugar
1 tablespoon fresh lemon juice
¼ teaspoon table salt
1 (4-inch) cinnamon stick

1. Mix all the ingredients in Ninja Foodi pressure cooker until the brown sugar dissolves. Assemble pressure lid, making sure the pressure release valve is in the Seal position. 2. Select Pressure and set to low (LO). Set time to 4 minutes. Press Start. 3. When pressure cooking is complete, allow pressure to natural release, about 15 minutes. 4. Unlatch the lid and open the cooker. Find and discard the cinnamon stick. Stir well before serving. If desired, store in a sealed container or covered bowl in the fridge for up to 3 days.

Cinnamon Roll-French Toast Casserole

Prep time: 10 minutes | Cook time: 25 minutes | Serves 4

Casserole:
4 cups cubed gluten-free bread, dried out overnight
2 cups whole milk
3 large eggs
1 teaspoon vanilla extract
2 tablespoons pure maple syrup
1 teaspoon ground cinnamon
⅛ teaspoon salt
¼ cup raisins
2 tablespoons chopped pecans
2 tablespoons unsalted butter, melted and cooled
1 cup water
Cream Cheese Drizzle:
1 tablespoon whole milk
1 tablespoon powdered sugar
2 tablespoons cream cheese

1. Add bread to a 7-cup glass dish greased with either oil or cooking spray. Set aside. 2. In a medium bowl, whisk together milk, eggs, vanilla, maple syrup, cinnamon, and salt. Pour over bread in glass dish. Evenly scatter raisins and pecans over bread and evenly drizzle butter over the top. 3. Add the reversible rack and water to Ninja Foodi pressure cooker. Place glass dish on top of rack. Assemble pressure lid, making sure the pressure release valve is in the Seal position. 4. Select Pressure and set to high (HI). Set time to 25 minutes. Press Start. Quick release pressure by moving the pressure release valve to the Vent position. 5. Remove glass bowl from the pot. Transfer to a rack and cool 10 minutes. 6. Combine milk, sugar, and cream cheese in a small bowl. Drizzle over casserole. Spoon casserole into four bowls and serve.

Spanish Tortilla with Red Bell Pepper Sauce

Prep time: 15 minutes | Cook time: 18 minutes | Serves 4

2 tablespoons olive oil
½ medium yellow onion, thinly sliced
1 large (12-ounce / 340-g) russet potato, peeled and cut into 1/16-inch slices, or 1½ cups hash browns such as Simply Potatoes
brand
Salt and freshly ground black pepper
8 large eggs
½ teaspoon smoked paprika
1 cup drained jarred roasted red peppers

1. Spray a 7 × 3-inch round metal baking pan with cooking spray and line the bottom with a round of parchment paper; spray the parchment, too. 2. Put the oil in the pot, select Sauté, and set to Medium (MD). When the oil is hot, add the onion and cook, stirring frequently, until beginning to soften, 3 minutes. Add the potato, 1 teaspoon salt, and several grinds of pepper and stir to combine. Cover loosely with the pressure lid set to Vent and cook, stirring frequently, until the potatoes are barely tender when pierced with a fork, 4 to 5 minutes. Press Cancel. 3. Scrape the onion and potato into the prepared pan. In a small bowl, whisk together the eggs with ¼ teaspoon of the paprika. Pour the egg mixture into the baking pan over the potato mixture. 4. Add the reversible rack and 1½ cups of water to Ninja Foodi pressure cooker. Place the baking pan, uncovered, on the rack. Assemble pressure lid, making sure the pressure release valve is in the Seal position. Select Pressure and set to high (HI). Set time to 10 minutes. Press Start. 5. While the tortilla is cooking, blend the roasted peppers with the remaining ¼ teaspoon smoked paprika and a few grinds of pepper until smooth. Set aside. 6. Let pressure release naturally for 10 minutes; quick-release any remaining pressure. Carefully remove the pan from the pot. Run a knife around the edges of the pan, place a dinner plate over the pan, and carefully invert the tortilla onto the plate. Discard the parchment paper. Cut the tortilla into wedges and serve with the sauce.

Baked Apples with Coconut Muesli

Prep time: 10 minutes | Cook time: 3 minutes | Serves 2

2 large unpeeled organic apples, cored
½ cup coconut muesli
2 tablespoons butter, cubed

2 teaspoons packed brown sugar
½ teaspoon ground cinnamon
⅓ cup water

1. Remove the tops of the apples. If necessary, slice the bottoms off just enough to help the apples sit flat in the pressure cooker. 2. In a bowl, mix together the muesli, butter, brown sugar, and cinnamon, mashing gently with a fork until combined. 3. Stuff each apple with the muesli mixture, then place them in the bottom of the pot. Add the water to the pot. Assemble pressure lid, making sure the pressure release valve is in the Seal position. Select Pressure and set to low (LO). Set time to 2 to 4 minutes. Press Start. When pressure cooking is complete, allow pressure to natural release, about 10 minutes. 4. Serve with Greek yogurt.

Aromatic Eggs Dish

Prep time: 2 minutes | Cook time: 5 minutes | Serves 4 to 6

1 cup water
8 eggs
¼ cup cream
1 teaspoon mayo sauce
1 tablespoon mustard

1 teaspoon ground white pepper
1 teaspoon minced garlic
½ teaspoon sea salt
¼ cup dill, chopped

1. Add the reversible rack and water to Ninja Foodi pressure cooker. 2. Place the eggs in the rack. 3. Assemble pressure lid, making sure the pressure release valve is in the Seal position. Select Pressure and set to high (HI). Set time to 5 minutes. Press Start. 4. Quick release pressure by moving the pressure release valve to the Vent position. 5. Transfer the eggs to the bowl of cold water and cool for 2 to 3 minutes. 6. Peel the eggs, remove the egg yolks and mash them. 7. In a medium bowl, combine the cream, mayo sauce, mustard, pepper, garlic, salt and mashed egg yolks. 8. Sprinkle the mixture with the dill. Mix well. 9. Transfer the egg yolk mixture to the pastry bag. 10. Fill the egg whites with the yolk mixture. Serve.

Breakfast Burrito

Prep time: 10 minutes | Cook time: 12 minutes | Serves 4

2 tablespoons olive oil
16 ounces (454 g) firm tofu, drained and diced
¼ cup diced red onion
½ cup diced tomato
¼ cup chopped fresh cilantro
¼ cup water
1 teaspoon salt
4 (10-inch) flour tortillas

1 cup canned black beans, warmed
1 medium avocado, peeled and sliced
½ cup vegan sour cream (optional)
½ cup shredded vegan Cheddar cheese (optional)

1. Add the oil to the cooking pot. Select Sauté and set to medium

(MD) Add the tofu, stir until well coated, and sauté until it begins to brown, about 5 minutes. Add the onion, tomato, cilantro, water, and salt. 2. Assemble pressure lid, making sure the pressure release valve is in the Seal position. Select Pressure and set to high (HI). Set time to 7 minutes. Press Start. When pressure cooking is complete, allow pressure to natural release. 3. Steam or microwave the tortillas until softened, then lay the tortillas on a flat surface to build the burritos. Place equal amounts of the tofu mixture, beans, and avocado in a line down the center of each tortilla. 4. Roll each burrito by first folding the sides of the tortilla over the filling. Then, while still holding the sides closed, fold the bottom of the tortilla over the filling. Next, roll the burrito while still holding the sides closed and pushing the filling down into the burrito if it starts to spill out. Repeat for remaining burritos. 5. Top with vegan sour cream and/or vegan cheese if desired.

Arugula and Feta Frittata

Prep time: 5 minutes | Cook time: 5 minutes | Serves 2

Unsalted butter, at room temperature, for greasing
3 eggs, beaten
¼ red onion, chopped
¼ cup loosely packed arugula

¼ cup feta cheese crumbles
¼ teaspoon garlic powder
Kosher salt
Freshly ground black pepper

1. Add the reversible rack and 1 cup of water to Ninja Foodi pressure cooker. Coat a 7-inch baking vessel (round cake pan, ramekin, or bowl) with butter and set aside. 2. In a medium bowl, stir together the eggs, onion, arugula, feta, and garlic powder, and season with salt and pepper. Add to the prepared pan. Cover with foil. 3. Carefully put the frittata mixture on top of the rack. 4. Assemble pressure lid, making sure the pressure release valve is in the Seal position. Select Pressure and set to high (HI). Set time to 5 minutes. When pressure cooking is complete, allow pressure to natural release, about 10 minutes. Remove the frittata. Serve hot.

Ham and Cheddar Breakfast Casserole

Prep time: 20 minutes | Cook time: 35 minutes | Serves 6

6 large eggs
½ cup 2% milk
½ teaspoon salt
¼ teaspoon pepper
4 cups frozen shredded hash

brown potatoes, thawed
1 cup cubed fully cooked ham
½ medium onion, chopped
2 cups shredded Cheddar cheese
1 cup water

1. Whisk together eggs, milk, salt and pepper. Combine the potatoes, ham, onion and cheese; transfer to a greased 2-quart souffle or round baking dish; pour egg mixture over top. 2. Add the reversible rack and 1½ cups of water to Ninja Foodi pressure cooker. Cover baking dish with foil. Place on the rack. Assemble pressure lid, making sure the pressure release valve is in the Seal position. 3. Select Pressure and set to high (HI). Set time to 35 minutes. Press Start. Let pressure release naturally for 10 minutes; quick-release any remaining pressure. Let stand 10 minutes before serving.

Banana Bread Inspired Amaranth

Prep time: 5 minutes | Cook time: 4 minutes | Serves 4

1 cup amaranth
2½ cups vanilla-flavored rice milk
2 cups bananas, sliced
2 tablespoons coconut sugar
½ teaspoon cinnamon
½ teaspoon nutmeg
¼ teaspoon salt
½ cup walnuts, chopped

1. In the Ninja Foodi pressure cooker, combine all the ingredients, except for the walnuts. Stir. 2. Assemble pressure lid, making sure the pressure release valve is in the Seal position. 3. Select Pressure and set to high (HI). Set time to 4 minutes. Press Start. 4. When pressure cooking is complete, allow pressure to natural release. 5. Stir in the walnuts before serving.

Bacon and Veggie-Packed Mini Breakfast Frittatas

Prep time: 15 minutes | Cook time: 14 minutes | Serves 4

2 tablespoons grass-fed butter or ghee, plus more for jars
½ cup white button or cremini mushrooms, cleaned and thinly sliced
1 large celery rib, thinly sliced
½ cup fresh spinach, washed, finely chopped
6 large eggs
¼ cup milk of choice
½ teaspoon sea salt
½ teaspoon garlic granules or garlic powder
¼ teaspoon onion powder
¼ teaspoon dried thyme
2 tablespoons chopped fresh flat-leaf parsley, plus more for garnish
½ cup shredded sharp or mild cheddar cheese
¼ cup shredded Parmesan, provolone or Gruyère cheese
4 slices cooked crispy bacon, crumbled
1½ cups water

1. Add your healthy fat of choice to the Ninja Foodi pressure cooker, select Sauté and set to medium (MD). Once the fat has melted, add the mushrooms and celery and sauté, stirring occasionally, for 7 minutes, or until lightly caramelized. Add the spinach and sauté, stirring occasionally, for 2 minutes, or just until wilted. 2. Butter 4 half-pint wide-mouth Mason jars or ramekins. Set them aside. 3. In a large bowl, whisk together the eggs and your milk of choice until the eggs are fully incorporated. Add the sautéed veggies, salt, garlic granules, onion powder, thyme, parsley, shredded cheeses and crumbled bacon. Evenly pour the mixture into the prepared jars. 4. Secure the metal lids on top of the Mason jars, or if you're using ramekins, cover the tops of the ramekins with unbleached parchment paper, then top them with foil and secure it around the edges. 5. Add the reversible rack and water to Ninja Foodi pressure cooker. Carefully transfer the jars on the rack. 6. Assemble pressure lid, making sure the pressure release valve is in the Seal position. Select Pressure and set to high (HI). Set time to 5 minutes. Press Start. 7. Quick release pressure by moving the pressure release valve to the Vent position. 8. Carefully remove the jars from the cooker and remove the lid from each jar. If the flat part of the metal lid has sealed, you may need to release the suction with the side of a can opener. 9. Allow the frittatas to rest for 5 minutes before serving.

New York Strip Steaks with Eggs

Prep time: 8 minutes | Cook time: 14 minutes per batch | Serves 4

Cooking oil spray
4 (4-ounce / 113-g) New York strip steaks
1 teaspoon granulated garlic, divided
1 teaspoon salt, divided
1 teaspoon freshly ground black pepper, divided
4 eggs
½ teaspoon paprika

1. Preheat the pressure cooker to 360°F (182°C). 2. Spray the cooking pot with cooking oil. Place 2 steaks into cook & crisp basket; do not oil or season them at this time. 3. Close crisping lid. Select Air Crisp and set time to 9 minutes. 4. After 5 minutes, open the lid and flip the steaks. Sprinkle each with ¼ teaspoon of granulated garlic, ¼ teaspoon of salt, and ¼ teaspoon of pepper. Resume cooking until the steaks register at least 145°F (63°C) on a food thermometer. 5. When the cooking is complete, transfer the steaks to a plate and tent with aluminum foil to keep warm. Repeat steps 2, 3, and 4 with the remaining steaks. 6. Spray 4 ramekins with olive oil. Crack 1 egg into each ramekin. Sprinkle the eggs with the paprika and remaining ½ teaspoon each of salt and pepper. Working in batches, place 2 ramekins into cooking pot. 7. Close crisping lid. Select Bake, set temperature to 330°F (166°C), and set time to 5 minutes. 8. When the cooking is complete and the eggs are cooked to 160°F (71°C), remove the ramekins and repeat step 7 with the remaining 2 ramekins. 9. Serve the eggs with the steaks.

Savory Sweet Potato Hash

Prep time: 15 minutes | Cook time: 18 minutes | Serves 6
2 medium sweet potatoes, peeled and cut into 1-inch cubes
½ green bell pepper, diced
½ red onion, diced
4 ounces (113 g) baby bella mushrooms, diced
2 tablespoons olive oil
1 garlic clove, minced
½ teaspoon salt
½ teaspoon black pepper
½ tablespoon chopped fresh rosemary

1. Preheat the pressure cooker to 380°F(193°C). 2. In a large bowl, toss all ingredients together until the vegetables are well coated and seasonings distributed. 3. Pour the vegetables into the cooking pot, making sure they are in a single even layer. 4. Close crisping lid. Select Roast and set time to 18 minutes, flipping halfway through. 5. Transfer to a serving bowl or individual plates and enjoy.

Pumpkin Spice Muffins
Prep time: 10 minutes | Cook time: 15 minutes | Serves 6
1 cup blanched finely ground almond flour
½ cup granular erythritol
½ teaspoon baking powder
¼ cup unsalted butter, softened
¼ cup pure pumpkin purée
½ teaspoon ground cinnamon
¼ teaspoon ground nutmeg
1 teaspoon vanilla extract
2 large eggs

1. Preheat the pressure cooker to 300°F (149°C). In a large bowl, mix almond flour, erythritol, baking powder, butter, pumpkin purée, cinnamon, nutmeg, and vanilla. 2. Gently stir in eggs. 3. Evenly pour the batter into six silicone muffin cups. Place muffin cups into the cooking pot. 4. Close crisping lid. Select Bake and set time to 15 minutes. 5. When completely cooked, a toothpick inserted in center will come out mostly clean. Serve warm.

Gruyere and Prosciutto Strata

Prep time: 15 minutes | Cook time: 25 minutes | Serves 5

1 teaspoon canola oil
2 ounces (57 g) thin slices prosciutto, chopped
1 large sweet onion, chopped
½ cup egg substitute
1¼ cups 2% milk

⅛ teaspoon ground mustard
Dash pepper
4 cups cubed French bread
¾ cup shredded Gruyere or Swiss cheese, divided

1. Add the oil to the Ninja Foodi pressure cooker, select Sauté and set to medium (MD). When oil is hot, cook and stir prosciutto until crisp, about 3 minutes. Remove from pan with a slotted spoon. Add onion to pressure cooker; cook and stir until tender, 4 to 5 minutes. 2. In a large bowl, whisk egg substitute, milk, mustard and pepper. Stir in bread, half the cheese, and onions. Reserve 2 tablespoons cooked prosciutto for topping; stir the remaining prosciutto into bread mixture. 3. Transfer to a greased 1½-quart baking dish. Wipe pressure cooker clean. Add the reversible rack and 1 cup water to Ninja Foodi pressure cooker. Cover baking dish with foil. Fold a (18 x 12 inch) piece of foil lengthwise into thirds, making a sling. Use the sling to lower the dish onto the rack. 4. Assemble pressure lid, making sure the pressure release valve is in the Seal position. Select Pressure and set to high (HI). Set time to 20 minutes. Press Start. Let pressure release naturally for 10 minutes; quick-release any remaining pressure. Using foil sling, carefully remove baking dish. Sprinkle with remaining cheese and prosciutto; cover and let stand 10 minutes.

Chocolate-Spiced Pumpkin Bread

Prep time: 10 minutes | Cook time: 55 minutes | Serves 8 to 10

8 tablespoons grass-fed butter, ghee or avocado oil, melted
½ cup pure maple syrup
1 cup pure pumpkin purée
2 large eggs (at room temperature)
1 teaspoon pure vanilla extract
1 cup cassava flour
¼ cup unsweetened cocoa powder

¼ cup grass-fed hydrolyzed collagen powder
2 teaspoons ground cinnamon
¼ teaspoon ground ginger
¼ teaspoon ground allspice
1 teaspoon baking soda
½ teaspoon sea salt
1 cup chopped quality chocolate
1 cup water

1. Use your healthy fat of choice to grease a 1½-quart casserole dish that fits Ninja Foodi pressure cooker. Line the bottom of the casserole dish with a circle of parchment paper. Set aside. 2. In a blender, in the order listed, combine all the ingredients, except the chopped chocolate and water. Process on low speed until smooth and fully blended, about 20 seconds, scraping down the sides, if needed. 3. Add the chopped chocolate and give it a stir with a spatula to fold in. Pour the batter into the prepared casserole dish. Cover the casserole dish with its glass lid. If your casserole dish doesn't come with a glass lid, you can cover the top of the dish with unbleached parchment paper, then top it with foil and secure it around the edges. 4. Add the reversible rack and water to Ninja Foodi pressure cooker. Carefully set the covered casserole dish on rack. Assemble pressure lid, making sure the pressure release valve

is in the Seal position. Select Pressure and set to high (HI). Set time to 55 minutes. Press Start. 5. Let pressure release naturally for 20 minutes; quick-release any remaining pressure. 6. Carefully lift the casserole dish out of the cooker. Carefully remove the hot lid from the dish, taking care not to drip any of the condensation on the top of the bread. Test with a toothpick to make sure the center is fully cooked; no more than a few moist crumbs should be on the toothpick. If it needs more time, re-cover with the lid (make sure to wipe off any condensation first) and return the dish to the cooker to cook on for another 5 minutes, then do a quick pressure release. 7. Allow the bread to cool at room temperature sitting on a cooling rack for 45 minutes. Gently run a knife around the edges of the bread to loosen it when you're ready to remove it from the dish. Turn the dish upside down on a plate to release the bread. Cut the bread into thick slices and serve immediately.

Bananas Foster Millet Bowl

Prep time: 2 minutes | Cook time: 15 minutes | Serves 4

1 cup millet
1 cup water
2 cups plant-based milk, divided, plus more for serving
½ teaspoon pure vanilla extract
½ teaspoon ground cinnamon
1 tablespoon vegan butter

1 tablespoon coconut sugar
2 bananas, peeled and quartered (cut in half lengthwise, then crosswise)
Pure maple syrup, to taste
½ cup slivered almonds, lightly toasted

1. In the inner pot, stir together the millet, 1 cup water, 1 cup milk, vanilla, and cinnamon. Assemble pressure lid, making sure the pressure release valve is in the Seal position. Select Pressure and set to high (HI). Set time to 12 minutes. 2. Let pressure release naturally for 10 minutes; quick-release any remaining pressure. Carefully remove the lid and stir in the remaining 1 cup milk. Select Keep Warm while cooking the bananas. 3. In a medium frying pan, melt the butter over medium heat. Whisk in the coconut sugar. Place the bananas cut-side down into the butter and sugar. Cook, turning once, until caramelized, about 3 minutes total. 4. Serve the millet porridge in bowls and top with the bananas, maple syrup, more milk, and slivered almonds. Enjoy immediately.

Apple and Pecan Oatmeal

Prep time: 5 minutes | Cook time: 7 minutes | Serves 2

1 cup old-fashioned oats
1¼ cups water
1 peeled and cored Granny Smith apple, diced
¼ teaspoon ground cinnamon

⅛ teaspoon salt
2 tablespoons light brown sugar
¼ teaspoon vanilla extract
¼ cup chopped pecans
4 tablespoons whole milk

1. Add oats, water, apple, cinnamon, and salt to the Ninja Foodi pressure cooker. Assemble pressure lid, making sure the pressure release valve is in the Seal position. 2. Press the Porridge button and adjust cook time to 7 minutes. Press Start. Let pressure release naturally for 5 minutes; quick-release any remaining pressure. Stir in brown sugar and vanilla. 3. Transfer oatmeal to two bowls. Garnish with pecans. Pour milk over oatmeal. Serve warm.

Steel-Cut Oats Cooked with Earl Grey Tea

Prep time: 2 minutes | Cook time: 3 minutes | Serves 4

Pressure Cooker:
3 cups brewed Earl Grey Tea (you can use black, decaf or rooibos)
1 cup steel-cut oats
For Serving:

1 teaspoon rosewater, vanilla extract or a few drops of lavender extract
Sweetener of choice, to taste
Nondairy milk

1. Add the brewed tea and oats to Ninja Foodi pressure cooker. Assemble pressure lid, making sure the pressure release valve is in the Seal position. Select Pressure and set to high (HI). Set time to 3 minutes. Press Start. When pressure cooking is complete, allow pressure to natural release. 2. Open and mix in an extra flavoring and your choice of sweetener. Serve topped with nondairy milk.

Pear Cardamom Steel-Cut Oats

Prep time: 5 minutes | Cook time: 3 minutes | Serves 2

1½ cups water
½ cup steel-cut oats
1 small pear, chopped
⅛ teaspoon cardamom (a large pinch) or 1 whole green cardamom pod

2 tablespoons toasted sliced almonds
Sweetener of choice, to taste (optional)
Nondairy milk, for serving

1. Add the water, oats, pear and cardamom to Ninja Foodi pressure cooker. Assemble pressure lid, making sure the pressure release valve is in the Seal position. Select Pressure and set to high (HI). Set time to 3 minutes. Press Start. 2. When pressure cooking is complete, allow pressure to natural release. 3. Open, and remove the cardamom pod (if using). Serve topped with almonds, the sweetener (if using) and a drizzle of nondairy milk. If the pears are very ripe you can skip the extra sweetener.

Coconut-Millet Porridge

Prep time: 10 minutes | Cook time: 22 minutes | Serves 4

Millet:
1 cup millet
1 (13½-ounce / 383-g) can lite or reduced-fat coconut milk
2¼ cups unsweetened plain almond milk or other nondairy milk
1½ teaspoons pure vanilla extract
1½ teaspoons ground cinnamon

¼ teaspoon ground ginger
4 large soft Medjool dates, pitted and finely chopped
¼ cup unsweetened shredded coconut
Topping Options:
¼ cup chopped pistachios plus
¼ cup chopped dried apricots plus 2 tablespoons chia seeds

1. Select Sauté, set to medium (MD) and, after a few minutes, add the millet to dry-toast. Toss occasionally until the millet is a shade darker, 5 to 7 minutes. Toasting unleashes millet's inherent nuttiness. 2. Carefully pour in the coconut milk and 1¼ cups of the almond milk. The mixture will briefly bubble. Add the vanilla, cinnamon, ginger, and dates. Stir to combine. 3. Assemble pressure lid, making sure the pressure release valve is in the Seal position. Select Pressure and set to high (HI). Set time to 12 minutes. Press Start. 4. When pressure cooking is complete, allow pressure to natural release. 5. Open the pot and stir to combine the porridge. The porridge will be very thick at this point. Add ½ cup of the remaining almond milk, stirring until the porridge is creamier and looser. Add another ½ cup milk as needed until you achieve your desired consistency. Then stir in the shredded coconut. Transfer the porridge to bowls and add your toppings of choice.

Egg and Potato Mayo Salad

Prep time: 10 minutes | Cook time: 5 minutes | Serves 2 to 4

1½ cups water
6 russet potatoes, peeled and diced
4 large eggs
1 cup mayonnaise
2 tablespoons fresh parsley,

chopped
¼ cup onion, chopped
1 tablespoon dill pickle juice
1 tablespoon mustard
Pinch of salt
Pinch of ground black pepper

1. Add the reversible rack and water to Ninja Foodi pressure cooker. 2. Place the potatoes and eggs on the rack. 3. Assemble pressure lid, making sure the pressure release valve is in the Seal position. Select Pressure and set to high (HI). Set time to 5 minutes. Press Start. 4. Quick release pressure by moving the pressure release valve to the Vent position. 5. Transfer the eggs to the bowl of cold water and cool for 2 to 3 minutes. 6. In a medium bowl, combine the mayonnaise, parsley, onion, dill pickle juice, and mustard. Mix well. Add salt and pepper. 7. Peel and slice the eggs. Toss the potatoes and eggs in the bowl. Stir and serve.

Spicy Tofu Scramble

Prep time: 10 minutes | Cook time: 14 minutes | Serves 2

16 ounces (454 g) firm tofu, drained
1 teaspoon fresh lemon juice
1 teaspoon salt
½ teaspoon freshly ground black pepper
½ teaspoon turmeric powder
1 tablespoon olive oil
¼ cup diced red onion

¼ cup diced red bell pepper
¼ cup diced tomato
1 clove garlic, minced
1 teaspoon ground cumin
½ teaspoon chipotle powder
½ teaspoon chili powder
¼ cup water
2 tablespoons chopped fresh cilantro

1. In a large bowl, mash the tofu with your hands or a fork, then stir in the lemon juice, salt, pepper, and turmeric. 2. Add the olive oil to the Ninja Foodi pressure cooker. Select the Sauté button and set to Medium (MD). Add the onion and bell pepper; sauté 3 minutes. Add the tomato, garlic, cumin, chipotle powder, and chili powder; sauté an additional 30 seconds. 3. Add the tofu mixture and water to the pot and stir. Assemble pressure lid, making sure the pressure release valve is in the Seal position. Select Pressure and set to high (HI). Set time to 10 minutes. Press Start. When pressure cooking is complete, allow pressure to natural release. 4. Stir in the cilantro and spoon the scramble into serving bowls. Serve warm.

Chocolate Chip Banana Bread

Prep time: 15 minutes | Cook time: 65 minutes | Serves 6

1¾ cups all-purpose flour
½ cup granulated sugar
½ cup packed light brown sugar
1 teaspoon baking soda
½ teaspoon salt
½ teaspoon ground cinnamon
2 large eggs, lightly beaten
½ cup melted unsalted butter,

cooled slightly
½ cup buttermilk
1 teaspoon vanilla extract
1½ cups mashed banana (about 3 bananas)
1 cup mini semisweet chocolate chips
1 cup water

1. In a large bowl, whisk together flour, granulated sugar, brown sugar, baking soda, salt, and cinnamon. 2. In a medium bowl, whisk together eggs, butter, buttermilk, and vanilla. 3. Make a well in the center of dry ingredients and mix in wet ingredients. The batter should still be lumpy with a few dry spots. 4. Fold in mashed banana and chocolate chips. 5. Grease a 7-inch PushPan with oil and flour. 6. Pour banana bread batter into PushPan. Place a paper towel on top of pan and tightly cover with foil. 7. Add the reversible rack and water to Ninja Foodi pressure cooker. Gently lower the PushPan on the rack using the foil sling. Assemble pressure lid, making sure the pressure release valve is in the Seal position. 8. Select Pressure and set to high (HI). Set time to 65 minutes. Press Start. 9. Quick release pressure by moving the pressure release valve to the Vent position. Carefully remove bread using the foil sling. Remove foil and paper towel. Use a clean paper towel to gently blot up any additional moisture that may have accumulated on top of chocolate chip banana bread. 10. Let cool on a cooling rack 10 minutes. Carefully remove the chocolate chip banana bread using push feature in pan.

Sweet Potato Apple Hash

Prep time: 5 minutes | Cook time: 10 minutes | Serves 2

1 tablespoon coconut oil
½ cup sweet yellow onion, diced
½ cup celery, finely diced
2 cups sweet potatoes, peeled and chopped
¼ cup vegetable broth

1 cup apple, chopped
½ teaspoon salt
½ teaspoon black pepper
½ teaspoon nutmeg
1 teaspoon thyme
¼ cup scallions, chopped

1. Add the coconut oil to the Ninja Foodi pressure cooker, select Sauté and set to medium (MD). 2. Once the oil is hot, add in the onion and celery. Sauté the mixture for 2 minutes before adding in the sweet potatoes. Stir and sauté an additional 3 minutes. 3. Add in the vegetable broth. 4. Assemble pressure lid, making sure the pressure release valve is in the Seal position. Select Pressure and set to high (HI). Set time to 2 minutes. Press Start. 5. Quick release pressure by moving the pressure release valve to the Vent position.. 6. Stir in the apples, salt, black pepper, nutmeg and thyme. 7. Reseal the cooker, bring it back up to pressure, and cook for an additional 2 minutes. 8. Quick release pressure by moving the pressure release valve to the Vent position. and carefully open the lid. 9. Garnish with chopped scallions before serving.

Maple Granola

Prep time: 5 minutes | Cook time: 40 minutes | Makes 2 cups

1 cup rolled oats
3 tablespoons pure maple syrup
1 tablespoon sugar
1 tablespoon neutral-flavored oil, such as refined coconut,

sunflower, or safflower
¼ teaspoon sea salt
¼ teaspoon ground cinnamon
¼ teaspoon vanilla extract

1. Preheat the pressure cooker to 250ºF (121ºC). 2. In a medium bowl, stir together the oats, maple syrup, sugar, oil, salt, cinnamon, and vanilla until thoroughly combined. Transfer the granola to cooking pot. 3. Close crisping lid. Select Bake and set time to 40 minutes, stirring every 10 minutes. 4. When the cooking is complete, place the granola on a plate to cool. It will become crisp as it cools. Store the completely cooled granola in an airtight container in a cool, dry place for 1 to 2 weeks.

Buffalo Chicken Breakfast Muffins

Prep time: 7 minutes | Cook time: 13 to 16 minutes | Serves 10

6 ounces (170 g) shredded cooked chicken
3 ounces (85 g) blue cheese, crumbled
2 tablespoons unsalted butter, melted
⅓ cup Buffalo hot sauce, such

as Frank's RedHot
1 teaspoon minced garlic
6 large eggs
Sea salt and freshly ground black pepper, to taste
Avocado oil spray

1. In a large bowl, stir together the chicken, blue cheese, melted butter, hot sauce, and garlic. 2. In a medium bowl or large liquid measuring cup, beat the eggs. Season with salt and pepper. 3. Preheat the pressure cooker to 300ºF (149ºC). Spray 10 silicone muffin cups with oil. Divide the chicken mixture among the cups, and pour the egg mixture over top. 4. Place the cups in the cooking pot. Close crisping lid. Select Bake and set time to 13 to 16 minutes, until the muffins are set and cooked through.

Bacon and Cheese Quiche

Prep time: 5 minutes | Cook time: 12 minutes | Serves 2

3 large eggs
2 tablespoons heavy whipping cream
¼ teaspoon salt

4 slices cooked sugar-free bacon, crumbled
½ cup shredded mild Cheddar cheese

1. Preheat the pressure cooker to 320ºF (160ºC). 2. In a large bowl, whisk eggs, cream, and salt together until combined. Mix in bacon and Cheddar. 3. Pour mixture evenly into two ungreased ramekins. Place into cooking pot. Close crisping lid. Select Bake and set time to 12 minutes. Quiche will be fluffy and set in the middle when done. 4. Let cool 5 minutes. Serve warm.

Maple-Pecan Steel-Cut Oatmeal

Prep time: 2 minutes | Cook time: 11 minutes | Serves 2

½ cup steel-cut oats
1½ cups water
¼ cup maple syrup, plus more for serving
2 tablespoons packed brown

sugar
¼ teaspoon ground cinnamon
Pinch kosher salt
1 tablespoon unsalted butter

1. Select Sauté and set to medium (MD). Add the oats and toast for about 2 minutes, stirring to avoid burning. Add the water, ¼ cup of maple syrup, the brown sugar, cinnamon, and a pinch of salt. 2. Assemble pressure lid, making sure the pressure release valve is in the Seal position. Select Pressure and set to high (HI). Set time to 11 to 13 minutes. Press Start. When pressure cooking is complete, allow pressure to natural release, about 10 minutes. 3. Stir the oats and taste, adding additional maple syrup or salt if desired. For softer oats, replace the lid unlocked and allow to sit 5 to 10 minutes. When ready to serve, stir in the butter. Divide the cooked oats between two bowls and top with pecans, if desired. Serve with fresh fruit or Greek yogurt.

Apple Streusel Oatmeal

Prep time: 5 minutes | Cook time: 8 minutes | Serves 2

1 cup water
1 cup unsweetened soy milk or almond milk
1 cup old-fashioned oats
2 medium Granny Smith apples,

peeled, cored, and diced
2 tablespoons light brown sugar
2 teaspoons ground cinnamon
2 tablespoons chopped pecans

1. In the Ninja Foodi pressure cooker, combine the water, soy milk, oats, apples, brown sugar, and cinnamon. Stir to combine. Assemble pressure lid, making sure the pressure release valve is in the Seal position. 2. Select Pressure and set to high (HI). Set time to 8 minutes. Press Start. When pressure cooking is complete, allow pressure to natural release. 3. Stir the oatmeal. Spoon the oats into serving bowls and top with pecans. Serve warm.

Cherry-Almond Oatmeal

Prep time: 10 minutes | Cook time: 12 minutes | Serves 6

4 cups vanilla almond milk
1 cup steel-cut oats
1 cup dried cherries
⅓ cup packed brown sugar

½ teaspoon salt
½ teaspoon ground cinnamon
Additional vanilla almond milk, optional

1. In Ninja Foodi pressure cooker, combine first 6 ingredients. Assemble pressure lid, making sure the pressure release valve is in the Seal position. Select Pressure and set to high (HI). Set time to 12 minutes. Press Start. Let pressure release naturally for 10 minutes; quick-release any remaining pressure. Serve with additional almond milk if desired.

Cheesy Hash Brown Casserole

Prep time: 10 minutes | Cook time: 20 minutes | Serves 4

8 ounces (227 g) frozen hash browns
6 precooked breakfast sausage patties
6 large eggs
¼ cup whole milk

½ teaspoon hot sauce
¼ teaspoon salt
⅛ teaspoon black pepper
½ cup shredded sharp Cheddar cheese
1½ cups water

1. Grease a 7-inch cake pan with cooking spray. Arrange frozen hash browns on the bottom of cake pan. 2. Place sausage patties in a single layer on top of hash browns with one in the center and five around edges. 3. In a small bowl, whisk together eggs, milk, hot sauce, salt, and pepper. Pour egg mixture over hash browns and sausage. Sprinkle cheese over top of hash brown casserole. 4. Place a paper towel on top of cake pan and tightly cover with foil. 5. Add the reversible rack and water to Ninja Foodi pressure cooker. 6. Create a foil sling with a long piece of foil folded lengthwise into thirds. Place it underneath cake pan. Use foil sling to gently lower pan on the rack. Fold foil sling over pan. 7. Assemble pressure lid, making sure the pressure release valve is in the Seal position. 8. Select Pressure and set to high (HI). Set time to 20 minutes. Press Start. 9. Let pressure release naturally for 5 minutes; quick-release any remaining pressure. 10. Carefully remove the casserole using the foil sling. Remove the foil and paper towel from the top of the pan. Serve immediately.

Three-Pepper Vegan Frittata

Prep time: 10 minutes | Cook time: 12 minutes | Serves 4

16 ounces (454 g) firm tofu, drained
½ cup unsweetened soy milk
4 teaspoons cornstarch
2 teaspoons nutritional yeast
1 teaspoon spicy mustard
½ teaspoon turmeric powder
1 teaspoon salt
2 tablespoons olive oil
1 cup peeled and diced red

potatoes
½ cup diced red onion
½ cup diced red bell pepper
½ cup diced green bell pepper
1 teaspoon minced jalapeño pepper
1 clove garlic, minced
¼ cup chopped fresh Italian flat-leaf parsley
¾ cup water

1. In a blender or food processor combine the tofu, soy milk, cornstarch, nutritional yeast, mustard, turmeric, and salt and process until smooth. Set aside. 2. Add the olive oil to the Ninja Foodi pressure cooker, select Sauté and set to medium (MD). Add the potatoes, onion, peppers, garlic, and parsley; sauté 3 to 5 minutes. 3. Transfer the cooked mixture to a 7-cup greased glass dish and pour the tofu mixture into the cooked potato mixture. 4. Place reversible rack in the pot. Pour in the water. Place the dish with the tofu mixture on the rack. Assemble pressure lid, making sure the pressure release valve is in the Seal position. Select Pressure and set to high (HI). Set time to 7 minutes. Press Start. When pressure cooking is complete, allow pressure to natural release. 5. Remove the dish from the pot and put aside 5 to 10 minutes to set. Slice and serve.

Hearty Blueberry Oatmeal

Prep time: 10 minutes | Cook time: 25 minutes | Serves 6

1½ cups quick oats
1¼ teaspoons ground cinnamon, divided
½ teaspoon baking powder
Pinch salt
1 cup unsweetened vanilla almond milk
¼ cup honey
1 teaspoon vanilla extract
1 egg, beaten
2 cups blueberries
Olive oil
1½ teaspoons sugar, divided
6 tablespoons low-fat whipped topping (optional)

1. In a large bowl, mix together the oats, 1 teaspoon of cinnamon, baking powder, and salt. 2. In a medium bowl, whisk together the almond milk, honey, vanilla and egg. 3. Pour the liquid ingredients into the oats mixture and stir to combine. Fold in the blueberries. 4. Preheat the pressure cooker to 360ºF (182ºC). Lightly spray cooking pot with oil. 5. Add half the blueberry mixture to the pot. 6. Sprinkle ⅛ teaspoon of cinnamon and ½ teaspoon sugar over the top. 7. Close crisping lid. Select Bake and set time to 25 minutes. Transfer the mixture to a shallow bowl. 8. Repeat with the remaining blueberry mixture, ½ teaspoon of sugar, and ⅛ teaspoon of cinnamon. 9. To serve, spoon into bowls and top with whipped topping.

Nuts and Fruit Oatmeal

Prep time: 5 minutes | Cook time: 7 minutes | Serves 2

1 cup old-fashioned oats
1¼ cups water
¼ cup freshly squeezed orange juice
1 medium pear, peeled, cored, and cubed
¼ cup dried cherries
¼ cup chopped walnuts
1 tablespoon honey
¼ teaspoon ground ginger
¼ teaspoon ground cinnamon
Pinch of salt

1. In the Ninja Foodi pressure cooker, add the oats, water, orange juice, pear, cherries, walnuts, honey, ginger, cinnamon, and salt. Stir to combine. Assemble pressure lid, making sure the pressure release valve is in the Seal position. 2. Select Pressure and set to high (HI). Set time to 7 minutes. Press Start. When pressure cooking is complete, allow pressure to natural release. 3. Stir oatmeal and spoon the cooked oats into two bowls. Serve warm.

Mango and Coconut Steel-Cut Oats

Prep time: 5 minutes | Cook time: 13 minutes | Serves 4

1 (13½-ounce / 383-g) can coconut milk
1¼ cups steel-cut oats
Salt
¼ to ⅓ cup loosely packed coconut sugar or brown sugar
1 large mango, pitted, peeled, and diced
½ cup unsweetened coconut flakes, lightly toasted
¼ cup chopped macadamia nuts

1. Combine the coconut milk, 1¼ cups warm water, the oats, and a generous pinch of salt in the Ninja Foodi pressure cooker. Assemble pressure lid, making sure the pressure release valve is in the Seal position. Select Pressure and set to high (HI). Set time to 13 minutes. Press Start. 2. Let pressure release naturally for 15 minutes; quick-release any remaining pressure. Stir the sugar into the oats. The oats will thicken a bit upon standing. 3. Top the oats with the mango, coconut flakes, and nuts. Serve warm.

Fresh Sweet and Spicy Tomato Jam with Toast

Prep time: 10 minutes | Cook time: 10 minutes | Serves 4 to 6

1 pound (454 g) tomatoes, cut into eighths
½ cup sugar
¼ cup white wine vinegar
¼ to ½ teaspoon crushed red
pepper flakes
¼ teaspoon salt
1 tablespoon water
Toast or crackers, for serving

1. In the Ninja Foodi pressure cooker, combine all the ingredients except for toast. 2. Assemble pressure lid, making sure the pressure release valve is in the Seal position. Select Pressure and set to high (HI). Set time to 10 minutes. Press Start. 3. Quick release pressure by moving the pressure release valve to the Vent position. 4. Remove the lid and use a potato masher to mash the tomatoes into small pieces. As the jam cools, it will thicken. When the jam is completely cool, transfer to a pint-size Mason jar with a lid. Store in the refrigerator for up to 3 weeks. 5. Spread the jam on toast or crackers.

Berry Muffins

Prep time: 15 minutes | Cook time: 12 to 17 minutes | Makes 8 muffins

1⅓ cups plus 1 tablespoon all-purpose flour, divided
¼ cup granulated sugar
2 tablespoons light brown sugar
2 teaspoons baking powder
2 eggs
⅔ cup whole milk
⅓ cup safflower oil
1 cup mixed fresh berries

1. In a medium bowl, stir together 1⅓ cups of flour, the granulated sugar, brown sugar, and baking powder until mixed well. 2. In a small bowl, whisk the eggs, milk, and oil until combined. Stir the egg mixture into the dry ingredients just until combined. 3. In another small bowl, toss the mixed berries with the remaining 1 tablespoon of flour until coated. Gently stir the berries into the batter. 4. Double up 16 foil muffin cups to make 8 cups. 5. Preheat the pressure cooker to 315ºF (157ºC). 6. Place 4 cups into the cooking pot and fill each three-quarters full with the batter. 7. Close crisping lid. Select Bake and set time to 17 minutes. 8. After about 12 minutes, check the muffins. If they spring back when lightly touched with your finger, they are done. If not, resume cooking. 9. When the cooking is done, transfer the muffins to a wire rack to cool. 10. Repeat steps 6, 7, and 8 with the remaining muffin cups and batter. 11. Let the muffins cool for 10 minutes before serving.

Egg White Cups

Prep time: 10 minutes | Cook time: 15 minutes | Serves 4

2 cups 100% liquid egg whites
3 tablespoons salted butter, melted
¼ teaspoon salt
¼ teaspoon onion powder

½ medium Roma tomato, cored and diced
½ cup chopped fresh spinach leaves

1. Preheat the pressure cooker to 300°F (149°C). In a large bowl, whisk egg whites with butter, salt, and onion powder. Stir in tomato and spinach, then pour evenly into four ramekins greased with cooking spray. 2. Place ramekins into cooking pot. Close crisping lid. Select Bake and set time to 15 minutes. Eggs will be fully cooked and firm in the center when done. Serve warm.

Johnny Cakes

Prep time: 10 minutes | Cook time: 10 to 12 minutes | Serves 4

½ cup all-purpose flour
1½ cups yellow cornmeal
2 tablespoons sugar
1 teaspoon baking powder
1 teaspoon salt

1 cup milk, whole or 2%
1 tablespoon butter, melted
1 large egg, lightly beaten
1 to 2 tablespoons oil

1. In a large bowl, whisk the flour, cornmeal, sugar, baking powder, and salt until blended. Whisk in the milk, melted butter, and egg until the mixture is sticky but still lumpy. 2. Preheat the pressure cooker to 350°F (177°C). Line the cooking pot with parchment paper. 3. For each cake, drop 1 heaping tablespoon of batter onto the parchment paper. The pot should hold 4 cakes. 4. Spritz the cakes with oil. Close crisping lid. Select Bake and set time to 5 to 6 minutes, turning and spritzing with oil halfway through. Repeat with a second batch of cakes.

Mississippi Spice Muffins

Prep time: 15 minutes | Cook time: 13 minutes | Makes 12 muffins

4 cups all-purpose flour
1 tablespoon ground cinnamon
2 teaspoons baking soda
2 teaspoons allspice
1 teaspoon ground cloves
1 teaspoon salt
1 cup (2 sticks) butter, room

temperature
2 cups sugar
2 large eggs, lightly beaten
2 cups unsweetened applesauce
¼ cup chopped pecans
1 to 2 tablespoons oil

1. In a large bowl, whisk the flour, cinnamon, baking soda, allspice, cloves, and salt until blended. 2. In another large bowl, combine the butter and sugar. Using an electric mixer, beat the mixture for 2 to 3 minutes until light and fluffy. Add the beaten eggs and stir until blended. 3. Add the flour mixture and applesauce, alternating between the two and blending after each addition. Stir in the pecans. 4. Preheat the pressure cooker to 325°F (163°C). Spritz 12 silicone muffin cups with oil. 5. Pour the batter into the prepared

muffin cups, filling each halfway. Place the muffins in the cooking pot. 6. Close crisping lid. Select Bake and set time to 13 minutes, shaking halfway through. The muffins are done when a toothpick inserted into the middle comes out clean.

Greek Feta Cheese Triangles

Prep time: 10 minutes | Cook time: 8 minutes | Serves 3

1 cup feta cheese
1 onion, chopped
½ teaspoon dried parsley

1 egg yolk
2 tablespoons olive oil
3 sheets filo pastry

1. Preheat the pressure cooker to 360°F (182°C). Cut each of the filo sheets into 3 equal-sized strips. Brush the strips with some olive oil. 2. In a bowl, mix onion, feta cheese, egg yolk, and parsley. Divide the mixture between the strips and fold each diagonally to make triangles. Arrange them in the cooking pot and brush the tops with the remaining olive oil. Close crisping lid. Select Bake and set time to 8 minutes. Serve warm.

Golden Avocado Tempura

Prep time: 5 minutes | Cook time: 10 minutes | Serves 4

½ cup bread crumbs
½ teaspoons salt
1 Haas avocado, pitted, peeled

and sliced
Liquid from 1 can white beans

1. Preheat the pressure cooker to 350°F (177°C). 2. Mix the bread crumbs and salt in a shallow bowl until well-incorporated. 3. Dip the avocado slices in the bean liquid, then into the bread crumbs. 4. Put the avocados in the cook & crisp basket, taking care not to overlap any slices. Close crisping lid. Select Air Crisp and set time to 10 minutes, giving the basket a good shake at the halfway point. 5. Serve immediately.

Three-Berry Dutch Pancake

Prep time: 10 minutes | Cook time: 12 to 16 minutes | Serves 4

2 egg whites
1 egg
½ cup whole-wheat pastry flour
½ cup 2% milk
1 teaspoon pure vanilla extract

1 tablespoon unsalted butter, melted
1 cup sliced fresh strawberries
½ cup fresh blueberries
½ cup fresh raspberries

1. In a medium bowl, use an eggbeater or hand mixer to quickly mix the egg whites, egg, pastry flour, milk, and vanilla until well combined. 2. Preheat the pressure cooker to 330°F (166°C). Use a pastry brush to grease the bottom of cooking pot with the melted butter. Immediately pour in the batter. Close crisping lid. Select Bake and set time to 12 to 16 minutes. 3. Remove the pan from the cooker; the pancake will fall. Top with the strawberries, blueberries, and raspberries. Serve immediately.

Classic British Breakfast

Prep time: 5 minutes | Cook time: 25 minutes | Serves 2

1 cup potatoes, sliced and diced	1 tablespoon olive oil
2 cups beans in tomato sauce	1 sausage
2 eggs	Salt, to taste

1. Preheat the pressure cooker to 390°F (199°C). 2. Break the eggs in cooking pot and sprinkle with salt. 3. Lay the beans on the pot, next to the eggs. 4. In a bowl, coat the potatoes with the olive oil. Sprinkle with salt. 5. Transfer the bowl of potato slices to the pot. Close crisping lid. Select Bake and set time to 10 minutes. 6. Swap out the bowl of potatoes for the pot containing the eggs and beans. Bake for another 10 minutes. Cover the potatoes with parchment paper. 7. Slice up the sausage and throw the slices on top of the beans and eggs. Bake for another 5 minutes. 8. Serve with the potatoes.

Veggie Frittata

Prep time: 7 minutes | Cook time: 21 to 23 minutes | Serves 2

Avocado oil spray	
¼ cup diced red onion	
¼ cup diced red bell pepper	Cheddar cheese, divided
¼ cup finely chopped broccoli	½ teaspoon dried thyme
4 large eggs	Sea salt and freshly ground
3 ounces (85 g) shredded sharp	black pepper, to taste

1. Preheat the pressure cooker to 350°F (177°C). Spray cooking pot well with oil. Put the onion, pepper, and broccoli in the pot. Close crisping lid. Select Bake and set time to 5 minutes. 2. While the vegetables cook, beat the eggs in a medium bowl. Stir in half of the cheese, and season with the thyme, salt, and pepper. 3. Add the eggs to the pan and top with the remaining cheese. Bake for 16 to 18 minutes, until cooked through.

Strawberry Tarts

Prep time: 15 minutes | Cook time: 10 minutes | Serves 6

2 refrigerated piecrusts	room temperature
½ cup strawberry preserves	3 tablespoons confectioners'
1 teaspoon cornstarch	sugar
Cooking oil spray	Rainbow sprinkles, for
½ cup low-fat vanilla yogurt	decorating
1 ounce (28 g) cream cheese, at	

1. Place the piecrusts on a flat surface. Using a knife or pizza cutter, cut each piecrust into 3 rectangles, for 6 total. Discard any unused dough from the piecrust edges. 2. In a small bowl, stir together the preserves and cornstarch. Mix well, ensuring there are no lumps of cornstarch remaining. 3. Scoop 1 tablespoon of the strawberry mixture onto the top half of each piece of piecrust. 4. Fold the bottom of each piece up to enclose the filling. Using the back of a fork, press along the edges of each tart to seal. 5.

Preheat the pressure cooker to 375°F (191°C). 6. Spray the cooking pot with cooking oil. Working in batches, spray the breakfast tarts with cooking oil and place them into the pot in a single layer. Do not stack the tarts. 7. Close crisping lid. Select Bake and set time to 10 minutes. 8. When the cooking is complete, the tarts should be light golden brown. Let the breakfast tarts cool fully before removing them from the basket. 9. Repeat steps 5, 6, 7, and 8 for the remaining breakfast tarts. 10. In a small bowl, stir together the yogurt, cream cheese, and confectioners' sugar. Spread the breakfast tarts with the frosting and top with sprinkles.

Meritage Eggs

Prep time: 5 minutes | Cook time: 8 minutes | Serves 2

2 teaspoons unsalted butter (or	(or unsweetened, unflavored
coconut oil for dairy-free), for	almond milk for dairy-free)
greasing the ramekins	3 tablespoons finely grated
4 large eggs	Parmesan cheese (or Kite Hill
2 teaspoons chopped fresh	brand chive cream cheese style
thyme	spread, softened, for dairy-free)
½ teaspoon fine sea salt	Fresh thyme leaves, for garnish
¼ teaspoon ground black pepper	(optional)
2 tablespoons heavy cream	

1. Preheat the pressure cooker to 400°F (204°C). Grease two (4-ounce / 113-g) ramekins with the butter. 2. Crack 2 eggs into each ramekin and divide the thyme, salt, and pepper between the ramekins. Pour 1 tablespoon of the heavy cream into each ramekin. Sprinkle each ramekin with 1½ tablespoons of the Parmesan cheese. 3. Place the ramekins in the cooking pot. Close crisping lid. Select Bake and set time to 8 minutes. 4. Garnish with a sprinkle of ground black pepper and thyme leaves, if desired. Best served fresh.

Italian Egg Cups

Prep time: 5 minutes | Cook time: 10 minutes | Serves 4

Olive oil	4 teaspoons grated Parmesan
1 cup marinara sauce	cheese
4 eggs	Salt and freshly ground black
4 tablespoons shredded	pepper, to taste
Mozzarella cheese	Chopped fresh basil, for garnish

1. Preheat the pressure cooker to 350°F (177°C). Lightly spray 4 individual ramekins with olive oil. 2. Pour ¼ cup of marinara sauce into each ramekin. 3. Crack one egg into each ramekin on top of the marinara sauce. 4. Sprinkle 1 tablespoon of Mozzarella and 1 tablespoon of Parmesan on top of each egg. Season with salt and pepper. 5. Cover each ramekin with aluminum foil. Place two of the ramekins in the cooking pot. 6. Close crisping lid. Select Bake and set time to 7 to 9 minutes, removing the aluminum foil after 5 minutes. If you prefer the yolk to be firmer, cook for 3 to 5 more minutes. 7. Repeat with the remaining two ramekins. Garnish with basil and serve.

Banana-Nut Muffins

Prep time: 5 minutes | Cook time: 15 minutes | Makes 10 muffins

Oil, for spraying
2 very ripe bananas
½ cup packed light brown sugar
⅓ cup canola oil or vegetable oil
1 large egg

1 teaspoon vanilla extract
¾ cup all-purpose flour
1 teaspoon baking powder
1 teaspoon ground cinnamon
½ cup chopped walnuts

1. Preheat the pressure cooker to 320ºF (160ºC). Spray 10 silicone muffin cups lightly with oil. 2. In a medium bowl, mash the bananas. Add the brown sugar, canola oil, egg, and vanilla and stir to combine. 3. Fold in the flour, baking powder, and cinnamon until just combined. 4. Add the walnuts and fold a few times to distribute throughout the batter. 5. Divide the batter equally among the prepared muffin cups and place them in the cooking pot. 6. Close crisping lid. Select Bake and set time to 15 minutes. 7. Let cool before serving.

Baked Peach Oatmeal

Prep time: 5 minutes | Cook time: 30 minutes | Serves 6

Olive oil cooking spray
2 cups certified gluten-free rolled oats
2 cups unsweetened almond milk
¼ cup raw honey, plus more for drizzling (optional)

½ cup nonfat plain Greek yogurt
1 teaspoon vanilla extract
½ teaspoon ground cinnamon
¼ teaspoon salt
1½ cups diced peaches, divided, plus more for serving (optional)

1. Preheat the pressure cooker to 380°F(193ºC). Lightly coat the cooking pot with olive oil cooking spray. 2. In a large bowl, mix together the oats, almond milk, honey, yogurt, vanilla, cinnamon, and salt until well combined. 3. Fold in ¾ cup of the peaches and then pour the mixture into the pot. 4. Sprinkle the remaining peaches across the top of the oatmeal mixture. Close crisping lid. Select Bake and set time to 30 minutes. 5. Allow to set and cool for 5 minutes before serving with additional fresh fruit and honey for drizzling, if desired.

Honey-Apricot Granola with Greek Yogurt

Prep time: 10 minutes | Cook time: 30 minutes | Serves 6

1 cup rolled oats
¼ cup dried apricots, diced
¼ cup almond slivers
¼ cup walnuts, chopped
¼ cup pumpkin seeds
¼ cup hemp hearts
¼ to ⅓ cup raw honey, plus more for drizzling

1 tablespoon olive oil
1 teaspoon ground cinnamon
¼ teaspoon ground nutmeg
¼ teaspoon salt
2 tablespoons sugar-free dark chocolate chips (optional)
3 cups nonfat plain Greek yogurt

1. Preheat the pressure cooker to 260°F(127ºC). 2. In a large bowl, combine the oats, apricots, almonds, walnuts, pumpkin seeds, hemp hearts, honey, olive oil, cinnamon, nutmeg, and salt, mixing so that the honey, oil, and spices are well distributed. 3. Pour the mixture into cooking pot and spread it into an even layer. 4. Close crisping lid. Select Bake and set time to 30 minutes, stirring every 10 minutes. 5. Allow the granola to cool completely before stirring in the chocolate chips (if using) and pouring into an airtight container for storage. 6. For each serving, top ½ cup Greek yogurt with ⅓ cup granola and a drizzle of honey, if needed.

Chimichanga Breakfast Burrito

Prep time: 10 minutes | Cook time: 10 minutes | Serves 2

2 large (10- to 12-inch) flour tortillas
½ cup canned refried beans (pinto or black work equally well)
4 large eggs, cooked scrambled
4 corn tortilla chips, crushed

½ cup grated Pepper Jack cheese
12 pickled jalapeño slices
1 tablespoon vegetable oil
Guacamole, salsa, and sour cream, for serving (optional)

1. Preheat the pressure cooker to 350°F (177ºC). 2. Place the tortillas on a work surface and divide the refried beans between them, spreading them in a rough rectangle in the center of the tortillas. Top the beans with the scrambled eggs, crushed chips, pepper jack, and jalapeños. Fold one side over the fillings, then fold in each short side and roll up the rest of the way like a burrito. 3. Brush the outside of the burritos with the oil, then transfer to the cooking pot, seam-side down. Close crisping lid. Select Bake and set time to 10 minutes, until the tortillas are browned and crisp and the filling is warm throughout. 4. Transfer the chimichangas to plates and serve warm with guacamole, salsa, and sour cream, if you like.

Poached Eggs on Whole Grain Avocado Toast

Prep time: 5 minutes | Cook time: 7 minutes | Serves 4

Olive oil cooking spray
4 large eggs
Salt
Black pepper

4 pieces whole grain bread
1 avocado
Red pepper flakes (optional)

1. Preheat the pressure cooker to 320°F(160ºC). Lightly coat four small oramekins with olive oil cooking spray. 2. Crack one egg into each ramekin, and season with salt and black pepper. 3. Place the ramekins into the cooking pot. Close crisping lid. Select Bake and set time to 7 minutes. 4. While the eggs are cooking, toast the bread in a toaster. 5. Slice the avocado in half lengthwise, remove the pit, and scoop the flesh into a small bowl. Season with salt, black pepper, and red pepper flakes, if desired. Using a fork, smash the avocado lightly. 6. Spread a quarter of the smashed avocado evenly over each slice of toast. 7. Remove the eggs from the pot, and gently spoon one onto each slice of avocado toast before serving.

Oat and Chia Porridge

Prep time: 10 minutes | Cook time: 5 minutes | Serves 4

2 tablespoons peanut butter
4 tablespoons honey
1 tablespoon butter, melted
4 cups milk
2 cups oats
1 cup chia seeds

1. Preheat the pressure cooker to 390°F (199°C). 2. Put the peanut butter, honey, butter, and milk in a bowl and stir to mix. Add the oats and chia seeds and stir. 3. Transfer the mixture to cooking pot. Close crisping lid. Select Bake and set time to 5 minutes. Give another stir before serving.

All-in-One Toast

Prep time: 10 minutes | Cook time: 10 minutes | Serves 1

1 strip bacon, diced
1 slice 1-inch thick bread
1 egg
Salt and freshly ground black pepper, to taste
¼ cup grated Colby cheese

1. Preheat the pressure cooker to 400°F (204°C). 2. Place the bacon in cook & crisp basket. Close crisping lid. Select Air Crisp and set time to 3 minutes, shaking the basket once or twice. Remove the bacon to a paper towel lined plate and set aside. 3. Use a sharp paring knife to score a large circle in the middle of the slice of bread, cutting halfway through, but not all the way through to the cutting board. Press down on the circle in the center of the bread slice to create an indentation. 4. Transfer the slice of bread, hole side up, to the cooking pot. Crack the egg into the center of the bread, and season with salt and pepper. 5. Close crisping lid. Select Bake, set temperature to 380°F (193°C), and set time to 5 minutes. Sprinkle the grated cheese around the edges of the bread, leaving the center of the yolk uncovered, and top with the cooked bacon. Press the cheese and bacon into the bread lightly. 6. Bake for one or two more minutes, just to melt the cheese and finish cooking the egg. Serve immediately.

Sausage and Egg Breakfast Burrito

Prep time: 5 minutes | Cook time: 30 minutes | Serves 6

6 eggs
Salt and pepper, to taste
Cooking oil
½ cup chopped red bell pepper
½ cup chopped green bell pepper
8 ounces (227 g) ground chicken sausage
½ cup salsa
6 medium (8-inch) flour tortillas
½ cup shredded Cheddar cheese

1. In a medium bowl, whisk the eggs. Add salt and pepper to taste. 2. Place a skillet on medium-high heat. Spray with cooking oil. Add the eggs. Scramble for 2 to 3 minutes, until the eggs are fluffy. Remove the eggs from the skillet and set aside. 3. If needed, spray the skillet with more oil. Add the chopped red and green bell peppers. Cook for 2 to 3 minutes, until the peppers are soft. 4. Add the ground sausage to the skillet. Break the sausage into smaller pieces using a spatula or spoon. Cook for 3 to 4 minutes, until the sausage is brown. 5. Add the salsa and scrambled eggs. Stir to combine. Remove the skillet from heat. 6. Spoon the mixture evenly onto the tortillas. 7. To form the burritos, fold the sides of each tortilla in toward the middle and then roll up from the bottom. You can secure each burrito with a toothpick. Or you can moisten the outside edge of the tortilla with a small amount of water. I prefer to use a cooking brush, but you can also dab with your fingers. 8. Preheat the pressure cooker to 400°F (204°C). Spray the burritos with cooking oil and place them in the cook & crisp basket. Do not stack. Close crisping lid. Select Air Crisp and set time to 10 minutes, flipping after 8 minutes. 9. Sprinkle the Cheddar cheese over the burritos. Cool before serving.

Blueberry Cobbler

Prep time: 5 minutes | Cook time: 15 minutes | Serves 4

⅓ cup whole-wheat pastry flour
¾ teaspoon baking powder
Dash sea salt
½ cup 2% milk
2 tablespoons pure maple syrup
½ teaspoon vanilla extract
Cooking oil spray
½ cup fresh blueberries
¼ cup granola

1. In a medium bowl, whisk the flour, baking powder, and salt. Add the milk, maple syrup, and vanilla and gently whisk, just until thoroughly combined. 2. Preheat the pressure cooker to 350°F (177°C). 3. Spray cooking pot with cooking oil and pour the batter into the pot. Top evenly with the blueberries and granola. 4. Close crisping lid. Select Bake and set time to 15 minutes. 5. Enjoy plain or topped with a little vanilla yogurt.

Two-Cheese Grits

Prep time: 10 minutes | Cook time: 10 to 12 minutes | Serves 4

⅔ cup instant grits
1 teaspoon salt
1 teaspoon freshly ground black pepper
¾ cup milk, whole or 2%
1 large egg, beaten
3 ounces (85 g) cream cheese, at room temperature
1 tablespoon butter, melted
1 cup shredded mild Cheddar cheese
1 to 2 tablespoons oil

1. In a large bowl, combine the grits, salt, and pepper. Stir in the milk, egg, cream cheese, and butter until blended. Stir in the Cheddar cheese. 2. Preheat the pressure cooker to 400°F (204°C). Spritz cooking pot with oil. 3. Pour the grits mixture into the pot. 4. Close crisping lid. Select Bake and set time to 10 to 12 minutes, stirring halfway through.

Parmesan Ranch Risotto

Prep time: 10 minutes | Cook time: 30 minutes | Serves 2

1 tablespoon olive oil
1 clove garlic, minced
1 tablespoon unsalted butter
1 onion, diced

¾ cup Arborio rice
2 cups chicken stock, boiling
½ cup Parmesan cheese, grated

1. Preheat the pressure cooker to 390°F (199°C). 2. Grease a round baking tin with olive oil and stir in the garlic, butter, and onion. 3. Transfer the tin to the cooking pot. Close crisping lid. Select Bake and set time to 4 minutes. Add the rice and bake for 4 more minutes. 4. Set the temperature to 320°F (160°C) and pour in the chicken stock. Cover and bake for 22 minutes. 5. Scatter with cheese and serve.

Chapter 3 Beef, Pork, and Lamb

Greek Stuffed Tenderloin

Prep time: 10 minutes | Cook time: 10 minutes | Serves 4

1½ pounds (680 g) venison or beef tenderloin, pounded to ¼ inch thick
3 teaspoons fine sea salt
1 teaspoon ground black pepper
2 ounces (57 g) creamy goat cheese
½ cup crumbled feta cheese (about 2 ounces / 57 g)

¼ cup finely chopped onions
2 cloves garlic, minced
For Garnish/Serving (Optional):
Prepared yellow mustard
Halved cherry tomatoes
Extra-virgin olive oil
Sprigs of fresh rosemary
Lavender flowers

1. Spray cooking pot with avocado oil. Preheat the pressure cooker to 400ºF (204ºC). 2. Season the tenderloin on all sides with the salt and pepper. 3. In a medium-sized mixing bowl, combine the goat cheese, feta, onions, and garlic. Place the mixture in the center of the tenderloin. Starting at the end closest to you, tightly roll the tenderloin like a jelly roll. Tie the rolled tenderloin tightly with kitchen twine. 4. Place the meat in the cooking pot. Close crisping lid. Select Roast and set time to 10 minutes, flipping halfway through, or until the internal temperature reaches 135ºF (57ºC) for medium-rare. 5. To serve, smear a line of prepared yellow mustard on a platter, then place the meat next to it and add halved cherry tomatoes on the side, if desired. Drizzle with olive oil and garnish with rosemary sprigs and lavender flowers, if desired. 6. Best served fresh.

Reuben Beef Rolls with Thousand Island Sauce

Prep time: 15 minutes | Cook time: 10 minutes per batch | Makes 10 rolls

½ pound (227 g) cooked corned beef, chopped
½ cup drained and chopped sauerkraut
1 (8-ounce / 227-g) package cream cheese, softened
½ cup shredded Swiss cheese
20 slices prosciutto
Cooking spray

Thousand Island Sauce:
¼ cup chopped dill pickles
¼ cup tomato sauce
¾ cup mayonnaise
Fresh thyme leaves, for garnish
2 tablespoons sugar
⅛ teaspoon fine sea salt
Ground black pepper, to taste

1. Preheat the pressure cooker to 400ºF (204ºC). 2. Combine the beef, sauerkraut, cream cheese, and Swiss cheese in a large bowl. Stir to mix well. 3. Unroll a slice of prosciutto on a clean work surface, then top with another slice of prosciutto crosswise. Scoop up 4 tablespoons of the beef mixture in the center. 4. Fold the top slice sides over the filling as the ends of the roll, then roll up the long sides of the bottom prosciutto and make it into a roll shape. Overlap the sides by about 1 inch. Repeat with remaining filling

and prosciutto. 5. Arrange the rolls in the cook & crisp basket, seam side down, and spritz with cooking spray. 6. Close crisping lid. Select Air Crisp and set time to 10 minutes, flipping halfway through. 7. Meanwhile, combine the ingredients for the sauce in a small bowl. Stir to mix well. 8. Serve the rolls with the dipping sauce.

Sausage and Peppers

Prep time: 7 minutes | Cook time: 35 minutes | Serves 4

Oil, for spraying
2 pounds (907 g) hot or sweet Italian sausage links, cut into thick slices
4 large bell peppers of any color, seeded and cut into slices
1 onion, thinly sliced

1 tablespoon olive oil
1 tablespoon chopped fresh parsley
1 teaspoon dried oregano
1 teaspoon dried basil
1 teaspoon balsamic vinegar

1. Preheat the pressure cooker to 350ºF (177ºC). Spray cooking pot lightly with oil. 2. In a large bowl, combine the sausage, bell peppers, and onion. 3. In a small bowl, whisk together the olive oil, parsley, oregano, basil, and balsamic vinegar. Pour the mixture over the sausage and peppers and toss until evenly coated. 4. Using a slotted spoon, transfer the mixture to the prepared pot, taking care to drain out as much excess liquid as possible. 5. Close crisping lid. Select Bake and set time to 35 minutes, stirring after 20 minutes.

Sausage and Pork Meatballs

Prep time: 15 minutes | Cook time: 8 to 12 minutes | Serves 8

1 large egg
1 teaspoon gelatin
1 pound (454 g) ground pork
½ pound (227 g) Italian sausage, casings removed, crumbled
⅓ cup Parmesan cheese
¼ cup finely diced onion
1 tablespoon tomato paste

1 teaspoon minced garlic
1 teaspoon dried oregano
¼ teaspoon red pepper flakes
Sea salt and freshly ground black pepper, to taste
Keto-friendly marinara sauce, for serving

1. Beat the egg in a small bowl and sprinkle with the gelatin. Allow to sit for 5 minutes. 2. In a large bowl, combine the ground pork, sausage, Parmesan, onion, tomato paste, garlic, oregano, and red pepper flakes. Season with salt and black pepper. 3. Stir the gelatin mixture, then add it to the other ingredients and, using clean hands, mix to ensure that everything is well combined. Form into 1½-inch round meatballs. 4. Preheat the pressure cooker to 400ºF (204ºC). Place the meatballs in the cook & crisp basket in a single layer, cooking in batches as needed. Close crisping lid. Select Air Crisp and set time to 8 to 12 minutes, flipping after 5 minutes, or until an instant-read thermometer reads 160ºF (71ºC).

Garlic Balsamic London Broil

Prep time: 30 minutes | Cook time: 25 to 27 minutes | Serves 8

2 pounds (907 g) London broil
3 large garlic cloves, minced
3 tablespoons balsamic vinegar
3 tablespoons whole-grain mustard

2 tablespoons olive oil
Sea salt and ground black pepper, to taste
½ teaspoon dried hot red pepper flakes

1. Score both sides of the cleaned London broil. 2. Thoroughly combine the remaining ingredients; massage this mixture into the meat to coat it on all sides. Let it marinate for at least 3 hours. 3. Preheat the pressure cooker to 400°F (204°C); Place the meat in cooking pot. Close crisping lid. Select Roast and set time to 25 to 27 minutes, flipping after 15 minutes. Bon appétit!

Kielbasa Sausage with Pineapple and Bell Peppers

Prep time: 15 minutes | Cook time: 10 minutes | Serves 2 to 4

¾ pound (340 g) kielbasa sausage, cut into ½-inch slices
1 (8-ounce / 227-g) can pineapple chunks in juice, drained

1 cup bell pepper chunks
1 tablespoon barbecue seasoning
1 tablespoon soy sauce
Cooking spray

1. Preheat the pressure cooker to 390°F (199°C). Spritz the cooking pot with cooking spray. 2. Combine all the ingredients in a large bowl. Toss to mix well. 3. Pour the sausage mixture in the cooking pot. 4. Close crisping lid. Select Roast and set time to 10 minutes, shaking halfway through. Serve.

Bulgogi Burgers

Prep time: 30 minutes | Cook time: 10 minutes | Serves 4

Burgers:
1 pound (454 g) 85% lean ground beef
¼ cup chopped scallions
2 tablespoons gochujang (Korean red chile paste)
1 tablespoon dark soy sauce
2 teaspoons minced garlic
2 teaspoons minced fresh ginger
2 teaspoons sugar

1 tablespoon toasted sesame oil
½ teaspoon kosher salt
Gochujang Mayonnaise:
¼ cup mayonnaise
¼ cup chopped scallions
1 tablespoon gochujang (Korean red chile paste)
1 tablespoon toasted sesame oil
2 teaspoons sesame seeds
4 hamburger buns

1. For the burgers: In a large bowl, mix the ground beef, scallions, gochujang, soy sauce, garlic, ginger, sugar, sesame oil, and salt. Marinate at room temperature for 30 minutes, or cover and refrigerate for up to 24 hours. 2. Divide the meat into four portions and form them into round patties. Make a slight depression in the middle of each patty with your thumb to prevent them from puffing up into a dome shape while cooking. 3. Preheat the pressure cooker to 350°F (177°C). Place the patties in a single layer in the cooking pot. Close crisping lid. Select Bake and set time to 10 minutes. 4. Meanwhile, for the gochujang mayonnaise: Stir together the mayonnaise, scallions, gochujang, sesame oil, and sesame seeds. 5. To serve, place the burgers on the buns and top with the mayonnaise.

Blackened Cajun Pork Roast

Prep time: 20 minutes | Cook time: 33 minutes | Serves 4

2 pounds (907 g) bone-in pork loin roast
2 tablespoons oil
¼ cup Cajun seasoning

½ cup diced onion
½ cup diced celery
½ cup diced green bell pepper
1 tablespoon minced garlic

1. Cut 5 slits across the pork roast. Spritz it with oil, coating it completely. Evenly sprinkle the Cajun seasoning over the pork roast. 2. In a medium bowl, stir together the onion, celery, green bell pepper, and garlic until combined. Set aside. 3. Preheat the pressure cooker to 360°F (182°C). 4. Place the pork roast in cooking pot and spritz with oil. 5. Close crisping lid. Select Roast and set time to 20 minutes, flipping every 5 minutes. 6. Increase the temperature to 390°F (199°C). 7. Roast for 8 minutes more and flip. Add the vegetable mixture to the pot and cook for a final 5 minutes. Let the roast sit for 5 minutes before serving.

Pork and Beef Egg Rolls

Prep time: 30 minutes | Cook time: 7 to 8 minutes per batch | Makes 8 egg rolls

¼ pound (113 g) very lean ground beef
¼ pound (113 g) lean ground pork
1 tablespoon soy sauce
1 teaspoon olive oil
½ cup grated carrots
2 green onions, chopped
2 cups grated Napa cabbage

¼ cup chopped water chestnuts
¼ teaspoon salt
¼ teaspoon garlic powder
¼ teaspoon black pepper
1 egg
1 tablespoon water
8 egg roll wraps
Oil for misting or cooking spray

1. In a large skillet, brown beef and pork with soy sauce. Remove cooked meat from skillet, drain, and set aside. 2. Pour off any excess grease from skillet. Add olive oil, carrots, and onions. Sauté until barely tender, about 1 minute. 3. Stir in cabbage, cover, and cook for 1 minute or just until cabbage slightly wilts. Remove from heat. 4. In a large bowl, combine the cooked meats and vegetables, water chestnuts, salt, garlic powder, and pepper. Stir well. If needed, add more salt to taste. 5. Beat together egg and water in a small bowl. 6. Fill egg roll wrappers, using about ¼ cup of filling for each wrap. Roll up and brush all over with egg wash to seal. 7. Preheat the pressure cooker to 390°F (199°C). Spray the rolls lightly with olive oil or cooking spray. 8. Place 4 egg rolls in cook & crisp basket. Close crisping lid. Select Air Crisp and set time to 7 to 8 minutes, turning halfway through. 8. Repeat to cook remaining egg rolls.

Bacon and Cheese Stuffed Pork Chops

Prep time: 10 minutes | Cook time: 12 minutes | Serves 4

½ ounce (14 g) plain pork rinds, finely crushed
½ cup shredded sharp Cheddar cheese
4 slices cooked sugar-free

bacon, crumbled
4 (4-ounce / 113-g) boneless pork chops
½ teaspoon salt
¼ teaspoon ground black pepper

1. In a small bowl, mix pork rinds, Cheddar, and bacon. 2. Make a 3-inch slit in the side of each pork chop and stuff with ¼ pork rind mixture. Sprinkle each side of pork chops with salt and pepper. 3. Preheat the pressure cooker to 400ºF (204ºC). Place pork chops into cooking pot, stuffed side up. Close crisping lid. Select Roast and set time to 12 minutes, until the internal temperature reaches 145ºF (63ºC) when done. Serve warm.

Carne Asada

Prep time: 5 minutes | Cook time: 15 minutes | Serves 4

3 chipotle peppers in adobo, chopped
⅓ cup chopped fresh oregano
⅓ cup chopped fresh parsley
4 cloves garlic, minced
Juice of 2 limes

1 teaspoon ground cumin seeds
⅓ cup olive oil
1 to 1½ pounds (454 g to 680 g) flank steak
Salt, to taste

1. Combine the chipotle, oregano, parsley, garlic, lime juice, cumin, and olive oil in a large bowl. Stir to mix well. 2. Dunk the flank steak in the mixture and press to coat well. Wrap the bowl in plastic and marinate under room temperature for at least 30 minutes. 3. Preheat the pressure cooker to 390ºF (199ºC). 4. Discard the marinade and place the steak in the cooking pot. Sprinkle with salt. 5. Close crisping lid. Select Roast and set time to 15 minutes, flipping halfway through. 6. Slice to serve.

Rosemary Ribeye Steaks

Prep time: 10 minutes | Cook time: 15 minutes | Serves 2

¼ cup butter
1 clove garlic, minced
Salt and ground black pepper, to taste

1½ tablespoons balsamic vinegar
¼ cup rosemary, chopped
2 ribeye steaks

1. Melt the butter in a skillet over medium heat. Add the garlic and fry until fragrant. 2. Remove the skillet from the heat and add the salt, pepper, and vinegar. Allow it to cool. 3. Add the rosemary, then pour the mixture into a Ziploc bag. 4. Put the ribeye steaks in the bag and shake well, coating the meat well. Refrigerate for an hour, then allow to sit for a further twenty minutes. 5. Preheat the pressure cooker to 400ºF (204ºC). 6. Transfer ribeye steaks to the cooking pot. 7. Close crisping lid. Select Roast and set time to 15 minutes. 8. Serve immediately.

Cinnamon-Beef Kofta

Prep time: 10 minutes | Cook time: 13 minutes per batch | Makes 12 koftas

1½ pounds (680 g) lean ground beef
1 teaspoon onion powder
¾ teaspoon ground cinnamon
¾ teaspoon ground dried turmeric

1 teaspoon ground cumin
¾ teaspoon salt
¼ teaspoon cayenne
12 (3½- to 4-inch-long) cinnamon sticks
Cooking spray

1. Preheat the pressure cooker to 375ºF (191ºC). Spritz the cooking pot with cooking spray. 2. Combine all the ingredients, except for the cinnamon sticks, in a large bowl. Toss to mix well. 3. Divide and shape the mixture into 12 balls, then wrap each ball around each cinnamon stick and leave a quarter of the length uncovered. 4. Arrange the beef-cinnamon sticks in the pot and spritz with cooking spray. 5. Close crisping lid. Select Bake and set time to 13 minutes, flipping halfway through. 6. Serve immediately.

Chorizo and Beef Burger

Prep time: 10 minutes | Cook time: 15 minutes | Serves 4

¾ pound (340 g) 80/20 ground beef
¼ pound (113 g) Mexican-style ground chorizo
¼ cup chopped onion

5 slices pickled jalapeños, chopped
2 teaspoons chili powder
1 teaspoon minced garlic
¼ teaspoon cumin

1. Preheat the pressure cooker to 375ºF (191ºC). In a large bowl, mix all ingredients. Divide the mixture into four sections and form them into burger patties. 2. Place burger patties into cooking pot, working in batches if necessary. 3. Close crisping lid. Select Bake and set time to 15 minutes, flipping halfway through. Serve warm.

Garlic-Marinated Flank Steak

Prep time: 30 minutes | Cook time: 8 to 10 minutes | Serves 6

½ cup avocado oil
¼ cup coconut aminos
1 shallot, minced
1 tablespoon minced garlic
2 tablespoons chopped fresh oregano, or 2 teaspoons dried

1½ teaspoons sea salt
1 teaspoon freshly ground black pepper
¼ teaspoon red pepper flakes
2 pounds (907 g) flank steak

1. In a blender, combine the avocado oil, coconut aminos, shallot, garlic, oregano, salt, black pepper, and red pepper flakes. Process until smooth. 2. Place the steak in a zip-top plastic bag or shallow dish with the marinade. Seal the bag or cover the dish and marinate in the refrigerator for at least 2 hours or overnight. 3. Remove the steak from the bag and discard the marinade. 4. Preheat the pressure cooker to 400ºF (204ºC). Place the steak in the cooking pot. Close crisping lid. Select Roast and set time to 8 to 10 minutes, flipping halfway through, or until the internal temperature reaches 120ºF (49ºC) for medium-rare (or as desired).

Greek Lamb Pita Pockets

Prep time: 15 minutes | Cook time: 6 minutes | Serves 4

Dressing:
1 cup plain yogurt
1 tablespoon lemon juice
1 teaspoon dried dill weed, crushed
1 teaspoon ground oregano
½ teaspoon salt
Meatballs:
½ pound (227 g) ground lamb
1 tablespoon diced onion
1 teaspoon dried parsley
1 teaspoon dried dill weed, crushed

¼ teaspoon oregano
¼ teaspoon coriander
¼ teaspoon ground cumin
¼ teaspoon salt
4 pita halves
Suggested Toppings:
1 red onion, slivered
1 medium cucumber, deseeded, thinly sliced
Crumbled feta cheese
Sliced black olives
Chopped fresh peppers

1. Preheat the pressure cooker to 390ºF (199ºC). 2. Stir the dressing ingredients together in a small bowl and refrigerate while preparing lamb. 3. Combine all meatball ingredients in a large bowl and stir to distribute seasonings. 4. Shape meat mixture into 12 small meatballs, rounded or slightly flattened if you prefer. 5. Transfer the meatballs in the cooking pot. Close crisping lid. Select Roast and set time to 6 minutes. Remove and drain on paper towels. 6. To serve, pile meatballs and the choice of toppings in pita pockets and drizzle with dressing.

Spicy Flank Steak with Zhoug

Prep time: 30 minutes | Cook time: 8 minutes | Serves 4

Marinade and Steak:
½ cup dark beer or orange juice
¼ cup fresh lemon juice
3 cloves garlic, minced
2 tablespoons extra-virgin olive oil
2 tablespoons Sriracha
2 tablespoons brown sugar
2 teaspoons ground cumin
2 teaspoons smoked paprika
1 tablespoon kosher salt
1 teaspoon black pepper
1½ pounds (680 g) flank steak,

trimmed and cut into 3 pieces
Zhoug:
1 cup packed fresh cilantro leaves
2 cloves garlic, peeled
2 jalapeño or serrano chiles, stemmed and coarsely chopped
½ teaspoon ground cumin
¼ teaspoon ground coriander
¼ teaspoon kosher salt
2 to 4 tablespoons extra-virgin olive oil

1. For the marinade and steak: In a small bowl, whisk together the beer, lemon juice, garlic, olive oil, Sriracha, brown sugar, cumin, paprika, salt, and pepper. Place the steak in a large resealable plastic bag. Pour the marinade over the steak, seal the bag, and massage the steak to coat. Marinate in the refrigerator for 1 hour or up to 24 hours, turning the bag occasionally. 2. Meanwhile, for the zhoug: In a food processor, combine the cilantro, garlic, jalapeños, cumin, coriander, and salt. Process until finely chopped. Add 2 tablespoons olive oil and pulse to form a loose paste, adding up to 2 tablespoons more olive oil if needed. Transfer the zhoug to a glass container. Cover and store in the refrigerator until 30 minutes before serving if marinating more than 1 hour. 3. Preheat the pressure cooker to 400ºF (204ºC). Remove the steak from the marinade and discard

the marinade. Place the steak in the cooking pot. Close crisping lid. Select Roast and set time to 8 minutes, or until the internal temperature reaches 150ºF / 66ºC (for medium). 4. Transfer the steak to a cutting board and let rest for 5 minutes. Slice the steak across the grain and serve with the zhoug.

Pigs in a Blanket

Prep time: 10 minutes | Cook time: 7 minutes | Serves 2

½ cup shredded Mozzarella cheese
2 tablespoons blanched finely ground almond flour
1 ounce (28 g) full-fat cream

cheese
2 (2-ounce / 57-g) beef smoked sausages
½ teaspoon sesame seeds

1. Place Mozzarella, almond flour, and cream cheese in a large microwave-safe bowl. Microwave for 45 seconds and stir until smooth. Roll dough into a ball and cut in half. 2. Press each half out into a 4 × 5-inch rectangle. Roll one sausage up in each dough half and press seams closed. Sprinkle the top with sesame seeds. 3. Preheat the pressure cooker to 400ºF (204ºC). Place each wrapped sausage into the cook & crisp basket. 4. Close crisping lid. Select Air Crisp and set time to 7 minutes. 5. Serve immediately.

Cheeseburger Casserole

Prep time: 5 minutes | Cook time: 50 minutes | Serves 4

¼ pound (113 g) reduced-sodium bacon
1 pound (454 g) 85% lean ground beef
1 clove garlic, minced
¼ teaspoon onion powder
4 eggs
¼ cup heavy cream

¼ cup tomato paste
2 tablespoons dill pickle relish
¼ teaspoon salt
¼ teaspoon freshly ground black pepper
1½ cups grated Cheddar cheese, divided

1. Preheat the pressure cooker to 350ºF (177ºC). Lightly coat a casserole dish with olive oil and set aside. 2. Arrange the bacon in a single layer in the cook & crisp basket. Close crisping lid. Select Air Crisp and set time to 10 minutes. Transfer the bacon to a plate lined with paper towels and let cool. Drain the grease. 3. Preheat the pressure cooker to 400ºF (204ºC). Crumble the beef into cooking pot. Scatter the garlic on top and sprinkle with the onion powder. Close crisping lid. Select Roast and set time to 15 to 20 minutes. 4. While the beef is baking, in a bowl whisk together the eggs, cream, tomato paste, pickle relish, salt, and pepper. Stir in 1 cup of the cheese. Set aside. 5. When the beef is done, transfer it to the prepared pan. Use the side of a spoon to break up any large pieces of beef. 6. Drain the grease and, when cool enough to handle, wash the pot. 7. Crumble the bacon and add it to the beef, spreading the meats into an even layer. Pour the egg mixture over the beef mixture and top with the remaining ½ cup of cheese. Bake at 350ºF (177ºC) for 20 to 25 minutes until the eggs are set and the top is golden brown.

Herb-Roasted Beef Tips with Onions

Prep time: 5 minutes | Cook time: 10 minutes | Serves 4

1 pound (454 g) rib eye steak, cubed	1 tablespoon fresh oregano
2 garlic cloves, minced	1 teaspoon salt
2 tablespoons olive oil	½ teaspoon black pepper
	1 yellow onion, thinly sliced

1. Preheat the pressure cooker to 380°F(193°C). 2. In a medium bowl, combine the steak, garlic, olive oil, oregano, salt, pepper, and onion. Mix until all of the beef and onion are well coated. 3. Put the seasoned steak mixture into the cooking pot. Close crisping lid. Select Roast and set time to 10 minutes, stirring halfway through. 4. Let rest for 5 minutes before serving with some favorite sides.

Parmesan-Crusted Pork Chops

Prep time: 5 minutes | Cook time: 12 minutes | Serves 4

1 large egg	pork chops
½ cup grated Parmesan cheese	½ teaspoon salt
4 (4-ounce / 113-g) boneless	¼ teaspoon ground black pepper

1. Whisk egg in a medium bowl and place Parmesan in a separate medium bowl. 2. Sprinkle pork chops on both sides with salt and pepper. Dip each pork chop into egg, then press both sides into Parmesan. 3. Preheat the pressure cooker to 400°F (204°C). Place pork chops into cooking pot. Close crisping lid. Select Roast and set time to 12 minutes, turning halfway through. Pork chops will be golden and have an internal temperature of at least 145°F (63°C) when done. Serve warm.

Spice-Coated Steaks with Cucumber and Snap Pea Salad

Prep time: 15 minutes | Cook time: 15 to 20 minutes | Serves 4

1 (1½-pound / 680-g) boneless top sirloin steak, trimmed and halved crosswise	3 tablespoons mayonnaise
1½ teaspoons chili powder	1½ tablespoons white wine vinegar
1½ teaspoons ground cumin	1 tablespoon minced fresh dill
¾ teaspoon ground coriander	1 small garlic clove, minced
⅛ teaspoon cayenne pepper	8 ounces (227 g) sugar snap peas, strings removed and cut in half on bias
⅛ teaspoon ground cinnamon	
1¼ teaspoons plus ⅛ teaspoon salt, divided	½ English cucumber, halved lengthwise and sliced thin
½ teaspoon plus ⅛ teaspoon ground black pepper, divided	2 radishes, trimmed, halved and sliced thin
1 teaspoon plus 1½ tablespoons extra-virgin olive oil, divided	2 cups baby arugula

1. Preheat the pressure cooker to 400°F (204°C). 2. In a bowl, mix chili powder, cumin, coriander, cayenne pepper, cinnamon, 1¼ teaspoons salt and ½ teaspoon pepper until well combined. 3. Add the steaks to another bowl and pat dry with paper towels. Brush with 1 teaspoon oil and transfer to the bowl of spice mixture. Roll over to coat thoroughly. 4. Arrange the coated steaks in the cooking pot, spaced evenly apart. Close crisping lid. Select Roast and set time to 15 to 20 minutes, or until an instant-read thermometer inserted in the thickest part of the meat registers at least 145°F (63°C). Flip halfway through to ensure even cooking. 5. Transfer the steaks to a clean work surface and wrap with aluminum foil. Let stand while preparing salad. 6. Make the salad: In a large bowl, stir together 1½ tablespoons olive oil, mayonnaise, vinegar, dill, garlic, ⅛ teaspoon salt, and ⅛ teaspoon pepper. Add snap peas, cucumber, radishes and arugula. Toss to blend well. 7. Slice the steaks and serve with the salad.

Short Ribs with Chimichurri

Prep time: 30 minutes | Cook time: 13 minutes | Serves 4

1 pound (454 g) boneless short ribs	1 tablespoon freshly squeezed lemon juice
1½ teaspoons sea salt, divided	½ teaspoon ground cumin
½ teaspoon freshly ground black pepper, divided	¼ teaspoon red pepper flakes
½ cup fresh parsley leaves	2 tablespoons extra-virgin olive oil
½ cup fresh cilantro leaves	Avocado oil spray
1 teaspoon minced garlic	

1. Pat the short ribs dry with paper towels. Sprinkle the ribs all over with 1 teaspoon salt and ¼ teaspoon black pepper. Let sit at room temperature for 45 minutes. 2. Meanwhile, place the parsley, cilantro, garlic, lemon juice, cumin, red pepper flakes, the remaining ½ teaspoon salt, and the remaining ¼ teaspoon black pepper in a blender or food processor. With the blender running, slowly drizzle in the olive oil. Blend for about 1 minute, until the mixture is smooth and well combined. 3. Preheat the pressure cooker to 400°F (204°C). Spray both sides of the ribs with oil. Place in the cooking pot. Close crisping lid. Select Roast and set time to 13 minutes, flipping after 8 minutes, until an instant-read thermometer reads 125°F (52°C) for medium-rare. 4. Allow the meat to rest for 5 to 10 minutes, then slice. Serve warm with the chimichurri sauce.

Spice-Rubbed Pork Loin

Prep time: 5 minutes | Cook time: 20 minutes | Serves 6

1 teaspoon paprika	1 (1½-pound / 680-g) boneless pork loin
½ teaspoon ground cumin	
½ teaspoon chili powder	½ teaspoon salt
½ teaspoon garlic powder	¼ teaspoon ground black pepper
2 tablespoons coconut oil	

1. In a small bowl, mix paprika, cumin, chili powder, and garlic powder. 2. Drizzle coconut oil over pork. Sprinkle pork loin with salt and pepper, then rub spice mixture evenly on all sides. 3. Preheat the pressure cooker to 400°F (204°C). Place pork loin into cooking pot. Close crisping lid. Select Roast and set time to 20 minutes, turning halfway through, or until the internal temperature reaches 145°F (63°C). Serve warm.

Meat and Rice Stuffed Bell Peppers

Prep time: 20 minutes | Cook time: 18 minutes | Serves 4

¾ pound (340 g) lean ground beef
4 ounces (113 g) lean ground pork
¼ cup onion, minced
1 (15-ounce / 425-g) can crushed tomatoes
1 teaspoon Worcestershire sauce
1 teaspoon barbecue seasoning
1 teaspoon honey
½ teaspoon dried basil
½ cup cooked brown rice
½ teaspoon garlic powder
½ teaspoon oregano
½ teaspoon salt
2 small bell peppers, cut in half, stems removed, deseeded
Cooking spray

1. Preheat the pressure cooker to 360°F (182°C). Spritz cooking pot with cooking spray. 2. Arrange the beef, pork, and onion in the bpot. Close crisping lid. Select Bake and set time to 8 minutes. Break the ground meat into chunks halfway through. 3. Meanwhile, combine the tomatoes, Worcestershire sauce, barbecue seasoning, honey, and basil in a saucepan. Stir to mix well. 4. Transfer the cooked meat mixture to a large bowl and add the cooked rice, garlic powder, oregano, salt, and ¼ cup of the tomato mixture. Stir to mix well. 5. Stuff the pepper halves with the mixture, then arrange the pepper halves in the pot and bake for 10 minutes or until the peppers are lightly charred. 6. Serve the stuffed peppers with the remaining tomato sauce on top.

Bo Luc Lac

Prep time: 50 minutes | Cook time: 8 minutes | Serves 4

For the Meat:
2 teaspoons soy sauce
4 garlic cloves, minced
1 teaspoon kosher salt
2 teaspoons sugar
¼ teaspoon ground black pepper
1 teaspoon toasted sesame oil
1½ pounds (680 g) top sirloin steak, cut into 1-inch cubes
Cooking spray
For the Salad:
1 head Bibb lettuce, leaves separated and torn into large pieces
¼ cup fresh mint leaves
½ cup halved grape tomatoes
½ red onion, halved and thinly sliced
2 tablespoons apple cider vinegar
1 garlic clove, minced
2 teaspoons sugar
¼ teaspoon kosher salt
¼ teaspoon ground black pepper
2 tablespoons vegetable oil
For Serving:
Lime wedges, for garnish
Coarse salt and freshly cracked black pepper, to taste

1. Combine the ingredients for the meat, except for the steak, in a large bowl. Stir to mix well. 2. Dunk the steak cubes in the bowl and press to coat. Wrap the bowl in plastic and marinate under room temperature for at least 30 minutes. 3. Preheat the pressure cooker to 400°F (204°C). Spritz the cooking pot with cooking spray. 4. Discard the marinade and transfer the steak cubes in the cooking pot. 5. Close crisping lid. Select Roast and set time to 4 minutes, shaking halfway through. 6. Meanwhile, combine the ingredients for the salad in a separate large bowl. Toss to mix well. 7. Pour the salad in a large serving bowl and top with the steak cubes. Squeeze the lime wedges over and sprinkle with salt and black pepper before serving.

Buttery Pork Chops

Prep time: 5 minutes | Cook time: 12 minutes | Serves 4

4 (4-ounce / 113-g) boneless pork chops
½ teaspoon salt
¼ teaspoon ground black pepper
2 tablespoons salted butter, softened

1. Preheat the pressure cooker to 400°F (204°C). Sprinkle pork chops on all sides with salt and pepper. Place chops into cooking pot in a single layer. Close crisping lid. Select Roast and set time to 12 minutes. Pork chops will be golden and have an internal temperature of at least 145°F (63°C) when done. 2. Top each chop with ½ tablespoon butter and let sit 2 minutes to melt. Serve warm.

Italian Pork Loin

Prep time: 30 minutes | Cook time: 16 minutes | Serves 3

1 teaspoon Celtic sea salt
½ teaspoon black pepper, freshly cracked
¼ cup red wine
2 tablespoons mustard
2 garlic cloves, minced
1 pound (454 g) pork top loin
1 tablespoon Italian herb seasoning blend

1. In a ceramic bowl, mix the salt, black pepper, red wine, mustard, and garlic. Add the pork top loin and let it marinate at least 30 minutes. 2. Preheat the pressure cooker to 370°F (188°C). Spritz the cooking pot with nonstick cooking spray. 3. Place the pork top loin in the pot; sprinkle with the Italian herb seasoning blend. Close crisping lid. Select Roast and set time to 15 to 16 minute, flipping and spraying with cooking oil after 10 minutes. Serve immediately.

Lemony Pork Loin Chop Schnitzel

Prep time: 15 minutes | Cook time: 15 minutes | Serves 4

4 thin boneless pork loin chops
2 tablespoons lemon juice
½ cup flour
¼ teaspoon marjoram
1 teaspoon salt
1 cup panko breadcrumbs
2 eggs
Lemon wedges, for serving
Cooking spray

1. Preheat the pressure cooker to 390°F (199°C). Spritz cooking pot with cooking spray. 2. On a clean work surface, drizzle the pork chops with lemon juice on both sides. 3. Combine the flour with marjoram and salt on a shallow plate. Pour the breadcrumbs on a separate shallow dish. Beat the eggs in a large bowl. 4. Dredge the pork chops in the flour, then dunk in the beaten eggs to coat well. Shake the excess off and roll over the breadcrumbs. 5. Arrange the chops in the pot and spritz with cooking spray. Close crisping lid. Select Roast and set time to 15 minutes, flipping halfway through. Squeeze the lemon wedges over the fried chops and serve immediately.

Panko Pork Chops

Prep time: 10 minutes | Cook time: 12 minutes | Serves 4

4 center-cut boneless pork chops, excess fat trimmed
¼ teaspoon salt
2 eggs
1½ cups panko bread crumbs
3 tablespoons grated Parmesan cheese
1½ teaspoons paprika

½ teaspoon granulated garlic
½ teaspoon onion powder
1 teaspoon chili powder
¼ teaspoon freshly ground black pepper
Olive oil spray

1. Sprinkle the pork chops with salt on both sides and let them sit while you prepare the seasonings and egg wash. 2. In a shallow medium bowl, beat the eggs. 3. In another shallow medium bowl, stir together the panko, Parmesan cheese, paprika, granulated garlic, onion powder, chili powder, and pepper. 4. Dip the pork chops in the egg and in the panko mixture to coat. Firmly press the crumbs onto the chops. 5. Preheat the pressure cooker to 400ºF (204ºC). 6. Spray the cooking pot with olive oil. Place the pork chops into the pot and spray them with olive oil. 7. Close crisping lid. Select Roast and set time to 12 minutes, flipping and spraying with more olive oil halfway through. 8. When the cooking is complete, the chops should be golden and crispy and a food thermometer should register 145ºF (63ºC). Serve immediately.

Chapter 4 Fish and Seafood

Honey Garlic Salmon

Prep time: 10 minutes | Cook time: 0 minutes | Serves 4

1 cup water	4 tablespoons soy sauce
1 pound (454 g) salmon fillets	2 tablespoons rice vinegar
½ teaspoon salt	4 cloves garlic, minced
¼ teaspoon black pepper	1 teaspoon sesame seeds
½ cup honey	

1. Add the reversible rack and water to Ninja Foodi pressure cooker. 2. Season salmon with salt and pepper and place on rack. 3. Assemble pressure lid, making sure the pressure release valve is in the Seal position. 4. Select Pressure and set to high (HI). Set time to 0 minutes. Press Start. 5. Let pressure release naturally for 10 minutes; quick-release any remaining pressure. 6. In a small bowl, whisk together honey, soy sauce, vinegar, garlic, and sesame seeds. 7. Pour sauce over salmon and serve.

Simple Poached Salmon

Prep time: 10 minutes | Cook time: 3 minutes | Serves 4

2 cups water	1 fresh rosemary sprig
1 cup white wine	1 bay leaf
1 medium onion, sliced	½ teaspoon salt
1 celery rib, sliced	¼ teaspoon pepper
1 medium carrot, sliced	4 (6-ounce / 170-g) salmon
2 tablespoons lemon juice	fillets
3 fresh thyme sprigs	Lemon wedges

1. Combine the first 11 ingredients in Ninja Foodi pressure cooker; top with salmon. Assemble pressure lid, making sure the pressure release valve is in the Seal position. Select Pressure and set to high (HI). Set time to 3 minutes. Press Start. Quick release pressure by moving the pressure release valve to the Vent position. A thermometer inserted in fish should read at least 145°F (63°C). 2. Serve warm or cold with lemon wedges.

Sea Scallops with Cherry Sauce

Prep time: 5 minutes | Cook time: 2 minutes | Serves 2

¼ cup cherry preserves	1 pound (454 g) fresh sea
1 teaspoon lemon juice	scallops
1 teaspoon tamari	½ teaspoon salt
1 tablespoon unsalted butter	1 cup water

1. In a small bowl, whisk together preserves, lemon juice, and tamari. Set aside. 2. Select Sauté and set to medium (MD). Add butter to pot and heat 30 seconds. Season scallops with salt, add to pot, and sear 30 seconds per side. Transfer to reversible rack. Top scallops with preserve mixture. 3. Add water to the cooker. Assemble pressure lid, making sure the pressure release valve is in the Seal position. 4. Select Pressure and set to high (HI). Set time to 0 minutes. Press Start. Quick release pressure by moving the pressure release valve to the Vent position. 5. Transfer scallops to two plates. Serve warm.

Salmon Cakes

Prep time: 15 minutes | Cook time: 9 minutes | Serves 4

½ pound (227 g) cooked salmon, shredded	1 tablespoon Worcestershire sauce
2 large eggs	½ tablespoon garlic powder
2 medium green onions, sliced	1 teaspoon salt
1 cup bread crumbs	½ teaspoon cayenne pepper
½ cup flat leaf parsley, chopped	¼ teaspoon celery seed
¼ cup soy sauce	4 tablespoons olive oil

1. In a large bowl, combine salmon, eggs, green onions, bread crumbs, parsley, soy sauce, Worcestershire, garlic powder, salt, cayenne, and celery seed. Mix together with clean hands until combined. 2. Add the oil to the Ninja Foodi pressure cooker, select Sauté and set to medium (MD). 3. Take golf ball-sized clumps of salmon mixture. Roll into balls and then flatten to form a cake. Place salmon cakes in an even layer in pot. 4. Let cook 2 minutes until golden brown. Flip and cook an additional 2 minutes. 5. Repeat with remaining salmon mixture. 6. Store salmon cakes under foil until ready to serve.

Butter Cod

Prep time: 10 minutes | Cook time: 7 minutes | Serves 4

4 (5-ounce / 142-g) cod fillets	4 tablespoons unsalted butter,
1 teaspoon salt	divided into 8 pats
½ teaspoon ground black pepper	4 teaspoons capers, drained
1 cup water	

1. Preheat oven to broiler for 500°F (260°C). 2. Pat cod fillets dry with a paper towel. Season with salt and pepper. 3. Add the reversible rack and water to Ninja Foodi pressure cooker. Place fillets on the rack. Assemble pressure lid, making sure the pressure release valve is in the Seal position. 4. Select Pressure and set to high (HI). Set time to 5 minutes. Press Start. Quick release pressure by moving the pressure release valve to the Vent position. 5. Transfer fillets to a baking sheet lined with parchment paper. Add two pats butter to each fillet. Broil fillets 2 minutes until tops are browned. 6. Transfer fish to four plates, garnish with capers, and serve warm.

Seafood Paella

Prep time: 10 minutes | Cook time: 12 minutes | Serves 6

2 cups chopped white fish and scallops
2 cups mussels and shrimp
4 tablespoons olive oil
1 onion, diced
1 red bell pepper, diced
1 green bell pepper, diced
2 cups rice
A few saffron threads
2 cups fish stock
Salt and ground black pepper, to taste

1. Add oil to the Ninja Foodi pressure cooker, select Sauté and set to medium (MD). 2. Add the onion and bell peppers and sauté for 4 minutes. 3. Add the fish, rice, and saffron, stir. Cook for 2 minutes more. 4. Pour in the fish stock and season with salt and pepper, stir. 5. Place the shellfish on top. 6. Assemble pressure lid, making sure the pressure release valve is in the Seal position. Select Pressure and set to high (HI). Set time to 6 minutes. Press Start. 7. Let pressure release naturally for 10 minutes; quick-release any remaining pressure. 8. Stir the dish and let sit for 5 minutes. Serve.

Cajun Fish Cakes

Prep time: 15 minutes | Cook time: 15 minutes | Serves 4
1 pound (454 g) cooked cod, shredded
1½ cups bread crumbs, divided
2 large eggs, lightly beaten
2 tablespoons full-fat sour
cream
2 teaspoons lemon juice
1 tablespoon Cajun seasoning
4 tablespoons olive oil

1. In a large bowl, combine cod, bread crumbs, eggs, sour cream, lemon juice, and Cajun seasoning. Mix together with clean hands until combined. 2. Add oil to the Ninja Foodi pressure cooker, select Sauté and set to medium (MD). 3. Take golf ball-sized clumps of cod mixture. Roll into balls and then flatten to form a cake. Place fish cakes in an even layer in pot. 4. Let cook 2 minutes until golden brown. Flip and cook an additional 2 minutes. 5. Repeat with remaining cod mixture. 6. Store Cajun fish cakes under foil until ready to serve.

Mussels with White Wine

Prep time: 10 minutes | Cook time: 6 minutes | Serves 4

3 pounds (1.4 kg) mussels, cleaned and debearded
6 tablespoons butter
4 shallots, chopped
1 cup white wine
1½ cups chicken stock

1. Add butter to the Ninja Foodi pressure cooker, select Sauté and set to medium (MD). 2. Once the butter has melted, add the shallots and sauté for 2 minutes. 3. Pour in the wine, stir and cook for another 1 minute. 4. Add the stock and mussels, stir well. Assemble pressure lid, making sure the pressure release valve is in the Seal position. 5. Select Pressure and set to high (HI). Set time to 3 minutes. Press Start. 6. Quick release pressure by moving the pressure release valve to the Vent position. 7. Remove mussels and serve.

Tortilla Shrimp Tacos

Prep time: 10 minutes | Cook time: 6 minutes | Serves 4

Spicy Mayo:
3 tablespoons mayonnaise
1 tablespoon Louisiana-style hot pepper sauce
Cilantro-Lime Slaw:
2 cups shredded green cabbage
½ small red onion, thinly sliced
1 small jalapeño, thinly sliced
2 tablespoons chopped fresh cilantro
Juice of 1 lime
¼ teaspoon kosher salt
Shrimp:
1 large egg, beaten
1 cup crushed tortilla chips
24 jumbo shrimp (about 1 pound / 454 g), peeled and deveined
⅛ teaspoon kosher salt
Cooking spray
8 corn tortillas, for serving

1. For the spicy mayo: In a small bowl, mix the mayonnaise and hot pepper sauce. 2. For the cilantro-lime slaw: In a large bowl, toss together the cabbage, onion, jalapeño, cilantro, lime juice, and salt to combine. Cover and refrigerate to chill. 3. For the shrimp: Place the egg in a shallow bowl and the crushed tortilla chips in another. Season the shrimp with the salt. Dip the shrimp in the egg, then in the crumbs, pressing gently to adhere. Place on a work surface and spray both sides with oil. 4. Preheat the pressure cooker to 360°F (182°C). 5. Working in batches, arrange a single layer of the shrimp in the cook & crisp basket. Close crisping lid. Select Air Crisp and set time to 6 minutes, flipping halfway. 6. To serve, place 2 tortillas on each plate and top each with 3 shrimp. Top each taco with ¼ cup slaw, then drizzle with spicy mayo.

Dukkah-Crusted Halibut

Prep time: 15 minutes | Cook time: 17 minutes | Serves 2

Dukkah:
1 tablespoon coriander seeds
1 tablespoon sesame seeds
1½ teaspoons cumin seeds
⅓ cup roasted mixed nuts
¼ teaspoon kosher salt
¼ teaspoon black pepper
Fish:
2 (5-ounce / 142-g) halibut fillets
2 tablespoons mayonnaise
Vegetable oil spray
Lemon wedges, for serving

1. For the dukkah: Preheat the pressure cooker to 400°F (204°C). Combine the coriander, sesame seeds, and cumin in a small baking pan. Place the pan in the cooking pot. Close crisping lid. Select Roast and set time to 5 minutes. Toward the end of the cooking time, you will hear the seeds popping. Transfer to a plate and let cool for 5 minutes. 2. Transfer the toasted seeds to a food processor or spice grinder and add the mixed nuts. Pulse until coarsely chopped. Add the salt and pepper and stir well. 3. For the fish: Spread each fillet with 1 tablespoon of the mayonnaise. Press a heaping tablespoon of the dukkah into the mayonnaise on each fillet, pressing lightly to adhere. 4. Spray the cooking pot with vegetable oil spray. Place the fish in the pot. Close crisping lid. Select Roast and set time to 12 minutes. 5. Serve the fish with lemon wedges.

Simple Buttery Cod

Prep time: 5 minutes | Cook time: 8 minutes | Serves 2

2 (4-ounce / 113-g) cod fillets
2 tablespoons salted butter, melted
1 teaspoon Old Bay seasoning
½ medium lemon, sliced

1. Preheat the pressure cooker to 350ºF (177ºC). Place cod fillets into a round baking dish. Brush each fillet with butter and sprinkle with Old Bay seasoning. Lay two lemon slices on each fillet. Cover the dish with foil and place into the cooking pot. 2. Close crisping lid. Select Bake and set time to 8 minutes, flipping halfway through. When cooked, internal temperature should be at least 145ºF (63ºC). Serve warm.

Tuna with Herbs

Prep time: 20 minutes | Cook time: 17 minutes | Serves 4

1 tablespoon butter, melted
1 medium-sized leek, thinly sliced
1 tablespoon chicken stock
1 tablespoon dry white wine
1 pound (454 g) tuna
½ teaspoon red pepper flakes, crushed
Sea salt and ground black pepper, to taste
½ teaspoon dried rosemary
½ teaspoon dried basil
½ teaspoon dried thyme
2 small ripe tomatoes, puréed
1 cup Parmesan cheese, grated

1. Melt ½ tablespoon of butter in a sauté pan over medium-high heat. Now, cook the leek and garlic until tender and aromatic. Add the stock and wine to deglaze the pan. 2. Preheat the pressure cooker to 370ºF (188ºC). 3. Grease a casserole dish with the remaining ½ tablespoon of melted butter. Place the fish in the casserole dish. Add the seasonings. Top with the sautéed leek mixture. Add the tomato purée. Transfer to the cooking pot. Close crisping lid. Select Bake and set time to 10 minutes. Top with grated Parmesan cheese; bake an additional 7 minutes until the crumbs are golden. Bon appétit!

Blackened Red Snapper

Prep time: 13 minutes | Cook time: 8 to 10 minutes | Serves 4

1½ teaspoons black pepper
¼ teaspoon thyme
¼ teaspoon garlic powder
⅛ teaspoon cayenne pepper
1 teaspoon olive oil
4 (4-ounce / 113-g) red snapper fillet portions, skin on
4 thin slices lemon
Cooking spray

1. Mix the spices and oil together to make a paste. Rub into both sides of the fish. 2. Preheat the pressure cooker to 390ºF (199ºC). Spray cooking pot with nonstick cooking spray and lay snapper steaks in pot, skin-side down. 3. Place a lemon slice on each piece of fish. 4. Close crisping lid. Select Roast and set time to 8 to 10 minutes. The fish will not flake when done, but it should be white through the center.

Crunchy Air Fried Cod Fillets

Prep time: 10 minutes | Cook time: 12 minutes | Serves 2

⅓ cup panko bread crumbs
1 teaspoon vegetable oil
1 small shallot, minced
1 small garlic clove, minced
½ teaspoon minced fresh thyme
Salt and pepper, to taste
1 tablespoon minced fresh parsley
1 tablespoon mayonnaise
1 large egg yolk
¼ teaspoon grated lemon zest, plus lemon wedges for serving
2 (8-ounce / 227-g) skinless cod fillets, 1¼ inches thick
Vegetable oil spray

1. Preheat the pressure cooker to 300ºF (149ºC). 2. Lightly spray the cooking pot with vegetable oil spray. 3. Toss the panko with the oil in a bowl until evenly coated. Stir in the shallot, garlic, thyme, ¼ teaspoon salt, and ⅛ teaspoon pepper. Microwave, stirring frequently, until the panko is light golden brown, about 2 minutes. Transfer to a shallow dish and let cool slightly; stir in the parsley. Whisk the mayonnaise, egg yolk, lemon zest, and ⅛ teaspoon pepper together in another bowl. 4. Pat the cod dry with paper towels and season with salt and pepper. Arrange the fillets, skinned-side down, on plate and brush tops evenly with mayonnaise mixture. Working with 1 fillet at a time, dredge the coated side in panko mixture, pressing gently to adhere. Arrange the fillets, crumb-side up, in the pot, spaced evenly apart. 5. Close crisping lid. Select Bake and set time to 12 to 16 minutes, flipping halfway through. Serve with the lemon wedges.

Salmon Burgers with Creamy Broccoli Slaw

Prep time: 15 minutes | Cook time: 10 minutes | Serves 4

For the salmon burgers
1 pound (454 g) salmon fillets, bones and skin removed
1 egg
¼ cup fresh dill, chopped
1 cup whole wheat bread crumbs
½ teaspoon salt
½ teaspoon cayenne pepper
2 garlic cloves, minced
4 whole wheat buns

For the broccoli slaw
3 cups chopped or shredded broccoli
½ cup shredded carrots
¼ cup sunflower seeds
2 garlic cloves, minced
½ teaspoon salt
2 tablespoons apple cider vinegar
1 cup nonfat plain Greek yogurt

Make the salmon burgers 1. Preheat the pressure cooker to 360ºF(182ºC). 2. In a food processor, pulse the salmon fillets until they are finely chopped. 3. In a large bowl, combine the chopped salmon, egg, dill, bread crumbs, salt, cayenne, and garlic until it comes together. 4. Form the salmon into 4 patties. Place them into thecooking pot, making sure that they don't touch each other. 5. Close crisping lid. Select Bake and set time to 10 minutes, flipping halfway through. Make the broccoli slaw 6. In a large bowl, combine all of the ingredients for the broccoli slaw. Mix well. 7. Serve the salmon burgers on toasted whole wheat buns, and top with a generous portion of broccoli slaw.

Chilean Sea Bass with Olive Relish

Prep time: 10 minutes | Cook time: 10 minutes | Serves 2

Olive oil spray
2 (6-ounce / 170-g) Chilean sea bass fillets or other firm-fleshed white fish
3 tablespoons extra-virgin olive oil
½ teaspoon ground cumin
½ teaspoon kosher salt
½ teaspoon black pepper
⅓ cup pitted green olives, diced
¼ cup finely diced onion
1 teaspoon chopped capers

1. Preheat the pressure cooker to 325°F (163°C). Spray cooking pot with the olive oil spray. Drizzle the fillets with the olive oil and sprinkle with the cumin, salt, and pepper. Place the fish in the pot. Close crisping lid. Select Bake and set time to 10 minutes. 2. Meanwhile, in a small bowl, stir together the olives, onion, and capers. 3. Serve the fish topped with the relish.

Spinach and Feta-Stuffed Tilapia

Prep time: 15 minutes | Cook time: 2 minutes | Serves 4

1 cup water
1 pound (454 g) tilapia fillets
½ teaspoon salt
¼ teaspoon black pepper
1 cup baby spinach, chopped
2 ounces (57 g) crumbled feta cheese
3 cloves garlic, minced

1. Add the reversible rack and water to Ninja Foodi pressure cooker. 2. Season tilapia with salt and pepper. 3. In a small bowl, combine spinach, feta, and garlic. 4. Fill the center of each tilapia fillet with the spinach mixture. Carefully roll up each fillet widthwise and secure with kitchen twine. Place rolled tilapia on the rack, seam-side up. 5. Assemble pressure lid, making sure the pressure release valve is in the Seal position. 6. Select Pressure and set to high (HI). Set time to 2 minutes. Press Start. 7. Quick release pressure by moving the pressure release valve to the Vent position. 8. Cut twine on rolled tilapia and serve with seam-side down so the fish stays rolled.

Halibut Poached in Red Wine with Roasted Peppers

Prep time: 10 minutes | Cook time: 17 minutes | Serves 4

1½ pounds (680 g) full-bodied, fruit-forward red wine
1 jarred roasted red pepper, chopped
½ cup drained canned chickpeas, rinsed
¼ cup pitted black olives
2 medium garlic cloves, peeled
and minced
2 teaspoons fresh oregano leaves, finely chopped
1 (2-inch) cinnamon stick
⅛ teaspoon saffron (optional)
4 (6- to 8-ounce / 170- to 227-g) skinless halibut fillets

1. Mix the wine, red pepper, chickpeas, olives, garlic, oregano, cinnamon stick, and saffron (if using) in Ninja Foodi pressure cooker. Assemble pressure lid, making sure the pressure release valve is in the Seal position. 2. Select Pressure and set to high (HI). Set time to 7 minutes. Press Start. 3. Quick release pressure by moving the pressure release valve to the Vent position. Unlatch the lid and open the cooker. Remove and discard the cinnamon stick. Stir well. 4. Select Sauté, set to medium (MD). 5. Bring the sauce to a simmer, stirring occasionally. Slip the fillets into the sauce and set the cover askew over the pot. Cook until the fish is opaque throughout, 4 to 6 minutes. Serve the fillets in bowls with lots of sauce around them.

Low-Country Boil

Prep time: 10 minutes | Cook time: 5 minutes | Serves 6

1 large sweet onion, peeled and chopped
4 cloves garlic, quartered
6 small red potatoes, cut into sixths
3 ears corn, cut into thirds
1½ pounds (680 g) fully cooked andouille sausage, cut into
1-inch sections
1 pound (454 g) frozen tail-on shrimp
1 tablespoon Old Bay Seasoning
2 cups chicken broth
1 lemon, cut into 6 wedges
½ cup chopped fresh parsley

1. Layer onions in an even layer in the cooking pot. Scatter the garlic on top of onions. Add red potatoes in an even layer, then do the same for the corn and sausage. Add the shrimp and sprinkle with Old Bay Seasoning. Pour in broth. 2. Squeeze lemon wedges into the pot and place squeezed lemon wedges in it. Assemble pressure lid, making sure the pressure release valve is in the Seal position. 3. Select Pressure and set to high (HI). Set time to 5 minutes. Press Start. Quick release pressure by moving the pressure release valve to the Vent position. Transfer ingredients to a serving platter and garnish with parsley.

Mussels in White Wine Sauce

Prep time: 5 minutes | Cook time: 8 minutes | Serves 4 to 6

6 tablespoons (¾ stick) salted butter
4 shallots, minced
9 cloves garlic, minced or pressed
¾ cup dry white wine
3 tablespoons parsley flakes
3 to 5 pounds (1.4 to 2.3 kg)
fresh mussels, rinsed and debearded
1½ cups chicken broth or garlic broth
Juice of 3 lemons
A fresh, crusty baguette, for serving

1. Add butter to the Ninja Foodi pressure cooker, select Sauté and set to high (HI).. Once the butter's melted, add the shallots and cook for about 2 minutes until beginning to brown, then add the garlic and sauté for 1 minute more. 2. Add the wine and stir, scraping up any browned bits from the bottom of the pot. Let simmer 1 to 2 minutes, until slightly thickened. 3. Stir in the parsley and add the mussels and pour the broth and lemon juice over everything. 4. Assemble pressure lid, making sure the pressure release valve is in the Seal position. Select Pressure and set to high (HI). Set time to 3 minutes. Press Start. Quick release pressure by moving the pressure release valve to the Vent position. 5. Serve immediately, sopping up any juices with the crusty baguette.

Catfish Bites with Creamy Slaw

Prep time: 10 minutes | Cook time: 3 minutes | Serves 4

Creamy Slaw:
1 (14-ounce / 397-g) bag coleslaw mix (shredded cabbage and carrots)
½ cup mayonnaise
⅓ cup sour cream
2 teaspoons granulated sugar
2 teaspoons dill pickle juice, from the jar

2 teaspoons Dijon mustard
½ teaspoon salt
¼ teaspoon ground black pepper
Catfish:
1 cup water
2 pounds (907 g) catfish fillets, rinsed and cut into 1-inch pieces
1 teaspoon salt
¼ teaspoon ground black pepper

1. In a small bowl, combine slaw ingredients and refrigerate covered until ready to serve. 2. Add the reversible rack and water to Ninja Foodi pressure cooker. Season catfish with salt and pepper. Place fish on the rack. Assemble pressure lid, making sure the pressure release valve is in the Seal position. 3. Select Pressure and set to high (HI). Set time to 3 minutes. Press Start. Quick release pressure by moving the pressure release valve to the Vent position. 4. Transfer catfish to four plates. Serve warm with chilled slaw.

Lemon Pepper Shrimp

Prep time: 15 minutes | Cook time: 8 minutes | Serves 2

Oil, for spraying
12 ounces (340 g) medium raw shrimp, peeled and deveined
3 tablespoons lemon juice

1 tablespoon olive oil
1 teaspoon lemon pepper
¼ teaspoon paprika
¼ teaspoon granulated garlic

1. Preheat the pressure cooker to 400°F (204°C). Spray cook & crisp basket lightly with oil. 2. In a medium bowl, toss together the shrimp, lemon juice, olive oil, lemon pepper, paprika, and garlic until evenly coated. 3. Place the shrimp in the prepared basket. 4. Close crisping lid. Select Air Crisp and set time to 6 to 8 minutes. Serve immediately.

Teriyaki Salmon Salad

Prep time: 10 minutes | Cook time: 3 to 4 minutes | Serves 2

¼ cup sesame oil
¼ cup soy sauce
¼ cup lime juice
2 tablespoons honey
2 tablespoons fish sauce
1 tablespoon sesame seeds
1 teaspoon grated peeled fresh ginger

1 teaspoon minced garlic
Grated zest of 1 lime
1 scallion, chopped, plus more for serving
2 (4- to 6-ounce / 113- to 170-g) skinless or skin-on salmon fillets
2 teaspoons cornstarch

1. In a gallon-size zip-top bag, combine the sesame oil, soy sauce, lime juice, honey, fish sauce, sesame seeds, ginger, garlic, lime zest, scallion, and salmon. Seal the bag and shake gently. Let the fish marinate in the refrigerator for 1 to 2 hours. 2. Remove the salmon from the marinade and transfer to a plate. Pour the marinade from the bag into the pot. select Sauté and set to medium (MD) and bring to a simmer. 3. Add the salmon to the pot (skin-side up, if using skin-on fillets). Spoon the marinade over the fish. 4. Assemble pressure lid, making sure the pressure release valve is in the Seal position. Select Pressure and set to high (HI). Set time to 4 minutes. Press Start. Quick release pressure by moving the pressure release valve to the Vent position. 5. Use a spatula to gently transfer the fish to a clean plate. Remove the skin if necessary. Transfer 2 teaspoons of the warm teriyaki liquid from the pot to a small bowl. Whisk in the cornstarch, then pour it back into the pot. Select Sauté and let the liquid simmer, stirring frequently, for 8 to 10 minutes, or until reduced to a glaze-like consistency. 6. To serve, toss salad greens with shredded cabbage and carrots, sliced bell pepper, edamame, mandarin orange sections, and slivered almonds and divide between two plates. Top each with a salmon fillet. 7. Brush or spoon the teriyaki sauce over the fish and salad.

Tuna Melt

Prep time: 3 minutes | Cook time: 10 minutes | Serves 1

Oil, for spraying
½ (5-ounce / 142-g) can tuna, drained
1 tablespoon mayonnaise
¼ teaspoon granulated garlic,

plus more for garnish
2 teaspoons unsalted butter
2 slices sandwich bread
2 slices Cheddar cheese

1. Preheat the pressure cooker to 400°F (204°C). Spray cooking pot lightly with oil. 2. In a medium bowl, mix together the tuna, mayonnaise, and garlic. 3. Spread 1 teaspoon of butter on each slice of bread and place one slice butter-side down in the pot. 4. Top with a slice of cheese, the tuna mixture, another slice of cheese, and the other slice of bread, butter-side up. 5. Close crisping lid. Select Roast and set time to for 10 minutes, flipping halfway through. 6. Sprinkle with additional garlic before cutting in half and serving.

Snapper with Shallot and Tomato

Prep time: 20 minutes | Cook time: 15 minutes | Serves 2

2 snapper fillets
1 shallot, peeled and sliced
2 garlic cloves, halved
1 bell pepper, sliced
1 small-sized serrano pepper, sliced
1 tomato, sliced

1 tablespoon olive oil
¼ teaspoon freshly ground black pepper
½ teaspoon paprika
Sea salt, to taste
2 bay leaves

1. Preheat the pressure cooker to 390°F (199°C). Place two parchment sheets on a working surface. Place the fish in the center of one side of the parchment paper. 2. Top with the shallot, garlic, peppers, and tomato. Drizzle olive oil over the fish and vegetables. Season with black pepper, paprika, and salt. Add the bay leaves. 3. Fold over the other half of the parchment. Now, fold the paper around the edges tightly and create a half moon shape, sealing the fish inside. Place into cooking pot. 4. Close crisping lid. Select Roast and set time to 15 minutes. Serve warm.

Tuna-Stuffed Tomatoes

Prep time: 5 minutes | Cook time: 5 minutes | Serves 2

2 medium beefsteak tomatoes, tops removed, seeded, membranes removed
2 (2.6-ounce / 74-g) pouches tuna packed in water, drained
1 medium stalk celery, trimmed and chopped

2 tablespoons mayonnaise
¼ teaspoon salt
¼ teaspoon ground black pepper
2 teaspoons coconut oil
¼ cup shredded mild Cheddar cheese

1. Preheat the pressure cooker to 320ºF (160ºC). 2. Scoop pulp out of each tomato, leaving ½-inch shell. 3. In a medium bowl, mix tuna, celery, mayonnaise, salt, and pepper. Drizzle with coconut oil. Spoon ½ mixture into each tomato and top each with 2 tablespoons Cheddar. 4. Place tomatoes into cooking pot. Close crisping lid. Select Bake and set time to 5 minutes. Cheese will be melted when done. Serve warm.

Tomato-Poached Halibut

Prep time: 15 minutes | Cook time: 5 minutes | Serves 4

1 tablespoon olive oil
2 poblano peppers, finely chopped
1 small onion, finely chopped
1 (14½-ounce / 411-g) can fire-roasted diced tomatoes, undrained
1 (14½-ounce / 411-g) can no-salt-added diced tomatoes, undrained
½ cup water

¼ cup chopped pitted green olives
3 garlic cloves, minced
¼ teaspoon pepper
⅛ teaspoon salt
4 (4-ounce / 113-g) halibut fillets
⅓ cup chopped fresh cilantro
4 lemon wedges
Crusty whole grain bread (optional)

1. Add oil to the Ninja Foodi pressure cooker, select Sauté and set to medium (MD). When oil is hot, cook and stir poblano peppers and onion until crisp-tender, 2 to 3 minutes. Stir in tomatoes, water, olives, garlic, pepper and salt. Top with fillets. 2. Assemble pressure lid, making sure the pressure release valve is in the Seal position. Select Pressure and set to high (HI). Set time to 3 minutes. Press Start. Quick release pressure by moving the pressure release valve to the Vent position. A thermometer inserted in fish should read at least 145ºF (63ºC). 3. Sprinkle with cilantro. Serve with lemon wedges and, if desired, bread.

Crispy Shrimp with Cilantro

Prep time: 40 minutes | Cook time: 10 minutes | Serves 4

1 pound (454 g) raw large shrimp, peeled and deveined with tails on or off
½ cup chopped fresh cilantro
Juice of 1 lime
½ cup all-purpose flour

1 egg
¾ cup bread crumbs
Salt and freshly ground black pepper, to taste
Cooking oil spray
1 cup cocktail sauce

1. Place the shrimp in a resealable plastic bag and add the cilantro and lime juice. Seal the bag. Shake it to combine. Marinate the shrimp in the refrigerator for 30 minutes. 2. Place the flour in a small bowl. 3. In another small bowl, beat the egg. 4. Place the bread crumbs in a third small bowl, season with salt and pepper, and stir to combine. 5. Preheat the pressure cooker to 400ºF (204ºC). 6. Remove the shrimp from the plastic bag. Dip each in the flour, the egg, and the bread crumbs to coat. Gently press the crumbs onto the shrimp. 7. Spray the cook & crisp basket with cooking oil. Place the shrimp in the basket. It is okay to stack them. Spray the shrimp with the cooking oil. 8. Close crisping lid. Select Air Crisp and set time to 8 minutes, flipping halfway through. 9. When the cooking is complete, the shrimp should be crisp. Let cool for 5 minutes. Serve with cocktail sauce.

Salmon with Mayonnaise Sauce

Prep time: 5 minutes | Cook time: 15 minutes | Serves 4 to 6

2 pounds (907 g) salmon fillets
½ cup mayonnaise
1 tablespoon lemon juice
4 cloves garlic, minced

1 teaspoon dry basil leaves
Salt and ground pepper, to taste
2 tablespoons olive oil
Green onion, chopped

1. In a bowl, combine the mayonnaise, lemon juice, garlic, and basil. 2. Season the salmon with salt and pepper. 3. Add oil to the Ninja Foodi pressure cooker, select Sauté and set to medium (MD). 4. Add the fillets and brown on both sides for 10 minutes. 5. Add the mayonnaise mixture to the pot and coat the fillets. 6. Cook for 5 minutes more. Flip the salmon from time to time. 7. Transfer to a serving plate and top with chopped green onion.

Fish Cakes

Prep time: 30 minutes | Cook time: 10 to 12 minutes | Serves 4

¾ cup mashed potatoes (about 1 large russet potato)
12 ounces (340 g) cod or other white fish
Salt and pepper, to taste
Oil for misting or cooking spray

1 large egg
¼ cup potato starch
½ cup panko bread crumbs
1 tablespoon fresh chopped chives
2 tablespoons minced onion

1. Preheat the pressure cooker to 360ºF (182ºC). Peel potatoes, cut into cubes, and cook on stovetop till soft. 2. Salt and pepper raw fish to taste. Mist with oil or cooking spray, and place into cooking pot. Close crisping lid. Select Bake and set time to for 6 to 8 minutes. 3. Transfer fish to a plate and break apart to cool. 4. Beat egg in a shallow dish. 5. Place potato starch in another shallow dish, and panko crumbs in a third dish. 6. When potatoes are done, drain in colander and rinse with cold water. 7. In a large bowl, mash the potatoes and stir in the chives and onion. Add salt and pepper to taste, then stir in the fish. 8. If needed, stir in a tablespoon of the beaten egg to help bind the mixture. 9. Shape into 8 small, fat patties. Dust lightly with potato starch, dip in egg, and roll in panko crumbs. Spray both sides with oil or cooking spray. Transfer to cooking pot and bake for 10 to 12 minutes more, until golden brown and crispy.

Breaded Shrimp Tacos

Prep time: 10 minutes | Cook time: 9 minutes | Makes 8 tacos

2 large eggs
1 teaspoon prepared yellow mustard
1 pound (454 g) small shrimp, peeled, deveined, and tails removed
½ cup finely shredded Gouda or Parmesan cheese

½ cup pork dust
For Serving:
8 large Boston lettuce leaves
¼ cup pico de gallo
¼ cup shredded purple cabbage
1 lemon, sliced
Guacamole (optional)

1. Preheat the pressure cooker to 400ºF (204ºC). 2. Crack the eggs into a large bowl, add the mustard, and whisk until well combined. Add the shrimp and stir well to coat. 3. In a medium-sized bowl, mix together the cheese and pork dust until well combined. 4. One at a time, roll the coated shrimp in the pork dust mixture and use your hands to press it onto each shrimp. Spray the coated shrimp with avocado oil and place them in the cook & crisp basket, leaving space between them. 5. Close crisping lid. Select Air Crisp and set time to 9 minutes, flipping after 4 minutes. 6. To serve, place a lettuce leaf on a serving plate, place several shrimp on top, and top with 1½ teaspoons each of pico de gallo and purple cabbage. Squeeze some lemon juice on top and serve with guacamole, if desired.

Lemon-Pepper Trout

Prep time: 5 minutes | Cook time: 15 minutes | Serves 4

4 trout fillets
2 tablespoons olive oil
½ teaspoon salt
1 teaspoon black pepper

2 garlic cloves, sliced
1 lemon, sliced, plus additional wedges for serving

1. Preheat the pressure cooker to 380°F(193ºC). 2. Brush each fillet with olive oil on both sides and season with salt and pepper. Place the fillets in an even layer in the cooking pot. 3. Place the sliced garlic over the tops of the trout fillets, then top the garlic with lemon slices. Close crisping lid. Select Roast and set time to 12 to 15 minutes, or until it has reached an internal temperature of 145°F(63ºC). 4. Serve with fresh lemon wedges.

Trout in Herb Sauce

Prep time: 5 minutes | Cook time: 5 minutes | Serves 4

Trout:
4 (½-pound / 227-g) fresh river trout
1 teaspoon sea salt
4 cups torn lettuce leaves, divided
1 teaspoon white wine vinegar
½ cup water
Herb Sauce:

½ cup minced fresh flat-leaf parsley
2 teaspoons Italian seasoning
1 small shallot, peeled and minced
2 tablespoons mayonnaise
½ teaspoon fresh lemon juice
¼ teaspoon sugar
Pinch of salt

2 tablespoons sliced almonds, toasted

1. For Trout: Rinse the trout inside and out; pat dry. Sprinkle with salt inside and out. Put 3 cups lettuce leaves in the pot. Arrange the trout over the top of the lettuce and top fish with the remaining lettuce. 2. Pour vinegar and water into pot. Assemble pressure lid, making sure the pressure release valve is in the Seal position. 3. Select Pressure and set to high (HI). Set time to 3 minutes. Press Start. Let pressure release naturally for 3 minutes; quick-release any remaining pressure. 4. Transfer fish to a serving plate. Peel and discard the skin from the fish. Remove and discard the heads if desired. 5. For Herb Sauce: In a small bowl, mix together the parsley, Italian seasoning, shallot, mayonnaise, lemon juice, sugar, and salt. Evenly divide among the fish, spreading it over them. Sprinkle toasted almonds over the top of the sauce. Serve.

Crab Cakes with Bell Peppers

Prep time: 5 minutes | Cook time: 10 minutes | Serves 4

8 ounces (227 g) jumbo lump crab meat
1 egg, beaten
Juice of ½ lemon
⅓ cup bread crumbs
¼ cup diced green bell pepper

¼ cup diced red bell pepper
¼ cup mayonnaise
1 tablespoon Old Bay seasoning
1 teaspoon flour
Cooking spray

1. Preheat the pressure cooker to 375ºF (190ºC). 2. Make the crab cakes: Place all the ingredients except the flour and oil in a large bowl and stir until well incorporated. 3. Divide the crab mixture into four equal portions and shape each portion into a patty with your hands. Top each patty with a sprinkle of ¼ teaspoon of flour. 4. Arrange the crab cakes in the cooking pot and spritz them with cooking spray. 5. Close crisping lid. Select Bake and set time to 10 minutes, flipping halfway through. 6. Divide the crab cakes among four plates and serve.

Lemony Salmon

Prep time: 30 minutes | Cook time: 10 minutes | Serves 4

1½ pounds (680 g) salmon steak
½ teaspoon grated lemon zest
Freshly cracked mixed peppercorns, to taste
⅓ cup lemon juice
Fresh chopped chives, for

garnish
½ cup dry white wine
½ teaspoon fresh cilantro, chopped
Fine sea salt, to taste

1. To prepare the marinade, place all ingredients, except for salmon steak and chives, in a deep pan. Bring to a boil over medium-high flame until it has reduced by half. Allow it to cool down. 2. After that, allow salmon steak to marinate in the refrigerator approximately 40 minutes. 3. Preheat the pressure cooker to 400ºF (204ºC). Discard the marinade and transfer the fish steak to the cooking pot. 4. Close crisping lid. Select Roast and set time to 9 to 10 minutes. To finish, brush hot fish steaks with the reserved marinade, garnish with fresh chopped chives, and serve right away!

Tuna Patties with Spicy Sriracha Sauce

Prep time: 10 minutes | Cook time: 10 minutes | Serves 4

2 (6-ounce / 170-g) cans tuna packed in oil, drained
3 tablespoons almond flour
2 tablespoons mayonnaise
1 teaspoon dried dill
½ teaspoon onion powder
Pinch of salt and pepper
Spicy Sriracha Sauce:
¼ cup mayonnaise
1 tablespoon Sriracha sauce
1 teaspoon garlic powder

1. Preheat the pressure cooker to 380ºF (193ºC). 2. In a large bowl, combine the tuna, almond flour, mayonnaise, dill, and onion powder. Season to taste with salt and freshly ground black pepper. Use a fork to stir, mashing with the back of the fork as necessary, until thoroughly combined. 3. Use an ice cream scoop to form the tuna mixture patties. Place the patties in a single layer in cooking pot. Press lightly with the bottom of the scoop to flatten into a circle about ½ inch thick. Close crisping lid. Select Bake and set time to 10 minutes, turning halfway through. 4. To make the Sriracha sauce: In a small bowl, combine the mayonnaise, Sriracha, and garlic powder. Serve the tuna patties topped with the Sriracha sauce.

Fish Curry

Prep time: 15 minutes | Cook time: 10 minutes | Serves 4

1½ pounds (680 g) fish fillets, cut into 2-inch pieces
2 tablespoons olive oil
4 cloves garlic, minced
2 medium onions, chopped
2 teaspoons fresh ginger, grated finely
½ teaspoon ground turmeric
1 teaspoon red chili powder
2 teaspoons ground cumin
2 teaspoons ground coriander
2 tablespoons curry powder
2 cups unsweetened coconut milk
1 cup tomatoes, chopped
2 Serrano peppers, seeded and chopped
Salt, to taste
1 tablespoon fresh lemon juice

1. Select Sauté, set to medium (MD), and heat the oil. 2. Add the garlic, onion, and ginger and sauté for 4 minutes. 3. Add the turmeric, chili powder, cumin, coriander, and curry. Stir and cook for 1 minute more. 4. Pour in the coconut milk and stir well. 5. Add the fish, tomatoes, and Serrano pepper, stir. Season with salt. 6. Assemble pressure lid, making sure the pressure release valve is in the Seal position. Select Pressure and set to low (LO). Set time to 5 minutes. Press Start. 7. Let pressure release naturally for 10 minutes; quick-release any remaining pressure. Open the lid. 8. Drizzle the dish with the lemon juice and serve.

Roasted Fish with Almond-Lemon Crumbs

Prep time: 10 minutes | Cook time: 7 to 8 minutes | Serves 4

½ cup raw whole almonds
1 scallion, finely chopped
Grated zest and juice of 1 lemon
½ tablespoon extra-virgin olive oil
¾ teaspoon kosher salt, divided
Freshly ground black pepper, to taste
4 (6 ounces / 170 g each) skinless fish fillets
Cooking spray
1 teaspoon Dijon mustard

1. In a food processor, pulse the almonds to coarsely chop. Transfer to a small bowl and add the scallion, lemon zest, and olive oil. Season with ¼ teaspoon of the salt and pepper to taste and mix to combine. 2. Spray the top of the fish with oil and squeeze the lemon juice over the fish. Season with the remaining ½ teaspoon salt and pepper to taste. Spread the mustard on top of the fish. Dividing evenly, press the almond mixture onto the top of the fillets to adhere. 3. Preheat the pressure cooker to 375ºF (191ºC). 4. Working in batches, place the fillets in the cooking pot in a single layer. Close crisping lid. Select Roast and set time to 7 to 8 minutes. 5. Serve immediately.

Mini Tuna Casseroles

Prep time: 15 minutes | Cook time: 15 minutes | Serves 6

1 cup water
1 (12-ounce / 340-g) can tuna, drained and flaked
1 (10½-ounce / 298-g) can cream of mushroom soup
½ pound (227 g) small shell pasta, cooked
1 cup shredded Cheddar cheese, divided
¾ cup frozen peas, thawed
¾ teaspoon salt
½ teaspoon garlic powder
½ teaspoon black pepper
24 potato chips

1. Add the reversible rack and water to Ninja Foodi pressure cooker. 2. In a large bowl, combine tuna, cream of mushroom soup, pasta, ½ cup Cheddar, peas, salt, garlic powder, and pepper. Mix. 3. Spray six ramekins with cooking spray. 4. Evenly divide tuna mixture into each ramekin and top with remaining cheese. Cover each ramekin tightly with foil and place on top of rack, stacked two by two. 5. Assemble pressure lid, making sure the pressure release valve is in the Seal position. 6. Select Pressure and set to high (HI). Set time to 15 minutes. Press Start. 7. Quick release pressure by moving the pressure release valve to the Vent position. 8. Carefully remove ramekins from the cooker and remove foil. 9. Sprinkle four crushed-up potato chips over each casserole before serving.

Spicy Buttery Shrimp

Prep time: 20 minutes | Cook time: 12 minutes | Serves 6 to 8

3 cups chicken broth
1 cup beer, preferably an amber ale
½ cup (1 stick) butter, cut into chunks
⅓ cup tomato paste
6 medium garlic cloves, peeled and minced
2 teaspoons dried thyme
1 teaspoon dried oregano

1 teaspoon fennel seeds
1 teaspoon red pepper flakes
½ teaspoon table salt
½ teaspoon celery seeds (optional)
3 pounds (1.4 kg) large shrimp, peeled and deveined
Crunchy bread, for serving

1. Stir the broth, beer, butter, tomato paste, garlic, thyme, oregano, fennel seeds, red pepper flakes, salt, and celery seed (if using) in cooking pot. Assemble pressure lid, making sure the pressure release valve is in the Seal position. 2. Select Pressure and set to high (HI). Set time to 7 minutes. Press Start. 3. Quick release pressure by moving the pressure release valve to the Vent position. Unlatch the lid and open the pot. 4. select Sauté and set to medium (MD). 5. Stir the sauce as it comes to a simmer. Add the shrimp, stir well, and set the lid askew over the pot. Cook until the shrimp are pink and firm, about 2 minutes. Pour the contents of the insert into a large serving bowl and serve with the crunchy bread to sop up the sauce.

Chapter 5 Pasta

Beef and Bow-Ties in Spicy Tomato-Almond Sauce

Prep time: 15 minutes | Cook time: 17 minutes | Serves 4

2 tablespoons vegetable, corn, or canola oil
1 small red onion, halved and sliced into thin half-moons
1 tablespoon minced peeled fresh ginger
1 pound (454 g) ground beef
1 (14-ounce / 397-g) can diced tomatoes
6 tablespoons almond butter
2 tablespoons honey

2 teaspoons mild paprika
1 teaspoon ground cinnamon
1 teaspoon ground cloves
1 teaspoon ground coriander
1 teaspoon ground cumin
1 teaspoon table salt
½ teaspoon cayenne
2¼ cups chicken broth
8 ounces (227 g) dried bow-tie or farfalle pasta

1. Add oil to the Ninja Foodi pressure cooker, select Sauté and set to medium (MD).2. Add the onion and ginger; cook, stirring often, until the onion begins to soften, about 3 minutes. Crumble in the ground beef; continue cooking, stirring frequently to break up any clumps, until the meat loses its raw, pink color, about 3 minutes. 3. Stir in the tomatoes and almond butter until the almond butter dissolves in the sauce, all the while scraping up every speck of browned stuff on the pot's bottom. Stir in the honey, paprika, cinnamon, cloves, coriander, cumin, salt, and cayenne until uniform. Turn off the Sauté function; stir in the broth and pasta. Assemble pressure lid, making sure the pressure release valve is in the Seal position. 4. Select Pressure and set to high (HI). Set time to 7 minutes. Press Start. 5. Quick release pressure by moving the pressure release valve to the Vent position. Stir well before serving.

Seafood Newburg Casserole

Prep time: 10 minutes | Cook time: 14 minutes | Serves 6

2½ cups chicken broth
½ cup dry sherry
2 tablespoons butter
1 tablespoon fresh minced tarragon leaves
½ teaspoon mild paprika
¼ teaspoon table salt
12 ounces (340 g) wide egg or

no-yolk noodles
¾ cup heavy cream
1 large egg yolk
½ pound (227 g) sea scallops, quartered
½ pound (227 g) small shrimp, peeled, deveined, and cut in half lengthwise

1. Select Sauté and set to medium (MD).2. Mix the broth, sherry, butter, tarragon, paprika, and salt in the pot. Cook until the butter melts, stirring occasionally, about 3 minutes. Stir in the noodles until coated. Assemble pressure lid, making sure the pressure release valve is in the Seal position. 3. Select Pressure and set to high (HI). Set time to 4 minutes. Press Start. 4. Quick release pressure by moving the pressure release valve to the Vent position.

Unlatch the lid and open the pot. 5. Select Sauté and set to low (LO). 6. Whisk the cream and egg yolk in a small bowl. Whisk about 1 cup of the hot mixture from the pot into this cream mixture, then stir this combined mixture back into the pot along with the scallops and shrimp. 7. Cook, stirring constantly, just until the shrimp are firm, not more than 2 minutes. Remove the hot insert from the pot to stop the cooking, and continue stirring until any bubbling stops and the noodles are well coated.

Seafood Pasta

Prep time: 10 minutes | Cook time: 14 minutes | Serves 4 to 6

1 tablespoon olive oil
1 medium onion, chopped
2 cloves garlic, chopped
2 tomatoes, chopped
1 red bell pepper, chopped
½ cup dry white wine
2 cups vegetable stock

2 cups macaroni
1½ cups frozen mixed seafood
1 teaspoon mixed herbs
1 tablespoon tomato purée
½ teaspoon salt
½ teaspoon ground black pepper
½ cup Parmesan cheese, grated

1. Add oil to the Ninja Foodi pressure cooker, select Sauté and set to medium (MD). 2. Add the onion and garlic and sauté for 2 minutes. 3. Add the tomatoes and bell pepper and cook for 2 minutes more. 4. Pour in the wine and stir well. Simmer for 5 minutes. 5. Add the stock, macaroni, seafood, herbs, and tomato purée. Season with salt and pepper. Stir well to combine. 6. Assemble pressure lid, making sure the pressure release valve is in the Seal position. Select Pressure and set to high (HI). Set time to 5 minutes. Press Start. 7. Quick release pressure by moving the pressure release valve to the Vent position. 8. Top with cheese and serve.

Cheesy Pesto Gnocchi Casserole

Prep time: 10 minutes | Cook time: 1 minute | Serves 4

1 (14½-ounce / 411-g) bag frozen gnocchi
1 cup diced smoked deli ham
1 cup chicken broth
½ cup evaporated milk
1 (4-ounce / 113-g) jar diced

pimientos, drained
3 tablespoons purchased pesto
4 ounces (113 g) shredded Swiss cheese
¼ cup heavy cream

1. Mix the gnocchi, ham, broth, evaporated milk, pimientos, and pesto in Ninja Foodi pressure cooker. Assemble pressure lid, making sure the pressure release valve is in the Seal position. 2. Select Pressure and set to high (HI). Set time to 1 minute. Press Start. 3. Let pressure release naturally for 1 minute; quick-release any remaining pressure. Unlatch the lid and open the cooker. Stir the cheese and cream into the casserole. Set the lid askew over the pot for 5 minutes to melt the cheese.

Spaghetti Puttanesca

Prep time: 10 minutes | Cook time: 20 minutes | Serves 4 to 6

3 tablespoons extra-virgin olive oil, divided
4 medium garlic cloves, finely chopped
1 teaspoon red pepper flakes
1 cup pitted Kalamata olives, roughly chopped
½ cup drained capers
1 (28-ounce / 794-g) can whole peeled tomatoes, drained (1 cup juices reserved) , and crushed
1 pound (454 g) spaghetti, broken in half
½ cup chopped fresh basil
1 ounce (28 g) Parmesan cheese, finely grated
Kosher salt and ground black pepper

1. Select Sauté and set to high (HI). Add 2 tablespoons of oil, the garlic and pepper flakes, then cook, stirring, until fragrant, about 30 seconds. Add the olives and capers, then cook, stirring, until the capers begin to brown, about 1 minute. 2. Add the tomatoes and cook, stirring occasionally, until most of the liquid has evaporated, about 8 minutes. Stir in the reserved tomato juices and 4 cups water, then distribute the mixture in an even layer. Add the pasta, placing the strands horizontally so they lay flat, then press them into the liquid until submerged. 3. Assemble pressure lid, making sure the pressure release valve is in the Seal position. Select Pressure and set to high (HI). Set time to 3 minutes. Press Start. Quick release pressure by moving the pressure release valve to the Vent position. 4. Select Sauté and set to high (HI). Stir the mixture to combine, then cook until the pasta is al dente and most of the liquid has been absorbed, 3 to 4 minutes. 5. Using potholders, carefully remove the insert from the housing. Let stand for 5 minutes. 6. Stir in the basil, Parmesan and the remaining 1 tablespoon oil. Taste and season with salt and black pepper.

Thai-Inspired Chicken and Rice Noodles

Prep time: 15 minutes | Cook time: 14 minutes | Serves 4

1 tablespoon peanut oil
2½ cups frozen sliced bell pepper strips
4 medium shallots, halved and thinly sliced lengthwise
2 pounds (907 g) unseasoned chicken breast, cut for stir-fry, any flavoring packets discarded
3 medium garlic cloves, peeled and minced
1¼ cups chicken broth
¼ cup fresh lime juice
¼ cup fish sauce
¼ cup packed light brown sugar
2 tablespoons sambal oelek
1 tablespoon tomato paste
8 ounces (227 g) dried rice stick noodles or rice noodles for pad Thai
½ cup loosely packed fresh basil leaves, roughly chopped
¼ cup chopped unsalted peanuts
Lime wedges, for garnish

1. Add oil to the Ninja Foodi pressure cooker, select Sauté and set to medium (MD). 2. Add the bell peppers and shallots. Cook, stirring often, until the shallot softens, about 4 minutes. Add the chicken and garlic. Cook, stirring frequently, until the chicken loses its raw, pink color, about 3 minutes. 3. Stir in the broth, turn off the Sauté function, and scrape up every speck of browned stuff on the pot's bottom. Stir in the lime juice, fish sauce, brown sugar, sambal oelek, and tomato paste until the brown sugar and tomato paste dissolve and the mixture is uniform in color. Stir in the rice noodles, basil, and peanuts. Assemble pressure lid, making sure the pressure release valve is in the Seal position. 4. Select Pressure and set to high (HI). Set time to 4 minutes. Press Start. 5. Quick release pressure by moving the pressure release valve to the Vent position. Unlatch the lid and open the cooker. Stir well and serve with lime wedges to squeeze over each portion.

Cheesy Chili Mac

Prep time: 10 minutes | Cook time: 17 minutes | Serves 6
2 tablespoons olive oil
1 medium yellow onion, chopped
2 (4½-ounce / 128-g) cans mild or hot chopped green chiles
1 medium garlic clove, peeled and minced
1½ pounds (680 g) lean ground beef
¼ cup standard chile powder
2 teaspoons ground cumin
½ teaspoon table salt
2 cups beef or chicken broth
1 (28-ounce / 794-g) can crushed tomatoes
1 (15-ounce / 425-g) can pink beans, drained and rinsed
8 ounces (227 g) dried ziti
4 ounces (113 g) shredded Cheddar

1. Add oil to the Ninja Foodi pressure cooker, select Sauté and set to medium (MD). 2. Add the onion and cook, stirring often, until it begins to soften, about 2 minutes. Add the chiles and garlic. Continue cooking, stirring once in a while, until the liquid has mostly evaporated, about 2 minutes. 3. Crumble in the ground beef. Cook, stirring often to break up any clumps, until the meat loses its raw, pink color, about 2 minutes. Stir in the chile powder, cumin, and salt until fragrant, just a couple of seconds. 4. Stir in the broth and scrape up every speck of browned stuff on the bottom of the pot. Turn off the Sauté function. Stir in the tomatoes, beans, and ziti until the pasta is coated. Assemble pressure lid, making sure the pressure release valve is in the Seal position. 5. Select Pressure and set to high (HI). Set time to 7 minutes. Press Start. 6. Quick release pressure by moving the pressure release valve to the Vent position. Unlatch the lid and open the pot. Stir in the cheese. Set the lid askew over the pot for 5 minutes to melt the cheese and mellow the flavors. Stir again before serving.

Lemon Herbed Pasta

Prep time: 5 minutes | Cook time: 4 minutes | Serves 4

12 ounces (340 g) gluten-free fusilli pasta
5 cups water
2 tablespoons unsalted butter
2 tablespoons Parmesan cheese
2 tablespoons lemon juice
1 tablespoon lemon zest
½ teaspoon salt
¼ cup chopped fresh parsley

1. Add pasta and water to the Ninja Foodi pressure cooker. Assemble pressure lid, making sure the pressure release valve is in the Seal position. 2. Select Pressure and set to high (HI). Set time to 4 minutes. Press Start. Let pressure release naturally for 3 minutes; quick-release any remaining pressure. Drain pasta and set aside. 3. Add remaining ingredients to pasta and toss until blended. Serve warm.

No-Layer Lasagna Casserole

Prep time: 10 minutes | Cook time: 17 minutes | Serves 2 to 4

1 tablespoon olive oil
1 pound (454 g) lean ground beef
2 medium garlic cloves, peeled and minced
2 teaspoons dried oregano
1 teaspoon fennel seeds
1 teaspoon dried thyme
½ teaspoon red pepper flakes
½ teaspoon table salt
1 (28-ounce / 794-g) can diced tomatoes
2 cups beef or chicken broth
8 ounces (227 g) dried lasagna noodles, broken into 2- to 3-inch pieces to fit into the cooker
8 ounces (227 g) shredded mozzarella

1. Add oil to the Ninja Foodi pressure cooker, select Sauté and set to medium (MD).2. Crumble in the ground beef and cook, stirring occasionally to break up the clumps, until lightly browned, about 6 minutes. 3. Stir in the garlic, oregano, fennel seeds, thyme, red pepper flakes, and salt until aromatic, a few seconds. Pour in the tomatoes and broth; scrape up every speck of browned stuff on the pot's bottom. Turn off the Sauté function. Stir in the broken lasagna noodles. Assemble pressure lid, making sure the pressure release valve is in the Seal position. 4. Select Pressure and set to high (HI). Set time to 7 minutes. Press Start. 5. Quick release pressure by moving the pressure release valve to the Vent position. Unlatch the lid and open the pot. Sprinkle the mozzarella over the casserole, then stir gently. Set the lid askew over the top of the pot for 5 minutes to melt the cheese and blend the flavors.

Speedy Penne Arrabbiata with Sheet Pan Meatballs

Prep time: 20 minutes | Cook time: 56 minutes | Serves 4 to 6

Meatballs:
¾ cup dried small red beans
1½ teaspoons fine sea salt
3 tablespoons extra-virgin olive oil
3 cloves garlic, minced
1 small yellow onion, finely chopped
4 ounces (113 g) cremini or button mushrooms, finely chopped
1 tablespoon tomato paste
1 tablespoon soy sauce, tamari, or coconut aminos
1 teaspoon Italian seasoning
2 cups low-sodium vegetable broth
¾ cup medium- or long-grain brown rice
1 large carrot, finely shredded
(use a coarse Microplane)
¾ cup panko bread crumbs
½ cup walnut halves and pieces, toasted and chopped
¼ teaspoon freshly ground black pepper
Arrabbiata Sauce:
¼ cup extra-virgin olive oil
2 cloves garlic, minced
1 (28-ounce / 794-g) can whole San Marzano tomatoes
4 pickled hot chile peppers or pepperoncini, minced
2 teaspoons Italian seasoning
1 teaspoon fine sea salt
½ teaspoon red pepper flakes
1 pound (454 g) penne pasta
3½ cups water
¼ cup chopped fresh flat-leaf parsley

Make the Meatballs: 1. In a bowl, combine the red beans with 3 cups water and 1 teaspoon of the salt. Soak for 10 to 12 hours, then drain in a colander. 2. Select Sauté, set to medium (MD), add the oil and garlic, and heat for 2 minutes, until the garlic is bubbling but not yet browned. Add the onion and sauté for 5 minutes, until the onion softens and the garlic turns golden brown. Add the mushrooms and sauté for 3 minutes more, until they are wilted and giving up their liquid. Add the tomato paste, soy sauce, and Italian seasoning, and sauté for 1 minute more. 3. Stir in the broth, beans, and rice, using a wooden spoon to nudge loose any browned bits from the bottom of the pot. Scrape down any grains of rice stuck to the sides of the pot, making sure the rice and beans are fully submerged in the broth. 4.Assemble pressure lid, making sure the pressure release valve is in the Seal position. Select Pressure and set to high (HI). Set time to 25 minutes. 5. Let pressure release naturally for 10 minutes; quick-release any remaining pressure. Open the pot and, wearing heat-resistant mitts, lift out the inner pot. Add the carrot, bread crumbs, walnuts, remaining ½ teaspoon salt, and pepper, and stir to combine. Let the mixture stand for 10 minutes to firm up and cool down a bit. 6. While the meatball mixture is cooling, preheat the oven to 375ºF (190ºC). Line a baking sheet with parchment paper or a silicone mat and grease it lightly with olive oil or nonstick cooking spray. 7. Use a small cookie scoop to portion the meatball mixture out onto the baking sheet. Bake the meatballs for 20 minutes, until they are lightly browned and crispy on the outside. Make the Sauce: 8. While the meatballs are baking, press the Cancel button to reset the cooking program. Then select the Sauté setting, add the oil and garlic, and heat for about 3 minutes, until the garlic turns golden but is not browned. Add the tomatoes and their liquid, crushing the tomatoes with your hands as you add them to the pot. 9. Stir in the chile peppers, Italian seasoning, salt, and red pepper flakes. Let the sauce cook for 10 minutes more, stirring occasionally. At this point, you can use the sauce as is, store it in the fridge for up to 1 week, freeze for up to 6 months, or add pasta and water for a one-pot dish. Make the One-Pot Dish: 10. Add the pasta and water to the sauce and stir well. Assemble pressure lid, making sure the pressure release valve is in the Seal position. Select Pressure and set to high (HI). Set time to 5 minutes. 11. Let pressure release naturally for 5 minutes; quick-release any remaining pressure. Open the pot and give the pasta and sauce a good stir. Spoon the pasta into bowls, top with the meatballs, sprinkle with parsley, and serve.

Red Curry Noodles

Prep time: 5 minutes | Cook time: 1 minute | Serves 4

2 cups water
1 (13½-ounce / 383-g) can coconut milk
¼ cup red curry paste
1 tablespoon freshly squeezed lime juice
1 tablespoon tamari or soy sauce
1 to 2 teaspoons toasted sesame oil
8 ounces (227 g) thick ramen noodles or wide brown rice noodles

1. In cooking pot, combine the water, coconut milk, curry paste, lime juice, tamari, and sesame oil. Add the noodles, breaking them into shorter strands if they're too long to lie flat on the bottom. Assemble pressure lid, making sure the pressure release valve is in the Seal position. Select Pressure and set to high (HI). Set time to 1 minute. Press Start. 2. Quick release pressure by moving the pressure release valve to the Vent position. 3. Once all the pressure has released, remove the lid. Toss everything together, breaking up any noodles that may have stuck together, and serve.

Linguine with White Clam Sauce

Prep time: 5 minutes | Cook time: 11 minutes | Serves 4 to 6

¼ cup extra-virgin olive oil
4 tablespoons (½ stick) salted butter
1 large shallot, minced
3 cloves garlic, minced or pressed
¼ cup dry white wine
2½ cups clam broth or chicken broth
Juice of ½ lemon
3 (6½-ounce / 184-g) cans

chopped clams in their juices, clams strained and juices reserved
1½ teaspoons dried sweet basil
1½ teaspoons dried oregano
1 teaspoon Old Bay seasoning
½ teaspoon black pepper
1 pound (454 g) linguine
½ cup grated Parmesan cheese, plus more for topping

1. Add oil and Melt butter in the Ninja Foodi pressure cooker, select Sauté and set to high (HI). 2. Add the shallot and sauté for 2 minutes, stirring, then add the garlic and sauté for 1 more minute. Add the white wine and let simmer for 1 minute longer. 3. Add the broth, lemon juice, clam juice (but not the clams), basil, oregano, Old Bay, and pepper and stir. 4. Break the linguine in half and just lay it on top but do not stir, just use a spoon to submerge it gently in the liquid (it's okay if some pieces stick up above the surface). 5. Assemble pressure lid, making sure the pressure release valve is in the Seal position. Select Pressure and set to high (HI). Set time to 6 minutes. Quick release pressure by moving the pressure release valve to the Vent position. 6. After removing the lid, don't worry if it looks a bit soupy as that will change! Stir in the clams and the Parmesan and let sit for about 5 minutes, stirring occasionally, until the clams are heated and the sauce has thickened. 7. Serve sprinkled with extra Parmesan cheese, if desired.

Creamy Mushroom Noodle Casserole

Prep time: 10 minutes | Cook time: 19 minutes | Serves 4 to 6

1 pound (454 g) white button mushrooms, thinly sliced
2 (12-ounce / 340-g) cans regular or low-fat evaporated milk
3 cups vegetable or chicken broth
1 teaspoon dried sage

½ teaspoon dried thyme
¼ teaspoon table salt
¼ teaspoon ground black pepper
12 ounces (340 g) wide egg or no-yolk noodles
¼ cup heavy cream
1 tablespoon cornstarch

1. Melt butter to the Ninja Foodi pressure cooker, select Sauté and set to medium (MD). 2. Add the mushrooms and cook, stirring often, until they give off some liquid and start to soften, about 5 minutes. 3. Stir in the evaporated milk, broth, sage, thyme, salt, and pepper until uniform. Turn off the Sauté function. Stir in the noodles. Not every noodle can be submerged; however, they should all be coated. Assemble pressure lid, making sure the pressure release valve is in the Seal position. 4. Select Pressure and set to high (HI). Set time to 4 minutes. Press Start. 5. Quick release pressure by moving the pressure release valve to the Vent position. Unlatch the lid and open the pot. 6. Select Sauté and set to medium (MD). 7. Whisk the cream and cornstarch into a small bowl until the cornstarch dissolves. Stir this slurry into the pot. Cook, stirring

constantly, until the sauce thickens considerably, 1 or 2 minutes. Turn off the Sauté function; remove the hot insert from the cooker to stop the cooking. Stir several more times, then serve warm.

Tuna Penne Noodle Casserole

Prep time: 10 minutes | Cook time: 10 minutes | Serves 4

12 ounces (340 g) gluten-free penne pasta
5 cups water
3 tablespoons unsalted butter
½ cup peeled and diced yellow onion
1 stalk celery, diced
1 cup canned sweet peas,

drained
1 (6-ounce / 170-g) can tuna, drained
1 (10½-ounce / 298-g) can condensed cream of mushroom soup
⅔ cup whole milk
¼ cup Parmesan cheese

1. Add pasta and water to the cooking pot. Assemble pressure lid, making sure the pressure release valve is in the Seal position. 2. Select Pressure and set to high (HI). Set time to 4 minutes. Press Start. Let pressure release naturally for 3 minutes; quick-release any remaining pressure. Drain pasta and set aside. 3. Select Sauté and set to medium (MD). Add butter, onion, and celery to pot and cook 5 minutes until onions are translucent. 4. Add remaining ingredients to pot and stir for 1 minute. Add pasta to pot. Stir until well combined. 5. Transfer mixture to a serving dish and serve warm.

Three-Cheese Pasta with Basil and Black Pepper

Prep time: 10 minutes | Cook time: 15 minutes | Serves 4 to 6

8 ounces (227 g) Asiago cheese, shredded
8 ounces (227 g) Fontina cheese, shredded
1½ teaspoons cornstarch
1 pound (454 g) cavatappi pasta
2 tablespoons salted butter, cut

into 2 pieces
½ cup heavy cream
½ cup finely chopped fresh basil
Ground black pepper
½ ounce (14 g) Parmesan cheese, finely grated

1. In a large bowl, toss together the Asiago, Fontina and cornstarch; set aside. In cooking pot, combine 5 cups water, the pasta and butter; stir to combine, then distribute in an even layer. 2. Assemble pressure lid, making sure the pressure release valve is in the Seal position. Select Pressure and set to high (HI). Set time to 3 minutes. Press Start. 3. Quick release pressure by moving the pressure release valve to the Vent position. 4. Select Sauté, set to medium (MD), and add the cream and bring to a simmer. One handful at a time, stir in the cheese mixture; after all the cheese has been added, continue to stir until fully melted. Return to a simmer and cook, stirring gently, until the mixture has thickened, about 1 minute. 5. Press Cancel to turn off the pot. Using potholders, carefully remove the insert from the housing. Let stand for 5 minutes. Stir in the basil and ½ to 1 teaspoon pepper. Transfer to a serving bowl and sprinkle with Parmesan and additional black pepper.

Cajun Spaghetti

Prep time: 15 minutes | Cook time: 11 minutes | Serves 4

1 tablespoon extra-virgin olive oil
1 yellow onion, diced
1 bell pepper (any color), seeded and diced
1 celery rib, diced
1 pound (454 g) andouille chicken sausage
2 tablespoons minced garlic
2 tablespoons Worcestershire sauce
1 tablespoon chili powder
½ teaspoon onion powder
½ teaspoon smoked paprika
¼ to ½ teaspoon cayenne pepper

1 teaspoon salt
¼ teaspoon freshly ground black pepper
1 pound (454 g) peeled and deveined shrimp
2 cups tomato sauce
1 (14½-ounce / 411-g) can fire-roasted diced tomatoes
1 cup water
1 pound (454 g) dried spaghetti noodles, cracked in half
Chopped fresh parsley, for garnish
Grated or shaved Parmesan cheese, for garnish

1. Add oil to the Ninja Foodi pressure cooker, select Sauté and set to medium (MD). After 1 minute, add the onion, bell pepper and celery. Sauté for 3 minutes. 2. Mix in the sausage and garlic and sauté for 3 more minutes. Press Cancel. Deglaze the pot with the Worcestershire. 3. Add the chili powder, onion powder, paprika, cayenne, salt and black pepper. Stir to combine. 4. Add the shrimp, tomato sauce, fire-roasted tomatoes and water. Stir, scraping up any browned bits from the bottom of the pot. Add the noodles, pressing them down into the sauce. 5. Assemble pressure lid, making sure the pressure release valve is in the Seal position. Select Pressure and set to high (HI). Set time to 5 minutes. Press Start. 6. Quick release pressure by moving the pressure release valve to the Vent position. Remove the lid and use tongs to toss the pasta and shrimp together. 7. Top with chopped fresh parsley and grated or shaved Parmesan cheese.

Barbecue Beef and Pasta Casserole

Prep time: 10 minutes | Cook time: 17 minutes | Serves 4

2 tablespoons vegetable, corn, or canola oil
1 large yellow onion, chopped
1 medium green bell pepper, stemmed, cored, and sliced into thin strips

1¼ pounds (567 g) lean ground beef
2 cups beef or chicken broth
1¼ cups barbecue sauce
8 ounces (227 g) dried rigatoni

1. Add oil to the Ninja Foodi pressure cooker, select Sauté and set to medium (MD). 2. Add the onion and bell pepper; cook, stirring often, until the onion begins to soften, about 4 minutes. Crumble in the ground beef and cook, stirring frequently to break up any clumps, until lightly browned, about 4 minutes. 3. Pour in the broth and scrape up every speck of browned stuff on the pot's bottom. Turn off the Sauté function. Stir in the barbecue sauce and pasta. Assemble pressure lid, making sure the pressure release valve is in the Seal position. 4. Select Pressure and set to high (HI). Set time to 7 minutes. Press Start. 5. Quick release pressure by moving the pressure release valve to the Vent position. Unlatch the lid and open the pot. Stir well before serving.

Cheesy Macaroni

Prep time: 10 minutes | Cook time: 5 minutes | Serves 4

1 pound (454 g) macaroni or other small pasta
5½ cups water, divided
½ to 1 teaspoon salt, plus more as needed
2 yellow potatoes or red potatoes, peeled and cut into chunks
2 carrots, scrubbed or peeled and cut into chunks (of similar

size to the potatoes)
½ cup nondairy milk
¼ cup nutritional yeast
1 tablespoon freshly squeezed lemon juice
2 teaspoons onion powder
1 teaspoon garlic powder
Pinch red pepper flakes or cayenne (optional)

1. In cooking pot, combine the macaroni, 4 cups of water, and a pinch of salt. 2. Place reversible rack in the pot and put the potatoes and carrots on top. Assemble pressure lid, making sure the pressure release valve is in the Seal position. Select Pressure and set to high (HI). Set time to 5 minutes. Press Start. 3. Quick release pressure by moving the pressure release valve to the Vent position. 4. Once all the pressure has released, remove the lid and carefully pull out the steaming basket with the potatoes and carrots. Transfer to a blender and add the milk, remaining 1½ cups of water, salt, nutritional yeast, lemon juice, onion powder, garlic powder, and red pepper flakes (if using). Purée until smooth. Stir the cheese sauce into the macaroni. Taste and season with more salt or other seasonings, if needed.

Lemon Alfredo Pasta

Prep time: 10 minutes | Cook time: 10 minutes | Serves 4 to 6

1½ cups chicken or vegetable stock
1 cup milk
¾ cup heavy cream
2 tablespoons grass-fed butter
¾ teaspoon sea salt
1½ pounds (680 g) gluten-free dried fettuccine pasta, broken in half
4 ounces (113 g) mascarpone cheese or cream cheese
1¼ cups shredded Parmesan cheese, plus more for garnish
Zest of 2 lemons
¼ cup finely chopped fresh flat-leaf parsley, for garnish (optional)

1. Combine the stock, milk, cream, butter, salt and pasta in the cooking pot, making sure the pasta is submerged in the liquid. 2. Assemble pressure lid, making sure the pressure release valve is in the Seal position. Select Pressure and set to high (HI). Set time to 5 minutes. Press Start. 3. Let pressure release naturally for 5 minutes; quick-release any remaining pressure. 4. Select Sauté, set to medium (MD) , and immediately give the pasta a stir to help it not stick together, then add the mascarpone and Parmesan. Allow to come to a simmer and quickly stir until the Parmesan is fully mixed in. Simmer for about 5 minutes, or until the sauce slightly thickens. Press Keep Warm. Add the lemon zest, gently stir to combine, then allow the fettuccine to rest for 10 minutes. 5. Serve immediately, garnished with shredded Parmesan and chopped fresh flat-leaf parsley (if using).

Chicken Noodle Paprikash

Prep time: 15 minutes | Cook time: 14 minutes | Serves 4

4 tablespoons (½ stick) butter

1 medium yellow onion, chopped

1 pound (454 g) unseasoned chicken breast, cut for stir-fry, any flavoring packets discarded

3 cups chicken broth

3 tablespoons mild paprika

½ teaspoon caraway seeds

¼ teaspoon grated nutmeg

¼ teaspoon table salt

¼ teaspoon ground black pepper

6 ounces (170 g) wide egg or no-yolk noodles

½ cup regular or low-fat sour cream

1. Melt butter in the Ninja Foodi pressure cooker, select Sauté and set to medium (MD). 2. Add the onion and cook, stirring often, until softened, about 3 minutes. Stir in the chicken strips and cook until they lose their pink color, about 2 minutes. 3. Stir in the broth, paprika, caraway seeds, nutmeg, salt, and pepper until aromatic, about 1 minute. Turn off the Sauté function. Stir in the noodles. Assemble pressure lid, making sure the pressure release valve is in the Seal position. 4. Select Pressure and set to high (HI). Set time to 4 minutes. Press Start. 5. Quick release pressure by moving the pressure release valve to the Vent position. Unlatch the lid and open the pot. Stir in the sour cream until smooth just before serving.

Chapter 6 Poultry

Cheesy Chicken and Rice

Prep time: 5 minutes | Cook time: 16 minutes | Serves 4

3 tablespoons olive oil
1 pound (454 g) boneless, skinless chicken thighs, cut into 1-inch pieces
1 cup white rice
½ teaspoon salt
¼ teaspoon black pepper
1½ cups chicken broth
1 cup shredded Cheddar cheese

1. Add to the Ninja Foodi pressure cooker, select Sauté and set to medium (MD). 2. Add chicken and rice. Season with salt and pepper. Let cook 5 minutes. 3. Pour in broth and deglaze bottom of pot. 4. Assemble pressure lid, making sure the pressure release valve is in the Seal position. 5. Select Pressure and set to high (HI). Set time to 10 minutes. Press Start. 6. When pressure cooking is complete, allow pressure to natural release. 7. Mix in cheese and serve.

Carolina Barbecued Chicken with Simple Slaw

Prep time: 10 minutes | Cook time: 20 minutes | Serves 4

Barbecued Chicken:
½ yellow onion, chopped
1 clove garlic, minced
¼ cup raw apple cider vinegar
¼ cup pure maple syrup
¼ cup water
1 tablespoon soy sauce or tamari
1 pound (454 g) boneless, skinless chicken breasts
1 teaspoon fine sea salt
Freshly ground black pepper
¼ cup tomato paste
1 teaspoon blackstrap molasses
1 teaspoon spicy brown mustard
½ teaspoon chili powder
½ teaspoon paprika
⅛ teaspoon cayenne pepper (optional)

¼ head green cabbage, shredded (about 8 ounces / 227 g)
Simple Slaw:
2 tablespoons freshly squeezed lemon juice
2 tablespoons pure maple syrup
1 tablespoon extra-virgin olive oil
½ teaspoon fine sea salt
Freshly ground black pepper
¼ head green cabbage, shredded (about 8 ounces / 227 g)
1 cup shredded carrot (about 1 large carrot)
¼ cup chopped fresh flat-leaf parsley
Butter lettuce or buns, for serving

1. To make the barbecued chicken, add the onion, garlic, vinegar, maple syrup, water, and soy sauce to the cooking pot and stir to combine. Arrange reversible rack on the bottom of the pot and place the chicken breasts on top. Season the breasts with ¼ teaspoon of the salt and several grinds of black pepper. Assemble pressure lid, making sure the pressure release valve is in the Seal position. Select Pressure and set to high (HI). Set time to 12 minutes. Press Start. 2. While the chicken is cooking, prepare the slaw. In a large bowl, combine the lemon juice, maple syrup, olive oil, salt, and several grinds of pepper and stir well. Add the cabbage, carrot, and parsley and toss to coat. Refrigerate the slaw to let the flavors meld while you finish preparing the chicken. 3. Quick release pressure by moving the pressure release valve to the Vent position. Press Cancel and use tongs to transfer the chicken to a cutting board to rest. Use oven mitts to remove the rack. 4. Select Sauté and set to medium (MD). Add the tomato paste, molasses, mustard, chili powder, paprika, cayenne, and the remaining ¾ teaspoon salt to the sauce. Stir well, then add the cabbage. Simmer the cabbage in the sauce until very tender, about 8 minutes. 5. Once the cabbage is tender, use two forks to shred the chicken. Add it to the pot and stir well. Taste and adjust the seasonings as needed; add more cayenne if you like it spicy. 6. To serve, scoop the barbecued chicken into lettuce cups or onto your favorite buns, with the chilled slaw on top. Serve any additional slaw on the side. Store leftovers in two separate airtight containers in the fridge. The chicken will keep for 3 or 4 days, but the slaw is best used within 1 day.

Chicken Paprikash

Prep time: 10 minutes | Cook time: 30 minutes | Serves 4

2 tablespoons salted butter
1 large yellow onion, finely chopped
Kosher salt and ground black pepper
2 tablespoons sweet paprika
1 tablespoon tomato paste
3 pounds (1.4 kg) bone-in, skin-on chicken thighs, skin removed and discarded
1 cup sour cream
1 tablespoon cornstarch
4 tablespoons chopped fresh dill, divided

1. Melt butter in the Ninja Foodi pressure cooker, select Sauté and set to high (HI).Add the onion, ½ teaspoon salt and ¼ teaspoon pepper, then cook, stirring occasionally, until the onion is golden brown, about 6 minutes. 2. Add the paprika and tomato paste and cook, stirring, until fragrant, about 1 minute. Stir in ½ cup water, scraping up the browned bits. Nestle the chicken in an even layer, skin side down, slightly overlapping the pieces if needed. Fast: 3. Assemble pressure lid, making sure the pressure release valve is in the Seal position. Select Pressure and set to high (HI). Set time to 10 minutes. Press Start. Let pressure release naturally for 10 minutes; quick-release any remaining pressure. Slow: With the pot still on Sauté function, bring the mixture to a boil. Assemble pressure lid, making sure the pressure release valve is in the Seal position. Select Slow Cook and set to high (HI). Set time to 3 to 4 hours; the chicken is done when a skewer inserted into the largest thigh meets no resistance. Press Cancel, then carefully open the pot. 4. Using tongs, transfer the chicken to a dish and tent with foil. In a small bowl, whisk together the sour cream and cornstarch. Whisk the mixture into the pot, then select Sauté, set to high (HI), and cook, whisking constantly, until the sauce begins to simmer and is lightly thickened. 5. Press Cancel to turn off the pot, then taste and season with salt and pepper. Stir in 2 tablespoons of dill. Using potholders, carefully remove the insert from the housing and pour the sauce over the chicken. Sprinkle with the remaining 2

tablespoons dill.

Citrus-Spiced Chicken

Prep time: 15 minutes | Cook time: 15 minutes | Serves 8

2 tablespoons olive oil	1 cup freshly squeezed orange
3 pounds (1.4 kg) boneless,	juice
skinless chicken thighs	⅛ cup freshly squeezed lemon
1 teaspoon smoked paprika	juice
½ teaspoon sea salt	⅛ cup freshly squeezed lime
⅛ teaspoon ground cinnamon	juice
⅛ teaspoon ground ginger	1 pound (454 g) carrots, peeled
⅛ teaspoon ground nutmeg	and diced large
½ cup white raisins	2 tablespoons water
½ cup slivered almonds	1 tablespoon arrowroot powder

1. Add oil to the Ninja Foodi pressure cooker, select Sauté and set to medium (MD). Fry chicken thighs for 2 minutes on each side until browned. 2. Add the paprika, salt, cinnamon, ginger, nutmeg, raisins, almonds, orange juice, lemon juice, lime juice, and carrots. Assemble pressure lid, making sure the pressure release valve is in the Seal position. 3. Select Pressure and set to high (HI). Set time to 10 minutes. Press Start. Let pressure release naturally for 5 minutes; quick-release any remaining pressure. Check the chicken using a meat thermometer to make sure the internal temperature is at least 165ºF (74ºC). 4. Use a slotted spoon to remove chicken, carrots, and raisins and transfer to a serving platter. 5. In a small bowl, whisk together water and arrowroot to create a slurry. Add to liquid in the cooker and stir to combine. Select Sauté, set to low (LO), and simmer unlidded for 3 minutes until sauce is thickened. Pour sauce over chicken and serve.

Easy Chicken and Rice

Prep time: 5 minutes | Cook time: 20 minutes | Serves 2

2 (8-ounce / 227-g) skin-on,	½ red onion, diced
bone-in chicken leg quarters	2 garlic cloves, minced
1 tablespoon ground adobo	¾ cup brown basmati rice
seasoning, plus more as desired	¾ cup chicken stock
½ tablespoon oil	¼ cup chopped fresh cilantro

1. Generously season the chicken on both sides with 1 tablespoon of adobo seasoning; set aside on a plate. 2. Preheat the pressure cooker on Sauté mode. When the display reads hot, add the oil. Add the onion and sauté until softened, 3 to 4 minutes. Add the garlic and cook for 1 minute until fragrant. 3. Stir in the rice and stock, scraping up the browned bits from the bottom of the pot with a wooden spoon and stirring them into the liquid. Season with adobo seasoning if you'd like. Press Cancel. Place the seasoned chicken on top. 4. Assemble pressure lid, making sure the pressure release valve is in the Seal position. Select Pressure and set to high (HI). Set time to 20 minutes. Press Start. When pressure cooking is complete, allow pressure to natural release, about 10 minutes. Open the vent at the top and remove the lid. Press Cancel. 5. Transfer the

chicken to a cutting board and use two forks to shred the meat from the skin and bones (which you should discard). Fluff the cooked rice, then stir in the shredded chicken and cilantro. Serve with the lime wedges (if using).

Huli Huli Chicken Thighs

Prep time: 5 minutes | Cook time: 10 minutes | Serves 8

1 cup crushed pineapple,	3 tablespoons lime juice
drained	1 garlic clove, minced
¾ cup ketchup	8 boneless skinless chicken
⅓ cup reduced-sodium soy	thighs (about 2 pounds / 907 g)
sauce	Hot cooked rice
3 tablespoons packed brown	Green onions, thinly sliced,
sugar	optional

1. Mix first six ingredients. Place chicken in cooking pot; top with pineapple mixture. Assemble pressure lid, making sure the pressure release valve is in the Seal position. Select Pressure and set to high (HI). Set time to 10 minutes. Press Start. Let pressure release naturally for 105 minutes; quick-release any remaining pressure. Serve with rice. If desired, top with green onions.

Saucy Barbecue Chicken Thighs

Prep time: 15 minutes | Cook time: 10 minutes | Serves 6

6 boneless skinless chicken	¼ cup water
thighs	¼ cup orange juice
½ teaspoon poultry seasoning	1 teaspoon garlic powder
1 medium onion, chopped	¾ teaspoon dried oregano
1 (14½-ounce / 411-g) can diced	½ teaspoon hot pepper sauce
tomatoes, undrained	¼ teaspoon pepper
1 (8-ounce / 227-g) can tomato	Hot cooked brown rice
sauce	(optional)
½ cup barbecue sauce	

1. Place chicken in cooking pot; sprinkle with poultry seasoning. Top with onion and tomatoes. In a small bowl, mix the tomato sauce, barbecue sauce, water, orange juice and seasonings; pour over top. 2. Assemble pressure lid, making sure the pressure release valve is in the Seal position. Select Pressure and set to high (HI). Set time to 10 minutes. Press Start. Quick release pressure by moving the pressure release valve to the Vent position. A thermometer inserted in chicken should read at least 170ºF (77ºC) If desired, serve with rice.

Sneaky Sloppy Joes

Prep time: 5 minutes | Cook time: 28 minutes | Serves 4

1 tablespoon extra-virgin olive	1½ teaspoons fine sea salt
oil	½ cup water
1 yellow onion, chopped	1 green bell pepper, seeded and
1 pound (454 g) ground turkey	chopped
1 teaspoon chili powder	½ cup tomato paste (about 6

ounces / 170 g)
1 butternut squash (about 1 pound / 454 g), peeled and cut into 1-inch cubes, or 8 ounces (227 g) frozen butternut squash pieces
2 tablespoons pure maple syrup
1½ tablespoons spicy brown mustard

Freshly ground black pepper
2 small sweet potatoes (each 11 ounces / 312 g or less), pierced with a fork to vent
Chopped green onions, tender white and green parts only, for garnish
Chopped fresh flat-leaf parsley, for garnish

1. Add oil to the Ninja Foodi pressure cooker, select Sauté and set to medium (MD). Once the oil is hot but not smoking, add the onion, turkey, chili powder, and 1 teaspoon of the salt and sauté until the turkey is browned and cooked through, breaking it up with a wooden spoon as you stir, about 8 minutes. Press Cancel to stop the cooking cycle. 2. Add the water and scrape up anything that has stuck to the bottom of the pot. Without stirring, add the bell pepper, tomato paste, butternut squash cubes, maple syrup, mustard, remaining ½ teaspoon salt, and several grinds of pepper. 3. Arrange reversible rack on top of the filling and place the sweet potatoes on the rack. Assemble pressure lid, making sure the pressure release valve is in the Seal position. Select Pressure and set to high (HI). Set time to 20 minutes. Press Start. 4. Let pressure release naturally for 10 minutes; quick-release any remaining pressure. Use oven mitts to lift the rack and potatoes out of the pot. Stir the filling, using a wooden spoon to mash up the squash. Select Sauté and set to medium (MD). Simmer away excess liquid until the sauce is to your liking. Adjust the seasoning as needed. 5. Carefully slice the hot sweet potatoes in half lengthwise and spoon filling over each half. Garnish with the green onions and parsley and serve immediately. Store leftover filling in an airtight container in the fridge for 3 or 4 days.

Mango-Pineapple Chicken Tacos

Prep time: 25 minutes | Cook time: 10 minutes | Serves 16

2 medium mangoes, peeled and chopped
1½ cups cubed fresh pineapple or canned pineapple chunks, drained
2 medium tomatoes, chopped
1 medium red onion, finely chopped
2 small Anaheim peppers, seeded and chopped

2 green onions, finely chopped
1 tablespoon lime juice
1 teaspoon sugar
4 pounds (1.8 kg) bone-in chicken breast halves, skin removed
3 teaspoons salt
¼ cup packed brown sugar
32 taco shells, warmed
¼ cup minced fresh cilantro

1. In a large bowl, combine the first eight ingredients. Place chicken in a cooking pot; sprinkle with salt and brown sugar. Top with mango mixture. Assemble pressure lid, making sure the pressure release valve is in the Seal position. Select Pressure and set to high (HI). Set time to 10 minutes. Press Start. 2. Let pressure release naturally for 10 minutes; quick-release any remaining pressure. Remove chicken; cool slightly. Strain cooking juices, reserving mango mixture and ½ cup juices. Discard remaining juices. When cool enough to handle, remove chicken from bones; discard bones. Shred chicken with two forks. 3. Select Sauté and set to high (HI). Return chicken and reserved mango mixture and cooking juices to pressure cooker; stir to heat through. Serve in taco shells; sprinkle with cilantro.

Chicken Marinara and Zucchini

Prep time: 5 minutes | Cook time: 15 minutes | Serves 4

2 large zucchini, diced large
4 chicken breast halves (about 2 pounds / 907 g)
3 cups marinara sauce

1 tablespoon Italian seasoning
½ teaspoon sea salt
1 cup shredded Mozzarella

1. Scatter zucchini into cooking pot. Place chicken on zucchini. Pour marinara sauce over chicken. Sprinkle with Italian seasoning and salt. Assemble pressure lid, making sure the pressure release valve is in the Seal position. 2. Select Pressure and set to high (HI). Set time to 15 minutes. Press Start. Let pressure release naturally for 10 minutes; quick-release any remaining pressure. Check chicken using a meat thermometer to ensure the internal temperature is at least 165ºF (74ºC). 3. Sprinkle chicken with Mozzarella. Press Keep Warm, lock lid back in place, and warm for 5 minutes to allow the cheese to melt. 4. Transfer chicken and zucchini to a serving platter.

Crispy Duck with Cherry Sauce

Prep time: 10 minutes | Cook time: 33 minutes | Serves 2 to 4

1 whole duck (up to 5 pounds / 2.3 kg), split in half, back and rib bones removed
1 teaspoon olive oil
Salt and freshly ground black pepper, to taste
Cherry Sauce:
1 tablespoon butter

1 shallot, minced
½ cup sherry
¾ cup cherry preserves
1 cup chicken stock
1 teaspoon white wine vinegar
1 teaspoon fresh thyme leaves
Salt and freshly ground black pepper, to taste

1. Preheat the pressure cooker to 400ºF (204ºC). 2. Trim some of the fat from the duck. Rub olive oil on the duck and season with salt and pepper. Place the duck halves in the cooking pot, breast side up and facing the center of the pot. 3. Close crisping lid. Select Roast and set time to 20 minutes. Turn and roast for another 6 minutes. 4. While duck is roasting, make the cherry sauce. Melt the butter in a large sauté pan. Add the shallot and sauté until it is just starting to brown, about 2 to 3 minutes. Add the sherry and deglaze the pan by scraping up any brown bits from the bottom of the pan. Simmer the liquid for a few minutes, until it has reduced by half. Add the cherry preserves, chicken stock and white wine vinegar. Whisk well to combine all the ingredients. Simmer the sauce until it thickens and coats the back of a spoon, about 5 to 7 minutes. Season with salt and pepper and stir in the fresh thyme leaves. 5. When the timer goes off, spoon some cherry sauce over the duck and continue to roast for 4 more minutes. Then, turn the duck halves back over so that the breast side is facing up. Spoon more cherry sauce over the top of the duck, covering the skin completely. Roast for 3 more minutes and then remove the duck to a plate to rest for a few minutes. 6. Serve the duck in halves, or cut each piece in half again for a smaller serving. Spoon any additional sauce over the duck or serve it on the side.

Cranberry Chicken Salad

Prep time: 10 minutes | Cook time: 6 to 10 minutes | Serves 2

1 pound (454 g) skinless, boneless chicken breasts
½ cup water
2 teaspoons kosher salt, plus more for seasoning
½ cup mayonnaise
2 tablespoons diced red onion
1 celery stalk, diced
½ cup chopped dried cranberries
¼ unpeeled organic green apple, shredded
¼ cup chopped walnuts
1 tablespoon freshly squeezed lime juice
Freshly ground black pepper

1. Put the chicken, water, and 2 teaspoons of salt in the cooking pot. Select Pressure and set to high (HI). Set time to 6 minutes. Press Start. 2. Let pressure release naturally for 5 minutes; quick-release any remaining pressure. Transfer the chicken to a cutting board and let rest for 5 to 10 minutes. Shred the meat, transfer to a salad bowl, and mix with ¼ cup of the chicken cooking liquid. 3. Add the mayonnaise and stir to coat well. Add the onion, celery, cranberries, apple, walnuts, and lime juice and season with salt and pepper. 4. Serve immediately, or refrigerate for several hours or overnight.

Chicken-Bacon Stew

Prep time: 25 minutes | Cook time: 15 minutes | Serves 2

1 tablespoon oil
1 pound (454 g) skin-on, bone-in chicken thighs and/or drumsticks
Kosher salt
Freshly ground black pepper
5 to 6 slices thick-cut bacon, chopped into ½-inch pieces
1 small onion, diced
2 medium carrots, peeled and
chopped
1 tablespoon tomato paste
½ teaspoon dried thyme
1 dried bay leaf
3 garlic cloves, chopped
¼ cup white wine (or stock)
1 cup chicken stock
1 large potato, cut into 1-inch cubes
2 teaspoons sherry vinegar

1. Add oil to the Ninja Foodi pressure cooker, select Sauté and set to medium (MD). When the display reads hot, add the oil. Pat the chicken pieces dry with paper towels and season with salt and pepper. 2. In the pot, brown the chicken on all sides, 4 minutes per side. Transfer to a plate and set aside. 3. Add the bacon and cook until it begins to crisp, 2 to 3 minutes. Add the onion, carrots, tomato paste, thyme, and bay leaf and sauté until softened, 3 to 4 minutes. Add the garlic and cook, stirring, for 1 minute. 4. Pour in the wine and deglaze the pot, scraping up the browned bits from the bottom and stirring them into the liquid. Cook for 2 minutes, or until the wine is reduced by half. 5. Add the stock and potato and stir well. Return the browned chicken to the pot. 6. Assemble pressure lid, making sure the pressure release valve is in the Seal position. Select Pressure and set to high (HI). Set time to 15 minutes. When pressure cooking is complete, allow pressure to natural release, about 10 minutes. 7. Remove the bay leaf and discard, then carefully transfer the chicken to a bowl. Remove and discard the skin and bones and shred the meat. 8. Return the chicken meat to the pot to reheat and stir well. Stir in the sherry vinegar. Taste and season with more salt and pepper as needed.

Honey-Sriracha Chicken

Prep time: 10 minutes | Cook time: 12 minutes | Serves 4

4 chicken breasts, diced
5 tablespoons soy sauce
2 to 3 tablespoons honey
¼ cup sugar
4 tablespoons cold water
1 tablespoon minced garlic
2 to 3 tablespoons Sriracha
2 tablespoons cornstarch

1. In the cooking pot, whisk together soy sauce, honey, sugar, 2 tablespoons of water, garlic, and Sriracha until combined. 2. Toss the chicken breasts in the mixture. Assemble pressure lid, making sure the pressure release valve is in the Seal position. 3. Select Pressure and set to high (HI). Set time to 9 minutes. 4. Meanwhile, in a small bowl combine 2 tablespoons of water and cornstarch. 5. Quick release pressure by moving the pressure release valve to the Vent position. 6. Pour the cornstarch mixture into the pot. 7. Select Sauté, set to low (LO), simmer and stir occasionally until the sauce begins to thicken. 8. Serve.

Best-Ever Chicken Wings

Prep time: 5 minutes | Cook time: 15 minutes | Serves 4

1 cup water or chicken stock
4 pounds (1.8 kg) chicken wings
4 tablespoons melted unsalted
butter
2 tablespoons of your favorite seasoning mix

1. Pour the water or chicken stock into the pot and insert reversible rack. Place the wings on the rack. 2. Assemble pressure lid, making sure the pressure release valve is in the Seal position. Select Pressure and set to high (HI). Set time to 10 minutes. 3. Quick release pressure by moving the pressure release valve to the Vent position. Remove the chicken from the pot and place on a broiler pan. Broil until the chicken is browned and crispy, about 5 minutes. 4. In a small bowl, mix together the melted butter and seasoning mix. Brush the wings with the butter mixture and serve immediately.

Pesto Chicken

Prep time: 5 minutes | Cook time: 15 minutes | Serves 4

1 cup water
1 pound (454 g) boneless, skinless chicken breasts, cut into strips
½ cup pesto
2 Roma tomatoes, sliced
¼ teaspoon salt
⅛ teaspoon black pepper

1. Add the reversible rack and water to Ninja Foodi pressure cooker. 2. In a 6-cup metal bowl, combine chicken, pesto, tomatoes, salt, and pepper. 3. Create a foil sling and carefully lower bowl on the rack. 4. Assemble pressure lid, making sure the pressure release valve is in the Seal position. 5. Select Pressure and set to high (HI). Set time to 15 minutes. 6. When pressure cooking is complete, allow pressure to natural release. Remove pan from pot using foil sling. 7. Serve hot.

Italian Crispy Chicken

Prep time: 10 minutes | Cook time: 20 minutes | Serves 4

2 (4-ounce / 113-g) boneless, skinless chicken breasts
2 egg whites, beaten
1 cup Italian bread crumbs
½ cup grated Parmesan cheese
2 teaspoons Italian seasoning

Salt and freshly ground black pepper, to taste
Cooking oil spray
¾ cup marinara sauce
½ cup shredded Mozzarella cheese

1. With your knife blade parallel to the cutting board, cut the chicken breasts in half horizontally to create 4 thin cutlets. On a solid surface, pound the cutlets to flatten them. You can use your hands, a rolling pin, a kitchen mallet, or a meat hammer. 2. Pour the egg whites into a bowl large enough to dip the chicken. 3. In another bowl large enough to dip a chicken cutlet in, stir together the bread crumbs, Parmesan cheese, and Italian seasoning, and season with salt and pepper. 4. Dip each cutlet into the egg whites and into the breadcrumb mixture to coat. 5. Preheat the pressure cooker to 375ºF (191ºC). 6. Spray the cook & crisp basket with cooking oil. Working in batches, place 2 chicken cutlets into the basket. Spray the top of the chicken with cooking oil. 7. Close crisping lid. Select Air Crisp and set time to 7 minutes. 8. When the cooking is complete, repeat steps 6 and 7 with the remaining cutlets. 9. Top the chicken cutlets with the marinara sauce and shredded Mozzarella cheese. 10. Air fry for another 3 minutes. 11. The cooking is complete when the cheese is melted and the chicken reaches an internal temperature of 165ºF (74ºC). Cool for 5 minutes before serving.

Broccoli Cheese Chicken

Prep time: 10 minutes | Cook time: 19 to 24 minutes | Serves 6

1 tablespoon avocado oil
¼ cup chopped onion
½ cup finely chopped broccoli
4 ounces (113 g) cream cheese, at room temperature
2 ounces (57 g) Cheddar cheese, shredded
1 teaspoon garlic powder

½ teaspoon sea salt, plus additional for seasoning, divided
¼ freshly ground black pepper, plus additional for seasoning, divided
2 pounds (907 g) boneless, skinless chicken breasts
1 teaspoon smoked paprika

1. Heat a medium skillet over medium-high heat and pour in the avocado oil. Add the onion and broccoli and cook, stirring occasionally, for 5 to 8 minutes, until the onion is tender. 2. Transfer to a large bowl and stir in the cream cheese, Cheddar cheese, and garlic powder, and season to taste with salt and pepper. 3. Hold a sharp knife parallel to the chicken breast and cut a long pocket into one side. Stuff the chicken pockets with the broccoli mixture, using toothpicks to secure the pockets around the filling. 4. In a small dish, combine the paprika, ½ teaspoon salt, and ¼ teaspoon pepper. Sprinkle this over the outside of the chicken. 5. Preheat the pressure cooker to 400ºF (204ºC). Place the chicken in a single layer in the cooking pot. Close crisping lid. Select Roast and set time to 14 to 16 minutes, until an instant-read thermometer reads 160ºF (71ºC). Place the chicken on a plate and tent a piece of aluminum foil over the chicken. Allow to rest for 5 to 10 minutes before serving.

Chipotle Aioli Wings

Prep time: 5 minutes | Cook time: 25 minutes | Serves 6

2 pounds (907 g) bone-in chicken wings
½ teaspoon salt
¼ teaspoon ground black pepper

2 tablespoons mayonnaise
2 teaspoons chipotle powder
2 tablespoons lemon juice

1. Preheat the pressure cooker to 400ºF (204ºC). In a large bowl, toss wings in salt and pepper, then place into cooking pot. Close crisping lid. Select Roast and set time to 25 minutes, shaking the basket twice. Wings will be done when golden and have an internal temperature of at least 165ºF (74ºC). 2. In a small bowl, whisk together mayonnaise, chipotle powder, and lemon juice. Place cooked wings into a large serving bowl and drizzle with aioli. Toss to coat. Serve warm.

Whole Turkey with Apricot Glaze

Prep time: 10 minutes | Cook time: 40 minutes | Serves 8 to 10

9 pounds (4 kg) turkey
6 ounces (170 g) apricot jam
½ teaspoon cumin
½ teaspoon turmeric
½ teaspoon coriander

1 teaspoon salt
1 teaspoon ground black pepper
2 cups chicken stock
1 onion, peeled and diced
1 carrot, diced

1. Rinse the turkey and dry with paper towels. 2. In a bowl, combine the jam, cumin, turmeric, coriander, salt and pepper. Mix well. 3. Rub all sides of the turkey with the paste. 4. Pour the broth into the cooking pot, add the onion and carrot. 5. Add the turkey. Assemble pressure lid, making sure the pressure release valve is in the Seal position. 6. Select Pressure and set to high (HI). Set time to 40 minutes. 7. Let pressure release naturally for 10 minutes; quick-release any remaining pressure. Serve. 8. If desired, broil in the oven for a few minutes for a browned top.

Chicken Nachos

Prep time: 2 minutes | Cook time: 15 minutes | Serves 6

2 pounds (907 g) boneless, skinless chicken thighs
1 tablespoon olive oil
1 (1-ounce / 28-g) package taco

seasoning mix
⅔ cup mild red salsa
⅓ cup mild Herdez salsa verde

1. Select Sauté, set to medium (MD) and heat the oil. 2. Add the chicken thighs and brown the meat nicely for a few minutes on each side. 3. In a medium bowl, combine the taco seasoning and salsa. 4. Pour the mixture in the pot and stir well. Assemble pressure lid, making sure the pressure release valve is in the Seal position. 5. Select Pressure and set to high (HI). Set time to 15 minutes. Press Start. 6. Let pressure release naturally for 10 minutes; quick-release any remaining pressure. Uncover the pot. 7. Shred the meat. Serve with tortilla chips.

Coconut Chicken Wings with Mango Sauce

Prep time: 15 minutes | Cook time: 20 minutes | Serves 4

16 chicken drumettes (party wings)
¼ cup full-fat coconut milk
1 tablespoon sriracha
1 teaspoon onion powder
1 teaspoon garlic powder
Salt and freshly ground black pepper, to taste
⅓ cup shredded unsweetened

coconut
½ cup all-purpose flour
Cooking oil spray
1 cup mango, cut into ½-inch chunks
¼ cup fresh cilantro, chopped
½ cup red onion, chopped
2 garlic cloves, minced
Juice of ½ lime

1. Place the drumettes in a resealable plastic bag. 2. In a small bowl, whisk the coconut milk and sriracha. 3. Drizzle the drumettes with the sriracha–coconut milk mixture. Season the drumettes with the onion powder, garlic powder, salt, and pepper. Seal the bag. Shake it thoroughly to combine the seasonings and coat the chicken. Marinate for at least 30 minutes, preferably overnight, in the refrigerator. 4. When the drumettes are almost done marinating, in a large bowl, stir together the shredded coconut and flour. 5. Dip the drumettes into the coconut-flour mixture. Press the flour mixture onto the chicken with your hands. 6. Preheat the pressure cooker to 400°F (204°C). 7. Spray cook & crisp basket with cooking oil. Place the drumettes in the basket. It is okay to stack them. Spray the drumettes with cooking oil, being sure to cover the bottom layer. 8. Close crisping lid. Select Air Crisp and set time to 20 minutes, shaking every 5 minutes. 9. When the cooking is complete, let the chicken cool for 5 minutes. 11. While the chicken cooks and cools, make the salsa. In a small bowl, combine the mango, cilantro, red onion, garlic, and lime juice. Mix well until fully combined. Serve with the wings.

Harissa-Rubbed Cornish Game Hens

Prep time: 30 minutes | Cook time: 21 minutes | Serves 4

Harissa:
½ cup olive oil
6 cloves garlic, minced
2 tablespoons smoked paprika
1 tablespoon ground coriander
1 tablespoon ground cumin
1 teaspoon ground caraway

1 teaspoon kosher salt
½ to 1 teaspoon cayenne pepper
Hens:
½ cup yogurt
2 Cornish game hens, any giblets removed, split in half lengthwise

1. For the harissa: In a medium microwave-safe bowl, combine the oil, garlic, paprika, coriander, cumin, caraway, salt, and cayenne. Microwave on high for 1 minute, stirring halfway through the cooking time. 2. For the hens: In a small bowl, combine 1 to 2 tablespoons harissa and the yogurt. Whisk until well combined. Place the hen halves in a resealable plastic bag and pour the marinade over. Seal the bag and massage until all of the pieces are thoroughly coated. Marinate at room temperature for 30 minutes or in the refrigerator for up to 24 hours. 3. Preheat the pressure cooker to 400°F (204°C). Arrange the hen halves in a single layer in the cooking pot. Close crisping lid. Select Roast and set time to 20 minutes. Use a meat thermometer to ensure the game hens have reached an internal temperature of 165°F (74°C).

Chicken and Broccoli Cheesy Rice

Prep time: 5 minutes | Cook time: 10 minutes | Serves 4

Nonstick cooking spray
4 cups low-sodium chicken broth
1 cup long-grain white rice
½ teaspoon fine sea salt
¼ teaspoon ground black pepper

2 boneless, skinless chicken breasts, cut into 1-inch pieces
4 cups broccoli florets
1½ cups shredded Cheddar cheese

1. Spray the cooking pot with nonstick cooking spray. Add the broth, rice, salt, pepper, chicken, and broccoli. 2. Assemble pressure lid, making sure the pressure release valve is in the Seal position. Select Pressure and set to high (HI). Set time to 10 minutes. Press Start. Quick release pressure by moving the pressure release valve to the Vent position. 3. Unlock and remove the lid. Stir in the cheese until melted.

Salsa Chicken Tacos

Prep time: 5 minutes | Cook time: 10 minutes | Serves 4

2 cups chunky salsa
1 cup chicken broth
1 (1-ounce / 28-g) packet taco seasoning
1 pound (454 g) boneless,

skinless chicken breasts
8 crunchy taco shells
2 cups shredded romaine lettuce
1 cup grated Mexican-blend cheese

1. In a medium bowl, combine chunky salsa, broth, and taco seasoning. Whisk to combine. Pour salsa mixture into cooking pot. 2. Add chicken breast to pot and stir. 3. Assemble pressure lid, making sure the pressure release valve is in the Seal position. 4. Select Pressure and set to high (HI). Set time to 10 minutes. 5. Let pressure release naturally for 10 minutes; quick-release any remaining pressure. 6. Use two forks to shred chicken. 7. Serve chicken in taco shells topped with shredded lettuce and cheese.

Tex-Mex Chicken Breasts

Prep time: 10 minutes | Cook time: 17 to 20 minutes | Serves 4

1 pound (454 g) low-sodium boneless, skinless chicken breasts, cut into 1-inch cubes
1 medium onion, chopped
1 red bell pepper, chopped
1 jalapeño pepper, minced

2 teaspoons olive oil
⅔ cup canned low-sodium black beans, rinsed and drained
½ cup low-sodium salsa
2 teaspoons chili powder

1. Preheat the pressure cooker to 400°F (204°C). 2. In cooking pot, mix the chicken, onion, bell pepper, jalapeño, and olive oil. Close crisping lid. Select Roast and set time to 10 minutes, stirring once during cooking. 3. Add the black beans, salsa, and chili powder. Roast for 7 to 10 minutes more, stirring once, until the chicken reaches an internal temperature of 165°F (74°C) on a meat thermometer. Serve immediately.

Chicken with Lettuce

Prep time: 15 minutes | Cook time: 14 minutes | Serves 4

1 pound (454 g) chicken breast tenders, chopped into bite-size pieces
½ onion, thinly sliced
½ red bell pepper, seeded and thinly sliced
½ green bell pepper, seeded and thinly sliced
1 tablespoon olive oil
1 tablespoon fajita seasoning
1 teaspoon kosher salt
Juice of ½ lime
8 large lettuce leaves
1 cup prepared guacamole

1. Preheat the pressure cooker to 400ºF (204ºC). 2. In a large bowl, combine the chicken, onion, and peppers. Drizzle with the olive oil and toss until thoroughly coated. Add the fajita seasoning and salt and toss again. 3. Working in batches if necessary, arrange the chicken and vegetables in a single layer in the cooking pot. Close crisping lid. Select Roast and set time to 14 minutes, shaking halfway through, or until the vegetables are tender and a thermometer inserted into the thickest piece of chicken registers 165ºF (74ºC). 4. Transfer the mixture to a serving platter and drizzle with the fresh lime juice. Serve with the lettuce leaves and top with the guacamole.

Ginger Turmeric Chicken Thighs

Prep time: 5 minutes | Cook time: 25 minutes | Serves 4

4 (4-ounce / 113-g) boneless, skin-on chicken thighs
2 tablespoons coconut oil, melted
½ teaspoon ground turmeric
½ teaspoon salt
½ teaspoon garlic powder
½ teaspoon ground ginger
¼ teaspoon ground black pepper

1. Preheat the pressure cooker to 400ºF (204ºC). Place chicken thighs in a large bowl and drizzle with coconut oil. Sprinkle with remaining ingredients and toss to coat both sides of thighs. 2. Place thighs skin side up into cooking pot. Close crisping lid. Select Roast and set time to 25 minutes, turning every 10 minutes. Chicken will be done when skin is golden brown and the internal temperature is at least 165ºF (74ºC). Serve warm.

Italian Flavor Chicken Breasts with Roma Tomatoes

Prep time: 10 minutes | Cook time: 60 minutes | Serves 8

3 pounds (1.4 kg) chicken breasts, bone-in
1 teaspoon minced fresh basil
1 teaspoon minced fresh rosemary
2 tablespoons minced fresh parsley
1 teaspoon cayenne pepper
½ teaspoon salt
½ teaspoon freshly ground black pepper
4 medium Roma tomatoes, halved
Cooking spray

1. Preheat the pressure cooker to 370ºF (188ºC). Spritz the cooking pot with cooking spray. 2. Combine all the ingredients, except for the chicken breasts and tomatoes, in a large bowl. Stir to mix well. 3. Dunk the chicken breasts in the mixture and press to coat well. 4. Transfer the chicken breasts in the pot. 5. Close crisping lid. Select Bake and set time to 25 minutes, flipping halfway through. 6. Remove the cooked chicken breasts from the cooker and set temperature to 350ºF (177ºC). 7. Place the tomatoes in the pot and spritz with cooking spray. Sprinkle with a touch of salt and bake for 10 minutes, shaking halfway through. 8. Serve the tomatoes with chicken breasts on a large serving plate.

African Piri-Piri Chicken Drumsticks

Prep time: 30 minutes | Cook time: 20 minutes | Serves 2

Chicken:
1 tablespoon chopped fresh thyme leaves
1 tablespoon minced fresh ginger
1 small shallot, finely chopped
2 garlic cloves, minced
⅓ cup piri-piri sauce or hot sauce
3 tablespoons extra-virgin olive oil
Zest and juice of 1 lemon
1 teaspoon smoked paprika
½ teaspoon kosher salt
½ teaspoon black pepper
4 chicken drumsticks
Glaze:
2 tablespoons butter or ghee
1 teaspoon chopped fresh thyme leaves
1 garlic clove, minced
1 tablespoon piri-piri sauce
1 tablespoon fresh lemon juice

1. For the chicken: In a small bowl, stir together all the ingredients except the chicken. Place the chicken and the marinade in a gallon-size resealable plastic bag. Seal the bag and massage to coat. Refrigerate for at least 2 hours or up to 24 hours, turning the bag occasionally. 2. Preheat the pressure cooker to 400ºF (204ºC). Place the chicken legs in the cooking pot. Close crisping lid. Select Roast and set time to 20 minutes, turning halfway through. 3. Meanwhile, for the glaze: Melt the butter in a small saucepan over medium-high heat. Add the thyme and garlic. Cook, stirring, until the garlic just begins to brown, 1 to 2 minutes. Add the piri-piri sauce and lemon juice. Reduce the heat to medium-low and simmer for 1 to 2 minutes. 4. Transfer the chicken to a serving platter. Pour the glaze over the chicken. Serve immediately.

Chipotle Drumsticks

Prep time: 5 minutes | Cook time: 25 minutes | Serves 4

1 tablespoon tomato paste
½ teaspoon chipotle powder
¼ teaspoon apple cider vinegar
¼ teaspoon garlic powder
8 chicken drumsticks
½ teaspoon salt
⅛ teaspoon ground black pepper

1. In a small bowl, combine tomato paste, chipotle powder, vinegar, and garlic powder. 2. Sprinkle drumsticks with salt and pepper, then place into a large bowl and pour in tomato paste mixture. Toss or stir to evenly coat all drumsticks in mixture. 3. Preheat the pressure cooker to 400ºF (204ºC). Place drumsticks into cooking pot. Close crisping lid. Select Roast and set time to 25 minutes, turning halfway through. Drumsticks will be dark red with an internal temperature of at least 165ºF (74ºC) when done. Serve warm.

Thai Game Hens with Cucumber and Chile Salad

Prep time: 25 minutes | Cook time: 25 minutes | Serves 6

2 (1¼-pound / 567-g) Cornish game hens, giblets discarded
1 tablespoon fish sauce
6 tablespoons chopped fresh cilantro
2 teaspoons lime zest
1 teaspoon ground coriander
2 garlic cloves, minced
2 tablespoons packed light brown sugar
2 teaspoons vegetable oil
Salt and ground black pepper, to taste
1 English cucumber, halved lengthwise and sliced thin
1 Thai chile, stemmed, deseeded, and minced
2 tablespoons chopped dry-roasted peanuts
1 small shallot, sliced thinly
1 tablespoon lime juice
Lime wedges, for serving
Cooking spray

1. Arrange a game hen on a clean work surface, remove the backbone with kitchen shears, then pound the hen breast to flat. Cut the breast in half. Repeat with the remaining game hen. 2. Loose the breast and thigh skin with your fingers, then pat the game hens dry and pierce about 10 holes into the fat deposits of the hens. Tuck the wings under the hens. 3. Combine 2 teaspoons of fish sauce, ¼ cup of cilantro, lime zest, coriander, garlic, 4 teaspoons of sugar, 1 teaspoon of vegetable oil, ½ teaspoon of salt, and ⅛ teaspoon of ground black pepper in a small bowl. Stir to mix well. 4. Rub the fish sauce mixture under the breast and thigh skin of the game hens, then let sit for 10 minutes to marinate. 5. Preheat the pressure cooker to 400°F (204°C). Spritz the cooking pot with cooking spray. 6. Arrange the marinated game hens in the preheated pot, skin side down. 7. Close crisping lid. Select Roast and set time to 25 minutes, turning after 15 minutes, or until the internal temperature reaches 165°F (74°C). 8. Meanwhile, combine all the remaining ingredients, except for the lime wedges, in a large bowl and sprinkle with salt and black pepper. Toss to mix well. 9. Transfer the fried hens on a large plate, then sit the salad aside and squeeze the lime wedges over before serving.

African Merguez Meatballs

Prep time: 30 minutes | Cook time: 10 minutes | Serves 4

1 pound (454 g) ground chicken
2 garlic cloves, finely minced
1 tablespoon sweet Hungarian paprika
1 teaspoon kosher salt
1 teaspoon sugar
1 teaspoon ground cumin
½ teaspoon black pepper
½ teaspoon ground fennel
½ teaspoon ground coriander
½ teaspoon cayenne pepper
¼ teaspoon ground allspice

1. In a large bowl, gently mix the chicken, garlic, paprika, salt, sugar, cumin, black pepper, fennel, coriander, cayenne, and allspice until all the ingredients are incorporated. Let stand for 30 minutes at room temperature, or cover and refrigerate for up to 24 hours. 2. Preheat the pressure cooker to 400°F (204°C). Form the mixture into 16 meatballs. Arrange them in a single layer in the cooking pot. Close crisping lid. Select Roast and set time to 10 minutes, turning halfway through. Use a meat thermometer to ensure the meatballs have reached an internal temperature of 165°F (74°C).

Cilantro Chicken Kebabs

Prep time: 30 minutes | Cook time: 10 minutes | Serves 4

Chutney:
½ cup unsweetened shredded coconut
½ cup hot water
2 cups fresh cilantro leaves, roughly chopped
¼ cup fresh mint leaves, roughly chopped
6 cloves garlic, roughly chopped
1 jalapeño, seeded and roughly chopped
¼ to ¾ cup water, as needed
Juice of 1 lemon
Chicken:
1 pound (454 g) boneless, skinless chicken thighs, cut crosswise into thirds
Olive oil spray

1. For the chutney: In a blender or food processor, combine the coconut and hot water; set aside to soak for 5 minutes. 2. To the processor, add the cilantro, mint, garlic, and jalapeño, along with ¼ cup water. Blend at low speed, stopping occasionally to scrape down the sides. Add the lemon juice. With the blender or processor running, add only enough additional water to keep the contents moving. Turn the blender to high once the contents are moving freely and blend until the mixture is puréed. 3. For the chicken: Place the chicken pieces in a large bowl. Add ¼ cup of the chutney and mix well to coat. Set aside the remaining chutney to use as a dip. Marinate the chicken for 15 minutes at room temperature. 4. Preheat the pressure cooker to 350°F (177°C). Spray the cook & crisp basket with olive oil spray. Arrange the chicken in the basket. Close crisping lid. Select Air Crisp and set time to 10 minutes. Use a meat thermometer to ensure that the chicken has reached an internal temperature of 165°F (74°C). 5. Serve the chicken with the remaining chutney.

Buffalo Chicken Wings

Prep time: 10 minutes | Cook time: 20 to 25 minutes | Serves 4

2 tablespoons baking powder
1 teaspoon smoked paprika
Sea salt and freshly ground black pepper, to taste
2 pounds (907 g) chicken wings or chicken drumettes
Avocado oil spray
⅓ cup avocado oil
½ cup Buffalo hot sauce, such as Frank's RedHot
¼ cup (4 tablespoons) unsalted butter
2 tablespoons apple cider vinegar
1 teaspoon minced garlic

1. In a large bowl, stir together the baking powder, smoked paprika, and salt and pepper to taste. Add the chicken wings and toss to coat. 2. Preheat the pressure cooker to 400°F (204°C). Spray the wings with oil. 3. Place the wings in the cooking pot in a single layer, working in batches. Close crisping lid. Select Roast and set time to 20 to 25 minutes. Check with an instant-read thermometer and remove when they reach 155°F (68°C). Let rest until they reach 165°F (74°C). 4. While the wings are cooking, whisk together the avocado oil, hot sauce, butter, vinegar, and garlic in a small saucepan over medium-low heat until warm. 5. When the wings are done cooking, toss them with the Buffalo sauce. Serve warm.

Bacon-Wrapped Stuffed Chicken Breasts

Prep time: 15 minutes | Cook time: 30 minutes | Serves 4

½ cup chopped frozen spinach, thawed and squeezed dry
¼ cup cream cheese, softened
¼ cup grated Parmesan cheese
1 jalapeño, seeded and chopped
½ teaspoon kosher salt
1 teaspoon black pepper

2 large boneless, skinless chicken breasts, butterflied and pounded to ½-inch thickness
4 teaspoons salt-free Cajun seasoning
6 slices bacon

1. In a small bowl, combine the spinach, cream cheese, Parmesan cheese, jalapeño, salt, and pepper. Stir until well combined. 2. Place the butterflied chicken breasts on a flat surface. Spread the cream cheese mixture evenly across each piece of chicken. Starting with the narrow end, roll up each chicken breast, ensuring the filling stays inside. Season chicken with the Cajun seasoning, patting it in to ensure it sticks to the meat. 3. Preheat the pressure cooker to 350°F (177°C). Wrap each breast in 3 slices of bacon. Place in the cooking pot. Close crisping lid. Select Bake and set time to 30 minutes. Use a meat thermometer to ensure the chicken has reached an internal temperature of 165°F (74°C). 4. Let the chicken stand 5 minutes before slicing each rolled-up breast in half to serve.

Turkey Breast with Stuffing and Gravy

Prep time: 10 minutes | Cook time: 50 minutes | Serves 4

5 tablespoons unsalted butter
1 small yellow onion, chopped
2 celery ribs, chopped
4 cups dry sage stuffing mix (such as Pepperidge Farm; 7 ounces / 198 g)
2¾ cups store-bought chicken broth, or homemade
1 (2½- to 2¾-pound / 1.1- to

1.2-kg) boneless, skin-on turkey breast half or tied turkey breast roast
Salt and freshly ground black pepper
1 tablespoon olive oil
2½ tablespoons all-purpose flour

1. Smear 1 tablespoon of the butter in a 7 × 3-inch round metal baking pan or butter the center of a 12-inch length of foil. 2. Put 1 tablespoon of the butter in the pot, select Sauté, and set to medium (MD). When the butter has melted, add the onion and celery and cook, stirring frequently, until tender, 4 minutes. Press Cancel. Pour the vegetables into a bowl, add the stuffing mix and 1¼ cups of the broth, and stir to moisten. Pour into the prepared baking pan and cover tightly with foil. If using foil instead of a baking pan, pour the stuffing into the center of the foil and bring the edges up to create a packet; set aside. 3. Season the turkey breast all over with salt and pepper and drizzle with the oil. Select Sauté, and set to medium (MD). When the pot is hot, place the turkey breast skin-side down in the pot and cook until golden brown, 3 minutes. Press Cancel. Remove the turkey breast from the pot. 4. Add the remaining 1½ cups broth to the pot and scrape up any browned bits on the bottom. 5. Place reversible rack into the pot and place the turkey breast skin-side up on the rack. Place the stuffing in the baking pan or foil packet on top of the turkey breast. Assemble pressure lid, making sure the pressure release valve is in the Seal position. Select Pressure and set to high (HI). Set time to 35 minutes. Press Start.

6. Let pressure release naturally for 10 minutes; quick-release any remaining pressure. Remove the stuffing pan from the pot. 7. Insert an instant-read thermometer into the thickest part of the breast; it should read 160°F (71°C). If it doesn't, cover the pot with a regular pot lid, select Sauté, set to low (LO), and simmer briefly until 160°F (71°C) is reached. Transfer the turkey breast to a cutting board and cover loosely with foil; leave the cooking liquid in the pot. 8. In a medium bowl, combine the remaining 3 tablespoons butter with the flour and stir until smooth. Select Sauté and set to medium (MD). Gradually whisk the flour mixture into the cooking liquid and cook until bubbly, 3 minutes. Season with salt and pepper. 9. Slice the turkey roast crosswise. Serve with the gravy and stuffing.

Cajun Chicken with Rice

Prep time: 10 minutes | Cook time: 25 minutes | Serves 4 to 6

1 tablespoon olive oil
1 onion, diced
3 cloves garlic, minced
1 pound (454 g) chicken breasts, sliced
2 cups chicken broth
1 tablespoon tomato paste

1½ cups white rice, rinsed
1 bell pepper, chopped
Cajun Spices:
¼ teaspoon cayenne pepper
2 teaspoons dried thyme
1 tablespoon paprika

1. Select Sauté, set to medium (MD) and heat the oil. 2. Add the onion and garlic and cook until fragrant. 3. Add the chicken breasts and Cajun spices, stir well. Sauté for another 3 minutes. 4. Pour the broth and tomato paste into the pot. Stir to dissolve the tomato paste. 5. Add the rice and bell pepper, stir. Assemble pressure lid, making sure the pressure release valve is in the Seal position. 6. Select Pressure and set to high (HI). Set time to 20 minutes. Press Start. 7. Let pressure release naturally for 10 minutes; quick-release any remaining pressure. 8. Serve.

Turkey Meatloaf

Prep time: 10 minutes | Cook time: 50 minutes | Serves 4

8 ounces (227 g) sliced mushrooms
1 small onion, coarsely chopped
2 cloves garlic
1½ pounds (680 g) 85% lean ground turkey
2 eggs, lightly beaten
1 tablespoon tomato paste

¼ cup almond meal
2 tablespoons almond milk
1 tablespoon dried oregano
1 teaspoon salt
½ teaspoon freshly ground black pepper
1 Roma tomato, thinly sliced

1. Preheat the pressure cooker to 350°F (177°C). Lightly coat cooking pot with olive oil and set aside. 2. In a food processor fitted with a metal blade, combine the mushrooms, onion, and garlic. Pulse until finely chopped. Transfer the vegetables to a large mixing bowl. 3. Add the turkey, eggs, tomato paste, almond meal, milk, oregano, salt, and black pepper. Mix gently until thoroughly combined. Transfer the mixture to the pot and shape into a loaf. Arrange the tomato slices on top. 4. Close crisping lid. Select Roast and set time to 50 minutes or until the meatloaf is nicely browned and a thermometer inserted into the thickest part registers 165°F (74°C). Let rest for about 10 minutes before slicing.

Turkey Verde and Rice

Prep time: 5 minutes | Cook time: 22 minutes | Serves 6 to 8

1½ pounds (680 g) turkey tenderloins
1 tablespoon olive oil
1 small onion, sliced
½ cup long-grain brown rice
½ cup salsa verde
1 cup chicken broth
½ teaspoon salt

1. Select Sauté, set to medium (MD) and heat the oil. 2. Add the onion. Stir and sauté for 3 to 4 minutes until the onion is translucent. 3. Add the rice, salsa verde, broth, and salt. Stir well. 4. Assemble pressure lid, making sure the pressure release valve is in the Seal position. Select Pressure and set to high (HI). Set time to 18 minutes. Press Start. 5. Let pressure release naturally for 10 minutes; quick-release any remaining pressure. 6. Transfer the turkey to a plate and slice the meat. Serve with rice.

Herb Roasted Whole Chicken

Prep time: 10 minutes | Cook time: 25 minutes | Serves 4

1 teaspoon dried thyme leaves
1 teaspoon dried oregano leaves
1 teaspoon dried basil leaves
1 teaspoon garlic powder
1 teaspoon salt
1 teaspoon ground black pepper
1 tablespoon olive oil
1 (5-pound / 2.3-kg) whole
chicken
1 small red apple, peeled, cored, and quartered
1 medium sweet onion, peeled and roughly chopped, divided
3 cloves garlic, peeled and halved
2 cups water

1. In a small bowl, combine thyme, oregano, basil, garlic powder, salt, and pepper. 2. Brush oil on the outside of chicken. Sprinkle mixture from small bowl evenly over chicken. Place apple quarters and half of onion in the cavity of the bird. 3. Add remaining onion and garlic to the cooking pot. Add water to pot. Insert reversible rack over vegetables. Place chicken on rack. Assemble pressure lid, making sure the pressure release valve is in the Seal position. 4. Select Pressure and set to high (HI). Set time to 25 minutes. Press Start. When pressure cooking is complete, allow pressure to natural release. Check chicken using a meat thermometer to ensure the internal temperature is at least 165ºF (74ºC).

Chicken Rogan Josh

Prep time: 15 minutes | Cook time: 30 minutes | Serves 4

2 tablespoons salted butter
2 medium yellow onions, finely chopped
4 medium garlic cloves, smashed and peeled
6 whole cardamom pods, lightly crushed
2 cinnamon sticks
2 tablespoons finely grated fresh ginger
2 tablespoons tomato paste
1½ teaspoons cumin seeds
1 teaspoon sweet paprika
¼ teaspoon ground allspice
¼ teaspoon cayenne pepper
Kosher salt and ground black pepper
3 pounds (1.4 kg) bone-in, skin-on chicken thighs, skin removed and discarded

½ cup whole-milk Greek yogurt   Chopped fresh cilantro, to serve

1. Melt butter in the Ninja Foodi pressure cooker, select Sauté and set to medium (MD). Add the onions, garlic, cardamom, cinnamon and ½ teaspoon salt. Cook, stirring often, until the onions have softened, about 5 minutes. 2. Add the ginger, tomato paste, cumin, paprika, allspice, cayenne, and 1 teaspoon each salt and black pepper, then cook, stirring, until fragrant, about 30 seconds. Stir in 1 cup water, scraping up any browned bits. Nestle the chicken in an even layer, slightly overlapping the pieces if needed. Fast: 3. Assemble pressure lid, making sure the pressure release valve is in the Seal position. Select Pressure and set to high (HI). Set time to 10 minutes. Press Start. Let pressure release naturally for 15 minutes; quick-release any remaining pressure. Press Cancel, then carefully open the pot. Slow: Select Sauté, set ti high (HI) and bring the mixture to a boil. Assemble pressure lid, making sure the pressure release valve is in the Seal position. Select Slow Cook and set to low (LO). Set time to 4 to 5 hours; the chicken is done when a skewer inserted into the largest thigh meets no resistance. Press Cancel, then carefully open the pot. 4. Remove and discard the cinnamon and cardamom pods. Using a slotted spoon, transfer the chicken to a serving dish and tent with foil. 5. Select Sauté and set to high (HI). Bring the cooking liquid to a boil and cook, stirring occasionally, until a spatula drawn though the mixture leaves a very brief trail, about 15 minutes. 6. Press Cancel to turn off the pot, then whisk in the yogurt. Taste and season with salt and black pepper. Using potholders, carefully remove the insert from the housing and pour the sauce over the chicken and sprinkle with cilantro.

Chicken Adobo

Prep time: 15 minutes | Cook time: 36 minutes | Serves 6

2 tablespoons vegetable, corn, or canola oil
6 (10- to 12-ounce / 283- to 340-g) bone-in skin-on chicken thighs
1 large yellow onion, chopped
⅔ cup chicken broth
¼ cup apple cider vinegar
¼ cup soy sauce
2 tablespoons granulated white
sugar
2 tablespoons sauce from a can of chipotle chiles in adobo sauce (optional)
6 medium garlic cloves, peeled and minced
2 teaspoons mild paprika
2 teaspoons ground black pepper
2 bay leaves

1. Add oil to the Ninja Foodi pressure cooker, select Sauté and set to medium (MD). 2. Add half the chicken thighs skin side down and brown well without turning, about 5 minutes. Transfer the thighs to a nearby bowl and brown the remaining thighs in the same way before transferring to the bowl. 3. Add the onion and cook, stirring often, until softened, about 5 minutes. Pour in the broth and scrape up any browned bits on the pot's bottom. Turn off the Sauté function and stir in the vinegar, soy sauce, sugar, adobo sauce (if using), garlic, paprika, pepper, and bay leaves. 4. Return the thighs skin side up to the pot, overlapping them to fit in the sauce. Add any juice from their bowl. Assemble pressure lid, making sure the pressure release valve is in the Seal position. 5. Select Pressure and set to high (HI). Set time to 16 minutes. Press Start. 6. When pressure cooking is complete, allow pressure to natural release, about 20 minutes. Unlatch the lid and open the pot. Serve the chicken and sauce in bowls.

Steam-Roasted Turkey Breast

Prep time: 10 minutes | Cook time: 25 minutes | Serves 6 to 8

2 tablespoons butter, softened to room temperature	½ teaspoon ground black pepper
1 teaspoon mild paprika	¼ teaspoon garlic powder
1 teaspoon kosher salt	1 (4½- to 5-pound / 2.0- to 2.3-
½ teaspoon dried sage	kg) bone-in, skin-on turkey
½ teaspoon onion powder	breast
	2 cups chicken broth or water

1. Use a fork to mash the butter, paprika, salt, sage, onion powder, pepper, and garlic powder into a paste in a small bowl. Smear this mixture all over the skin of the turkey breast. 2. Pour the broth or water into cooking pot. Set reversible rack in the pot. Set the turkey breast skin side up on the rack. Assemble pressure lid, making sure the pressure release valve is in the Seal position. 3. Select Steam and set to high (HI). Set time to 25 minutes. Press Start. 4. When pressure cooking is complete, allow pressure to natural release, about 45 minutes. Unlatch the lid and open the cooker. Use large kitchen tongs and a large metal spatula to transfer the hot turkey breast to a nearby cutting board. Cool for 5 minutes, then carve into ¼- to ½-inch-wide slices.

One-Dish Chicken and Rice

Prep time: 10 minutes | Cook time: 40 minutes | Serves 4

1 cup long-grain white rice, rinsed and drained	3 cloves garlic, minced
1 cup cut frozen green beans (do not thaw)	1 tablespoon toasted sesame oil
1 tablespoon minced fresh ginger	1 teaspoon kosher salt
	1 teaspoon black pepper
	1 pound (454 g) chicken wings, preferably drumettes

1. Preheat the pressure cooker to 375°F (191°C). In a baking pan, combine the rice, green beans, ginger, garlic, sesame oil, salt, and pepper. Stir to combine. Place the chicken wings on top of the rice mixture. 2. Cover the pan with foil. Make a long slash in the foil to allow the pan to vent steam. Place the pan in the cooking pot. Close crisping lid. Select Bake and set time to 30 minutes. 3. Remove the foil. Bake for 10 minutes, or until the wings have browned and rendered fat into the rice and vegetables, turning halfway through the cooking time.

Renaissance Festival Turkey Legs

Prep time: 10 minutes | Cook time: 25 minutes | Serves 2

2 tablespoons light brown sugar	¼ teaspoon cayenne pepper
2 tablespoons tamari	1 teaspoon salt
2 tablespoons ketchup	2 turkey legs
1 tablespoon olive oil	1 cup water
1 teaspoon garlic powder	

1. In a gallon-sized plastic storage bag, combine brown sugar, tamari, ketchup, olive oil, garlic powder, cayenne pepper, and salt.

Squeeze around the ingredients without spilling until combined. Add turkey legs and seal bag. Refrigerate at least 30 minutes or up to overnight. 2. Add the reversible rack and water to Ninja Foodi pressure cooker. Place turkey legs and leftover marinade on the rack. Assemble pressure lid, making sure the pressure release valve is in the Seal position. 3. Select Pressure and set to high (HI). Set time to 20 minutes. Press Start. Let pressure release naturally for 10 minutes; quick-release any remaining pressure. Check turkey using a meat thermometer to ensure the internal temperature is at least 165°F (74°C). 4. Preheat oven to broiler for 500°F (260°C). 5. Transfer legs to a baking sheet lined with parchment paper. Broil 5 minutes. Serve warm.

Juicy Paprika Chicken Breast

Prep time: 5 minutes | Cook time: 30 minutes | Serves 4

Oil, for spraying	1 tablespoon packed light brown
4 (6-ounce / 170-g) boneless, skinless chicken breasts	sugar
1 tablespoon olive oil	½ teaspoon cayenne pepper
1 tablespoon paprika	½ teaspoon onion powder
	½ teaspoon granulated garlic

1. Preheat the pressure cooker to 360°F (182°C). Spray cooking pot lightly with oil. 2. Brush the chicken with the olive oil. 3. In a small bowl, mix together the paprika, brown sugar, cayenne pepper, onion powder, and garlic and sprinkle it over the chicken. 4. Place the chicken in the prepared basket. 5. Close crisping lid. Select Bake and set time to 30 minutes, flipping halfway through, or until the internal temperature reaches 165°F (74°C). Serve.

Tex-Mex Chicken Roll-Ups

Prep time: 10 minutes | Cook time: 14 to 17 minutes | Serves 8

2 pounds (907 g) boneless, skinless chicken breasts or thighs	black pepper, to taste
1 teaspoon chili powder	6 ounces (170 g) Monterey Jack cheese, shredded
½ teaspoon smoked paprika	4 ounces (113 g) canned diced green chiles
½ teaspoon ground cumin	Avocado oil spray
Sea salt and freshly ground	

1. Place the chicken in a large zip-top bag or between two pieces of plastic wrap. Using a meat mallet or heavy skillet, pound the chicken until it is about ¼ inch thick. 2. In a small bowl, combine the chili powder, smoked paprika, cumin, and salt and pepper to taste. Sprinkle both sides of the chicken with the seasonings. 3. Sprinkle the chicken with the Monterey Jack cheese, then the diced green chiles. 4. Roll up each piece of chicken from the long side, tucking in the ends as you go. Secure the roll-up with a toothpick. 5. Preheat the pressure cooker to 350°F (177°C). Spray the outside of the chicken with avocado oil. Place the chicken in a single layer in the cooking pot. Close crisping lid. Select Roast and set time to 14 to 17 minutes, flipping halfway through, until an instant-read thermometer reads 160°F (71°C). 6. Allow it to rest for about 5 minutes before serving.

Spanish Chicken and Mini Sweet Pepper Baguette

Prep time: 10 minutes | Cook time: 20 minutes | Serves 2

1¼ pounds (567 g) assorted small chicken parts, breasts cut into halves
¼ teaspoon salt
¼ teaspoon ground black pepper
2 teaspoons olive oil
½ pound (227 g) mini sweet peppers
¼ cup light mayonnaise
¼ teaspoon smoked paprika
½ clove garlic, crushed
Baguette, for serving
Cooking spray

1. Preheat the pressure cooker to 375ºF (191ºC). Spritz the cooking pot with cooking spray. 2. Toss the chicken with salt, ground black pepper, and olive oil in a large bowl. 3. Arrange the sweet peppers and chicken in the pot. Close crisping lid. Select Bake and set time to 10 minutes. Then transfer the peppers on a plate. 4. Flip the chicken and bake for 10 more minutes or until well browned. 5. Meanwhile, combine the mayo, paprika, and garlic in a small bowl. Stir to mix well. 6. Assemble the baguette with chicken and sweet pepper, then spread with mayo mixture and serve.

Chinese-Take-Out Lacquered Chicken Legs

Prep time: 5 minutes | Cook time: 15 minutes | Serves 4 to 6

1 cup reduced-sodium soy sauce
¼ cup unseasoned rice vinegar
12 skin-on chicken legs
¼ cup granulated white sugar

1. Pour the soy sauce and vinegar into cooking pot. Set a reversible rack in the pot. Pile the chicken legs on the rack. Assemble pressure lid, making sure the pressure release valve is in the Seal position. 2. Select Steam and set to high (HI). Set time to 12 minutes. 3. Quick release pressure by moving the pressure release valve to the Vent position. Unlatch the lid and open the cooker. Use kitchen tongs to transfer the chicken legs to a large, lipped baking sheet. Remove the steaming basket from the pot. Stir the sugar into the liquids in the pot. 4. Position the rack 4 inches from the broiler heat source; heat the broiler for a minute or two. Baste the legs with the sauce in the pot, then broil them until coated and crunchy, about 2 minutes, turning a couple of times and basting each time with more of the pot liquid. Serve warm.

Easy Spicy Chicken Wings

Prep time: 2 minutes | Cook time: 16 minutes | Serves 4

3 pounds (1.4 kg) chicken wings
2 tablespoons olive oil
¼ cup light brown sugar
½ teaspoon garlic powder
½ teaspoon cayenne pepper
½ teaspoon black pepper
½ teaspoon paprika
½ teaspoon salt
1½ cups chicken broth or water

1. Rinse and dry the chicken wings with a paper towel. Put in the large bowl. 2. In a medium bowl, combine the olive oil, sugar, garlic powder, cayenne pepper, black pepper, paprika, and salt. Mix well. 3. Rub all sides of the chicken with the spice mix. 4.

Pour the chicken broth into the cooking pot and add the wings. 5. Assemble pressure lid, making sure the pressure release valve is in the Seal position. Select Pressure and set to high (HI). Set time to 10 minutes. Press Start. 6. Quick release pressure by moving the pressure release valve to the Vent position. Carefully unlock the lid. 7. If you want a crisp skin, slide under the broiler for 5 to 6 minutes. 8. Serve.

Turkey with Bean Chili

Prep time: 10 minutes | Cook time: 35 minutes | Serves 4

1 pound (454 g) ground turkey
1 tablespoon olive oil
2 cups onion, diced
½ cup Anaheim pepper, diced
½ cup red bell pepper, diced
1 cup cannellini beans, soaked for 8 hours
2½ cups chicken stock
1 teaspoon oregano
2 tablespoons chili powder
1 tablespoon salt
½ teaspoon black pepper
3 tablespoons cilantro leaves, chopped

1. Add oil to the Ninja Foodi pressure cooker, select Sauté and set to medium (MD). 2. Add the onion, Anaheim pepper, and bell pepper and sauté until the vegetables are translucent. 3. Add the ground turkey, beans, chicken stock, oregano, chili powder, salt, and black pepper. Stir well. Assemble pressure lid, making sure the pressure release valve is in the Seal position. 4. Select Pressure and set to high (HI). Set time to 30 minutes. 5. Let pressure release naturally for 10 minutes; quick-release any remaining pressure. Open the pot. 6. Top with cilantro leaves and serve.

Chicken Jalfrezi

Prep time: 15 minutes | Cook time: 15 minutes | Serves 4

Chicken:
1 pound (454 g) boneless, skinless chicken thighs, cut into 2 or 3 pieces each
1 medium onion, chopped
1 large green bell pepper, stemmed, seeded, and chopped
2 tablespoons olive oil
1 teaspoon ground turmeric
1 teaspoon garam masala
1 teaspoon kosher salt
½ to 1 teaspoon cayenne pepper
Sauce:
¼ cup tomato sauce
1 tablespoon water
1 teaspoon garam masala
½ teaspoon kosher salt
½ teaspoon cayenne pepper
Side salad, rice, or naan bread, for serving

1. For the chicken: Preheat the pressure cooker to 350ºF (177ºC). In a large bowl, combine the chicken, onion, bell pepper, oil, turmeric, garam masala, salt, and cayenne. Stir and toss until well combined. 2. Place the chicken and vegetables in the cooking pot. Close crisping lid. Select Bake and set time to 15 minutes, stirring and tossing halfway through. Use a meat thermometer to ensure the chicken has reached an internal temperature of 165ºF (74ºC). 3. Meanwhile, for the sauce: In a small microwave-safe bowl, combine the tomato sauce, water, garam masala, salt, and cayenne. Microwave on high for 1 minute. Remove and stir. Microwave for another minute; set aside. 4. When the chicken is cooked, remove and place chicken and vegetables in a large bowl. Pour the sauce over all. Stir and toss to coat the chicken and vegetables evenly. 5. Serve with rice, naan, or a side salad.

Barbecue Chicken

Prep time: 10 minutes | Cook time: 18 to 20 minutes | Serves 4

⅓ cup no-salt-added tomato sauce
2 tablespoons low-sodium grainy mustard
2 tablespoons apple cider vinegar
1 tablespoon honey

2 garlic cloves, minced
1 jalapeño pepper, minced
3 tablespoons minced onion
4 (5-ounce / 142-g) low-sodium boneless, skinless chicken breasts

1. Preheat the pressure cooker to 370°F (188°C). 2. In a small bowl, stir together the tomato sauce, mustard, cider vinegar, honey, garlic, jalapeño, and onion. 3. Brush the chicken breasts with some sauce and place into cooking pot. Close crisping lid. Select Bake and set time to 10 minutes. 4. Turn and brush chicken with more sauce. Bake for 5 minutes more. 5. Turn the chicken again; brush with more sauce. Bake for 3 to 5 minutes more. Discard any remaining sauce. Serve immediately.

Hoisin Turkey Burgers

Prep time: 30 minutes | Cook time: 20 minutes | Serves 4

Olive oil
1 pound (454 g) lean ground turkey
¼ cup whole-wheat bread

crumbs
¼ cup hoisin sauce
2 tablespoons soy sauce
4 whole-wheat buns

1. In a large bowl, mix together the turkey, bread crumbs, hoisin sauce, and soy sauce. 2. Form the mixture into 4 equal patties. Cover with plastic wrap and refrigerate the patties for 30 minutes. 3. Preheat the pressure cooker to 370°F (188°C). Spray the cooking pot lightly with olive oil. 4. Place the patties in the pot in a single layer. Spray the patties lightly with olive oil. 5. Close crisping lid. Select Bake and set time to 15 to 20 minutes, flipping and lightly spraying with olive oil after 10 minutes. 6. Place the patties on buns and top with your choice of low-calorie burger toppings like sliced tomatoes, onions, and cabbage slaw.

Mediterranean Stuffed Chicken Breasts

Prep time: 5 minutes | Cook time: 20 to 25 minutes | Serves 4

4 small boneless, skinless chicken breast halves (about 1½ pounds / 680 g)
Salt and freshly ground black pepper, to taste
4 ounces (113 g) goat cheese
6 pitted Kalamata olives, coarsely chopped

Zest of ½ lemon
1 teaspoon minced fresh rosemary or ½ teaspoon ground dried rosemary
½ cup almond meal
¼ cup balsamic vinegar
6 tablespoons unsalted butter

1. Preheat the pressure cooker to 360°F (182°C). 2. With a boning knife, cut a wide pocket into the thickest part of each chicken breast half, taking care not to cut all the way through. Season the chicken evenly on both sides with salt and freshly ground black pepper. 3. In a small bowl, mix the cheese, olives, lemon zest, and rosemary. Stuff the pockets with the cheese mixture and secure with toothpicks. 4. Place the almond meal in a shallow bowl and dredge the chicken, shaking off the excess. Coat lightly with olive oil spray. 5. Working in batches if necessary, arrange the chicken breasts in a single layer in the cooking pot. Close crisping lid. Select Bake and set time to 20 to 25 minutes, flipping halfway through. 6. While the chicken is baking, prepare the sauce. In a small pan over medium heat, simmer the balsamic vinegar until thick and syrupy, about 5 minutes. Set aside until the chicken is done. When ready to serve, warm the sauce over medium heat and whisk in the butter, 1 tablespoon at a time, until melted and smooth. Season to taste with salt and pepper. 7. Serve the chicken breasts with the sauce drizzled on top.

Ranch Chicken Wings

Prep time: 10 minutes | Cook time: 40 minutes | Serves 4

2 tablespoons water
2 tablespoons hot pepper sauce
2 tablespoons unsalted butter, melted
2 tablespoons apple cider vinegar

1 (1-ounce / 28-g) envelope ranch salad dressing mix
1 teaspoon paprika
4 pounds (1.8 kg) chicken wings, tips removed
Cooking oil spray

1. In a large bowl, whisk the water, hot pepper sauce, melted butter, vinegar, salad dressing mix, and paprika until combined. 2. Add the wings and toss to coat. At this point, you can cover the bowl and marinate the wings in the refrigerator for 4 to 24 hours for best results. However, you can just let the wings stand for 30 minutes in the refrigerator. 3. Preheat the pressure cooker to 400°F (204°C). 4. Spray cook & crisp basket with cooking oil. Working in batches, put half the wings into the basket; it is okay to stack them. Refrigerate the remaining wings. 5. Close crisping lid. Select Air Crisp and set time to 20 minutes, shaking every 5 minutes. 6. Repeat steps 4, 5, and 6 with the remaining wings. 7. When the cooking is complete, serve warm.

Nice Goulash

Prep time: 5 minutes | Cook time: 17 minutes | Serves 2

2 red bell peppers, chopped
1 pound (454 g) ground chicken
2 medium tomatoes, diced
½ cup chicken broth

Salt and ground black pepper, to taste
Cooking spray

1. Preheat the pressure cooker to 365°F (185°C). Spritz cooking pot with cooking spray. 2. Set the bell pepper in the pot. Close crisping lid. Select Broil and set time to 5 minutes, shaking halfway through. 3. Add the ground chicken and diced tomatoes in the pot and stir to mix well. Broil for 6 more minutes or until the chicken is lightly browned. 4. Pour the chicken broth over and sprinkle with salt and ground black pepper. Stir to mix well. Broil for an additional 6 minutes. 5. Serve immediately.

Chicken Shawarma

Prep time: 30 minutes | Cook time: 15 minutes | Serves 4

Shawarma Spice:
2 teaspoons dried oregano
1 teaspoon ground cinnamon
1 teaspoon ground cumin
1 teaspoon ground coriander
1 teaspoon kosher salt
½ teaspoon ground allspice
½ teaspoon cayenne pepper

Chicken:
1 pound (454 g) boneless, skinless chicken thighs, cut into large bite-size chunks
2 tablespoons vegetable oil
For Serving:
Tzatziki
Pita bread

1. For the shawarma spice: In a small bowl, combine the oregano, cayenne, cumin, coriander, salt, cinnamon, and allspice. 2. For the chicken: In a large bowl, toss together the chicken, vegetable oil, and shawarma spice to coat. Marinate at room temperature for 30 minutes or cover and refrigerate for up to 24 hours. 3. Preheat the pressure cooker to 350ºF (177ºC). Place the chicken in the cooking pot. Close crisping lid. Select Bake and set time to 15 minutes, or until the chicken reaches an internal temperature of 165ºF (74ºC). 4. Transfer the chicken to a serving platter. Serve with tzatziki and pita bread.

Nacho Chicken Fries

Prep time: 20 minutes | Cook time: 6 to 7 minutes per batch | Serves 4 to 6

1 pound (454 g) chicken tenders
Salt, to taste
¼ cup flour
2 eggs
¾ cup panko bread crumbs
¾ cup crushed organic nacho cheese tortilla chips

Oil for misting or cooking spray
Seasoning Mix:
1 tablespoon chili powder
1 teaspoon ground cumin
½ teaspoon garlic powder
½ teaspoon onion powder

1. Stir together all seasonings in a small cup and set aside. 2. Cut chicken tenders in half crosswise, then cut into strips no wider than about ½ inch. 3. Preheat the pressure cooker to 390ºF (199ºC). 4. Salt chicken to taste. Place strips in large bowl and sprinkle with 1 tablespoon of the seasoning mix. Stir well to distribute seasonings. 5. Add flour to chicken and stir well to coat all sides. 6. Beat eggs together in a shallow dish. 7. In a second shallow dish, combine the panko, crushed chips, and the remaining 2 teaspoons of seasoning mix. 8. Dip chicken strips in eggs, then roll in crumbs. Mist with oil or cooking spray. Transfer to cook & crisp basket. 9. Chicken strips will cook best if done in two batches. They can be crowded and overlapping a little but not stacked in double or triple layers. 10. Close crisping lid. Select Air Crisp and set time to 6 to 7 minutes, shaking and misting with oil after 4 minutes. 11. Repeat step 10 to cook remaining chicken fries.

Chapter 7 Staples, Sauces, Dips, and Dressings

Black Beans

Prep time: 10 minutes | Cook time: 25 minutes | Serves 4

1 pound (454 g) dried black beans, rinsed and sorted
1 large green bell pepper, seeded and chopped
1 medium onion, chopped
1 teaspoon dried oregano
1 bay leaf
4 ounces (113 g) salt pork, cut into 1-inch pieces, or 1 ham

hock (optional)
1 (14-ounce / 397-g) can diced tomatoes, drained
4 cups chicken or vegetable broth
¼ cup distilled white vinegar
1 teaspoon granulated sugar
2 teaspoons fine sea salt (optional)

1. Rinse the beans and discard any that float. Combine the beans, bell pepper, onion, oregano, bay leaf, pork (if using), tomatoes, and broth in the inner cooking pot. The liquid should cover the beans by about 1½ inches. Add water, if needed, to achieve this. 2. Assemble pressure lid, making sure the pressure release valve is in the Seal position. Select Pressure and set to high (HI). Set time to 25 minutes. Press Start. Let pressure release naturally for 10 minutes; quick-release any remaining pressure. 3. Unlock and remove the lid and taste the beans for doneness. If done, use a fork to press the beans against the side of the pot to mash them. This will thicken the liquid. Stir in the vinegar, sugar, salt (if not using pork or ham)

Thick and Rich Jackfruit Ragu

Prep time: 15 minutes | Cook time: 20 minutes | Serves 6

1 to 2 tablespoons olive oil (or dry sauté or add a little water/ vegetable broth)
1 small onion, minced
4 cloves garlic, minced
2 small carrots, chopped small
1 medium stalk celery, chopped small
1 (20-ounce / 567-g) can jackfruit in brine (do not use the kind in syrup)

1 (28-ounce / 794-g) can tomato purée
2 tablespoons tomato paste
1 tablespoon balsamic vinegar
2 teaspoons dried oregano
1 teaspoon dried basil
1 bay leaf
½ teaspoon salt
¼ teaspoon dried rosemary
¼ teaspoon ground black pepper

1. Add oil (if using) to the Ninja Foodi pressure cooker, select Sauté and set to medium (MD). Sauté the onion until transparent, 5 minutes. Then add the garlic, carrots and celery and sauté for 4 minutes more. 2. Rinse the jackfruit in a strainer and then smash it in your hands to get it to break into shreds. You can remove any large seedpods and discard. They will be obvious once you start smashing. 3. Add the jackfruit shreds, tomato purée, tomato paste,

balsamic vinegar, oregano, basil, bay leaf, salt, rosemary and black pepper. Assemble pressure lid, making sure the pressure release valve is in the Seal position. Select Pressure and set to high (HI). Set time to 10 minutes. 4. When pressure cooking is complete, allow pressure to natural release. 5. Before serving, taste and add extra salt, pepper, herbs and balsamic vinegar if needed. Remove and discard the bay leaf. Serve over toasted bread, pasta or polenta.

Tomato and Basil Sauce

Prep time: 10 minutes | Cook time: 16 minutes | Serves 4
1 tablespoon olive oil
3 cloves garlic, minced
2½ pounds (1.1 kg) Roma tomatoes, diced
½ cup chopped basil
¼ cup vegetable broth
Salt, to taste

1. Add oil to the Ninja Foodi pressure cooker, select Sauté and set to medium (MD). 2. Add the garlic and sauté for 1 minute. 3. Add the tomatoes, basil, and broth. Mix well. 4. Select Pressure and set to high (HI). Set time to 10 minutes. 5. Quick release pressure by moving the pressure release valve to the Vent position. 6. Select Sauté again and cook on medium for 5 minutes more. 7. Using an immersion blender, blend until smooth. 8. Taste and season with salt if necessary. Serve.

Carolina Mustard Barbecue Sauce

Prep time: 5 minutes | Cook time: 5 minutes | Makes about 3 cups

2 cups yellow mustard
⅔ cup apple cider vinegar
½ cup honey
½ cup amber beer or water
2 tablespoons ketchup
2 teaspoons garlic powder
2 teaspoons onion powder

2 teaspoons kosher salt
Pinch freshly ground black pepper
2 tablespoons butter
½ teaspoon cayenne pepper (optional)

1. Put the mustard, vinegar, honey, beer, ketchup, garlic powder, onion powder, salt, pepper, butter, and cayenne pepper (if using) in the cooker and stir well. Assemble pressure lid, making sure the pressure release valve is in the Seal position. Select Pressure and set to high (HI). Set time to 5 minutes. When pressure cooking is complete, allow pressure to natural release, about 5 minutes. 2. Using an immersion or countertop blender, purée the sauce until smooth. Taste and adjust the seasonings, adding more salt, vinegar, or honey as desired. If you'd like to thicken the sauce, select Sauté, set on low (LO) and simmer with the lid off, stirring often, until it reaches your desired consistency. When cool, pour into clean jars, leaving about ½ inch headroom. 3. Cover and store in the refrigerator for up to 12 days or in the freezer for up to 6 months.

Baked Beans

Prep time: 5 minutes | Cook time: 14 minutes | Serves 8

4 bacon slices (optional)
1 (15-ounce / 425-g) can kidney beans, rinsed and drained
1 (15-ounce / 425-g) can pinto beans, rinsed and drained
1 (15-ounce / 425-g) can great northern beans, rinsed and

drained
¾ cup water
½ cup ketchup
⅓ cup unpacked brown sugar
1 tablespoon ground mustard
1 teaspoon chili powder

1. Add the bacon (if using) to the inner cooking pot. Select Sauté and set to Medium. Cook the bacon for 3 minutes on each side, until almost crisp. Transfer the bacon to a paper towel–lined plate to drain, then chop it into bite-size pieces. Drain the fat from the pot. 2. Return the bacon to the pot and add the kidney beans, pinto beans, great northern beans, water, ketchup, sugar, mustard, and chili powder. Assemble pressure lid, making sure the pressure release valve is in the Seal position. Select Pressure and set to high (HI). Set time to 8 minutes. 3. Let pressure release naturally for 15 minutes; quick-release any remaining pressure. Unlock and remove the lid and stir well before serving.

Salted Caramel Sauce

Prep time: 5 minutes | Cook time: 15 minutes |Makes 1½ cups

1 (13½-ounce / 383-g) can full-fat coconut milk
⅔ cup coconut sugar

½ teaspoon sea salt
1 teaspoon pure vanilla extract

1. Select Sauté and set to medium (MD). Combine the coconut milk and coconut sugar in the pot and give the mixture a quick stir. 2. Let the mixture bubble and begin to brown for at least 10 minutes, and up to 15 minutes. Select Cancel, then add the salt and vanilla. 3. Allow the caramel to cool and thicken for another 20 minutes. Remove from the pot and store in a glass container.

Steamed Butternut or Spaghetti Squash
Prep time: 5 minutes | Cook time: 7 minutes | Makes about 5 cups
1 butternut or spaghetti squash, no larger than 3½ pounds (1.6 kg)

1. Add the reversible rack and 1½ cups water to Ninja Foodi pressure cooker. 2. Trim off the stem end of the squash, cut the squash lengthwise into quarters, and scoop out and discard the seeds. Place the squash quarters on the rack in the pot, arranging the pieces in a single layer. 3. Assemble pressure lid, making sure the pressure release valve is in the Seal position. Select Steam and set to high (HI). Set time to 7 minutes. 4. Quick release pressure by moving the pressure release valve to the Vent position. Open the pot and, using tongs, transfer the squash to a plate or cutting board. Set aside until cool enough to handle, about 5 minutes. Use a spoon to scoop the flesh from the skin of the butternut squash, or a fork to separate the strands of the spaghetti squash. Discard the skin. 5. Use immediately, or let cool to room temperature, transfer to an airtight container, and refrigerate for up to 3 days. The texture of spaghetti squash tends to suffer when frozen, while pureed butternut squash freezes well, for up to 3 months.

Basic Lentils

Prep time: 3 minutes | Cook time: 15 minutes | Makes about 6 cups
1 cup lentils (any variety)
1½ cups water
½ teaspoon fine sea salt

1. In a 1½-quart stainless-steel bowl, stir together the lentils, 1½ cups of the water, and the salt. 2. Add the reversible rack and 2 cups water to cooker. Put the bowl on the rack. Select Pressure and set to high (HI). Set time to 15 minutes. 3. Quick release pressure by moving the pressure release valve to the Vent position. Open the pot and, wearing heat-resistant mitts, remove the bowl of lentils from the cooker. 4. If any liquid remains in the bowl with the lentils, drain the lentils into a colander. Transfer the lentils to an airtight container, let cool for about 1 hour, then cover and refrigerate for up to 5 days. To freeze, transfer the lentils to a 1-quart ziplock plastic freezer bag, seal well, and freeze for up to 6 months.

Simple Adzuki Beans

Prep time: 2 minutes | Cook time: 10 minutes | Serves 4
1 cup adzuki beans
1½ cups water or vegetable
stock
1 (3-inch) piece of kombu

1. Combine the beans, water, and kombu in the cooking pot. Assemble pressure lid, making sure the pressure release valve is in the Seal position. Select Pressure and set to high (HI). Set time to 10 minutes. When pressure cooking is complete, allow pressure to natural release. Let the beans sit in the pot for at least 10 minutes. 2. Taste a few beans to make sure they are thoroughly cooked. Carefully remove the lid, remove the kombu (eat, set aside for stock, or compost), and serve.

Creamy Tomato and Basil Pasta Sauce

Prep time: 10 minutes | Cook time: 5 minutes | Makes for 2 pounds pasta

2 (28-ounce / 794-g) cans whole tomatoes, drained
½ cup regular or low-fat evaporated milk
½ small yellow onion, chopped
¼ cup loosely packed fresh basil

leaves, roughly chopped
1 tablespoon fresh rosemary leaves, chopped (optional)
½ teaspoon table salt
¼ cup heavy cream
2 tablespoons tomato paste

1. Wash and dry your hands. Crush the canned tomatoes one by one into a 6-quart cooker. Add the evaporated milk, onion, basil, rosemary (if using), and salt. Stir well. Assemble pressure lid, making sure the pressure release valve is in the Seal position. 2. Select Pressure and set to high (HI). Set time to 5 minutes. 3. Quick release pressure by moving the pressure release valve to the Vent position. Unlatch the lid and open the cooker. Stir in the cream and tomato paste. Either use an immersion blender to purée the sauce right in the pot, or pour the contents of the pot into a large blender, cover, and blend until smooth, scraping down the canister's inside at least once.

Oil-Free Chickpea Sliceable Cheese

Prep time: 2 minutes | Cook time: 9 minutes | Makes about 3 cups

2 cups water
1½ cups cooked chickpeas
2 tablespoons nutritional yeast
2 teaspoons sea salt
1½ teaspoons lactic acid
½ teaspoon granulated onion
½ teaspoon granulated garlic
3 tablespoons tapioca starch
2 tablespoons kappa carrageenan

1. In the jar of a strong blender, combine the water, chickpeas, nutritional yeast, salt, lactic acid, granulated onion and garlic. Blend well. 2. Add the tapioca starch and kappa carrageenan, and blend for 5 to 10 seconds until smooth. 3. Pour the mixture into cooking pot. Select Sauté and set to medium (MD). Bring to a simmer over medium heat, whisking continually. Continue cooking, whisking continuously, for about 7 to 9 minutes, until the mixture has thickened nicely and is very glossy. 4. Pour the cheese into a container that can hold a minimum of 2 cups in volume. 5. If properly cooked, the cheese will start to set right away. Allow the cheese to set at room temperature for 30 minutes. Then cover and refrigerate the cheese to finish setting for 3 to 4 hours. 6. If the cheese doesn't set up properly that means you haven't cooked it long enough. If this happens to you, throw it back into the saucepan and cook for a few minutes more! It will remelt and then you can pour it back into the mold for it to solidify. 7. Remove the cheese from the mold and serve. Store leftovers in the fridge. The cheese should last 10 to 14 days in the fridge.

Fiery Arrabbiata Sauce

Prep time: 10 minutes | Cook time: 18 minutes | Makes about 7 cups

2 (28-ounce / 794-g) cans whole peeled San Marzano tomatoes
2 tablespoons extra-virgin olive oil, plus more for finishing
½ medium yellow onion, diced
1 small carrot, diced
4 garlic cloves, chopped
1 to 2 teaspoons crushed red pepper flakes, to taste (1 teaspoon for moderate heat, 2 teaspoons for spicy)
½ cup fresh basil, chopped, plus
2 tablespoons, finely slivered
1 sprig fresh oregano or 1 teaspoon dried oregano
¼ teaspoon kosher salt (½ teaspoon if using fresh tomatoes)
Freshly cracked black pepper
2 tablespoons tomato paste
1½ teaspoons reduced-sodium tamari or soy sauce (optional)
1 tablespoon high-quality balsamic vinegar

1. Pour the canned whole tomatoes into a large bowl (with the sauce) and crush the tomatoes with your hands by squeezing them through your fingers until no large pieces remain. 2. Select Sauté, set to medium (MD) and let the pot heat up for a few minutes before adding the olive oil. Once the oil is hot, add the onion and carrot. Cook until the vegetables are mostly softened, about 4 minutes. 3. Add the garlic and pepper flakes. Cook for 1 minute, stirring frequently to prevent burning. 4. Select the Cancel setting and pour in the crushed tomatoes, the ½ cup chopped basil, the oregano, salt, and black pepper to taste. Stir gently to combine all of the ingredients. Spoon the tomato paste on top but do not stir, to prevent burning. 5. Assemble pressure lid, making sure the pressure release valve is in the Seal position. Select Pressure and set to high (HI). Set time to 10 minutes. 6. Quick release pressure by moving the pressure release valve to the Vent position. 7. Open

the pot, remove the oregano sprig, and stir in the tamari (if using) and balsamic vinegar. Using an immersion blender, blend the sauce until it has a thick, chunky texture. Taste for seasonings and adjust accordingly. 8. When ready to serve, add the remaining 2 tablespoons basil and, if desired, a drizzle of extra-virgin olive oil. 9. Serve the sauce immediately, or allow the sauce to cool to room temperature, transfer to airtight containers, and refrigerate for up to 1 week. You can also freeze the sauce for up to 6 months. To reheat, warm the sauce gently in a saucepan, stirring until heated through, adding water as needed to thin.

Fire-Roasted Tomato and Butternut Squash Sauce

Prep time: 15 minutes | Cook time: 10 minutes | Serves 4 to 6

2 (14½-ounce / 411-g) cans fire-roasted diced tomatoes
1 cup water
1 yellow onion, diced
3 cloves garlic, chopped
3 cups peeled, seeded and cubed butternut squash
1 teaspoon salt, plus more to taste
1 teaspoon pure maple syrup
1 tablespoon balsamic vinegar
1 teaspoon dried oregano
1 teaspoon dried thyme
Pinch of crushed red pepper flakes
½ teaspoon freshly ground black pepper, plus more to taste
3 tablespoons tomato paste

1. In the cooking pot, combine all the ingredients, except the tomato paste, and mix well. 2. Assemble pressure lid, making sure the pressure release valve is in the Seal position. Select Pressure and set to high (HI). Set time to 10 minutes. 3. Quick release pressure by moving the pressure release valve to the Vent position. Remove the lid. 4. Stir in the tomato paste. Use an immersion blender to purée the sauce until smooth. Adjust the salt and pepper, if needed.

Chili Sauce

Prep time: 5 minutes | Cook time: 8 minutes | Serves 4

4 medium-sized Ancho chili peppers
½ teaspoon ground cumin
½ teaspoon dried oregano
2 teaspoons kosher salt
1½ teaspoons sugar
1½ cups water
2 tablespoons apple cider vinegar
2 cloves garlic, crushed
2 tablespoons heavy cream

1. Cut the peppers in half and remove the stems and seeds. Chop into small pieces. 2. Add the peppers, cumin, oregano, salt, and sugar to the cooking pot. 3. Pour in the water and stir well. 4. Assemble pressure lid, making sure the pressure release valve is in the Seal position. Select Pressure and set to high (HI). Set time to 8 minutes. 5. Let pressure release naturally for 10 minutes; quick-release any remaining pressure. 6. Transfer the mixture to a food processor. Add the vinegar, garlic, and heavy cream. Pulse until smooth and creamy. 7. Serve.

Pumpkin Purée

Prep time: 5 minutes | Cook time: 10 minutes | Makes 2 to 3 cups

1 (2-pound / 907-g) pie pumpkin   1 cup water

1. Slice the pumpkin in half along its equator; remove the stem and seeds. 2. Add the reversible rack and water to Ninja Foodi pressure cooker. Place the pumpkin, cut side down, on top of the rack. 3. Assemble pressure lid, making sure the pressure release valve is in the Seal position. Select Pressure and set to high (HI). Set time to 10 minutes. 4. Quick release pressure by moving the pressure release valve to the Vent position. Using pot holders or tongs, carefully remove the pumpkin. 5. Gently scoop the flesh into a large bowl or food processor. Using an immersion blender or the food processor, pulse until smooth. 6. Store in the refrigerator for up to 1 week.

Easy Jamaican Curry Powder

Prep time: 2 minutes | Cook time: 0 minutes | Makes scant 6 tablespoons

2 tablespoons ground turmeric   ½ teaspoon ground ginger
2 tablespoons ground coriander   ¼ teaspoon cayenne pepper, or
1 tablespoon ground cumin   to taste
1 teaspoon ground cardamom

1. Combine the turmeric, coriander, cumin, cardamom, ginger and cayenne pepper in a bowl. Store in an airtight container for about 3 months.

Restaurant-Style Hummus

Prep time: 5 minutes | Cook time: 40 minutes | Makes 3½ to 4 cups

8 ounces (227 g) dried chickpeas (about 1 cup plus 2 tablespoons)   (about 2 small lemons)
1 teaspoon baking soda   4 garlic cloves, roughly chopped
2 teaspoons kosher salt, plus more to taste   1½ teaspoons ground cumin
¾ cup tahini   8 to 12 tablespoons ice water
6 tablespoons fresh lemon juice   Optional Garnishes:
     Extra-virgin olive oil, smoked paprika, chopped Italian flat-leaf parsley

1. Add the dried chickpeas to the cooking pot and cover with 6 cups water. Stir in the baking soda and 1 teaspoon of the salt. 2. Assemble pressure lid, making sure the pressure release valve is in the Seal position. Select Pressure and set to high (HI). Set time to 40 minutes. 3. Let pressure release naturally for 15 minutes; quick-release any remaining pressure. 4. Open the pot. The chickpeas should be very tender. Drain the chickpeas in a colander (discard the cooking liquid). 5. Transfer the chickpeas to a food processor and blend for 2 minutes until you have a thick paste-like purée, scraping down the sides with a silicone spatula as needed. 6. To the food processor, add the tahini, lemon juice, garlic, cumin, and the remaining 1 teaspoon salt. With the motor running, stream in the ice water, 1 tablespoon at a time, until the hummus is thick yet

smooth and creamy. Taste for seasonings and add more salt, lemon juice, garlic, or cumin as needed. If the hummus is still too thick for your liking, add a tablespoon or two more of ice water. 7. Transfer the hummus to a serving bowl and cover with plastic wrap to keep it from drying out. Ideally, let it rest for 30 minutes before serving. If desired, drizzle a generous amount of extra-virgin olive oil on top of the hummus and garnish with chopped parsley and smoked paprika. Store leftovers in the fridge in an airtight container for up to 1 week. Let the hummus come to room temperature before serving.

Red Garden Salsa

Prep time: 5 minutes | Cook time: 10 minutes | Makes 5 cups

2 cups diced fresh tomatoes   adobo sauce (optional)
1 medium red onion, diced   3 garlic cloves, minced
1 green bell pepper, stemmed, seeded, and diced   1 (8-ounce / 227-g) can tomato sauce
1 jalapeño pepper, stemmed, seeded, and diced   1 tablespoon apple cider vinegar
2 canned chipotle chiles in   3 teaspoons ground cumin
     3 teaspoons kosher salt

1. To the pot of the pressure cooker, add the tomatoes, onion, bell pepper, jalapeño, chipotles (if using), garlic, and tomato sauce. 2. Assemble pressure lid, making sure the pressure release valve is in the Seal position. Select Pressure and set to high (HI). Set time to 10 minutes. When pressure cooking is complete, allow pressure to natural release, about 10 minutes. 3. Stir the vinegar, cumin, and salt into the pot. Taste and adjust the seasonings if necessary. Transfer 3 cups of the salsa to a bowl, then use an immersion or countertop blender to purée the rest of the salsa until mostly smooth. Return the reserved salsa to the pot. 4. Store in a covered jar in the refrigerator for up to 4 days or in the freezer for 3 to 4 months.

Red Hot Enchilada Sauce

Prep time: 10 minutes | Cook time: 10 minutes | Makes 3 to 4 cups

6 garlic cloves, peeled   1 teaspoon chili powder (I use a nice New Mexico blend), plus more as needed
2 poblano peppers, chopped
2 tomatoes, chopped
1 or 2 canned chipotle peppers in adobo sauce   1 teaspoon ground cumin
½ red onion, chopped   1 teaspoon salt
½ cup vegetable stock   1 teaspoon apple cider vinegar
1 tablespoon adobo sauce from the can   ½ teaspoon smoked paprika
     8 ounces (227 g) tomato paste

1. In cooking pot, combine the garlic, poblanos, tomatoes, chipotles, red onion, stock, adobo sauce, chili powder, cumin, salt, vinegar, and paprika. Stir well. Spoon the tomato paste on top, without mixing it in. Assemble pressure lid, making sure the pressure release valve is in the Seal position. Select Pressure and set to high (HI). Set time to 10 minutes. 2. When pressure cooking is complete, allow pressure to natural release. 3. Carefully remove the lid. Using an immersion blender. There may still be a few small intact pieces of basil.

Lentil Tomato Sauce

Prep time: 10 minutes | Cook time: 14 minutes | Makes 4 cups

1 cup finely chopped onion
½ cup finely minced crimini mushrooms
½ cup finely chopped carrot
4 cloves garlic, minced
½ cup green or brown (not French) lentils, rinsed and picked over
¼ cup chopped fresh flat-leaf
parsley
¼ cup chopped fresh basil
1 bay leaf
1 cup vegetable stock
3 cups diced fresh or canned tomatoes
Salt and freshly ground black pepper

1. Select Sauté and set to medium (MD). Add the onion and mushrooms and dry sauté for 2 minutes. Add the carrot and garlic and dry sauté another 30 seconds, adding a bit of the stock if the vegetables start to stick. Add the lentils, half the parsley, half the basil, the bay leaf, and stock. 2. Assemble pressure lid, making sure the pressure release valve is in the Seal position. Select Pressure and set to high (HI). Set time to 10 minutes. When pressure cooking is complete, allow pressure to natural release. Remove the lid, carefully tilting it away from you. 3. Add the tomatoes. Assemble pressure lid, making sure the pressure release valve is in the Seal position. Bring to high pressure again, and cook for 4 minutes. When pressure cooking is complete, allow pressure to natural release. Remove the lid, carefully tilting it away from you. 4. Add the remaining parsley and basil. Use the Sauté function to cook to desired thickness. Remove the bay leaf and add salt and pepper to taste. Refrigerate for 3 days or freeze for up to 3 months.

Chunky Corn and Tempeh Sauce

Prep time: 10 minutes | Cook time: 7 minutes | Makes 4 cups

½ cup vegetable stock
2 teaspoons tamari
1 clove garlic, minced
1 small hot chile, minced (optional)
1 teaspoon crushed or ground coriander seeds
8 ounces (227 g) tempeh, minced, diced, or crumbled
Vegetable cooking spray
(optional)
1 cup diced onion
3 cups fresh or frozen corn kernels (2 large or 3 small ears)
5 plum tomatoes, peeled and chopped
1 tablespoon arrowroot powder, if needed
Salt and freshly ground black pepper

1. Combine the stock, tamari, garlic, chile, if using, and coriander in a medium dish. Stir in the tempeh and marinate for at least 15 minutes, or up to 1 hour. 2. Select Sauté and set to medium (MD). Spray with cooking spray, if using. Add the onion and cook for 1 minute. Add the tempeh with its marinade. 3. Assemble pressure lid, making sure the pressure release valve is in the Seal position. Select Pressure and set to high (HI). Set time to 4 minutes. Quick release pressure by moving the pressure release valve to the Vent position. 4. Add the corn and tomatoes. Lock the lid back on the cooker. Bring to high pressure and cook for 2 minutes. Quick release pressure again. 5. If the sauce looks too runny, add the arrowroot powder and stir well. Add salt and pepper to taste.

No-Effort Soy Yogurt

Prep time: 3 minutes | Cook time: 12 hours | Makes 4 cups

1 (32-ounce / 907-g) container plain unsweetened soy milk
1 packet vegan yogurt starter (I use Cultures for Health Vegan
Yogurt Starter)
1 tablespoon tapioca starch (optional)

1. Whisk together the soy milk, starter and starch (if using) in a very clean mixing bowl. Either pour the mixture directly into the cooking pot. 2. Assemble pressure lid, making sure the pressure release valve is in the Seal position. Select Yogurt. Set time to 8 hours, but I find the yogurt gets firmer without an added thickener if you let it culture for 12 or more hours. Be aware that the yogurt will also become tangier the longer it cultures. 3. Store in the fridge for up to 10 days.

Homemade BBQ Sauce

Prep time: 2 minutes | Cook time: 10 minutes | Makes about 1 cup

1 cup tomato sauce
⅓ cup apple cider vinegar
1 tablespoon pure maple syrup
2 tablespoons vegan Worcestershire sauce (gluten-free, if needed)
1 teaspoon ground cumin
1 teaspoon garlic powder
¼ teaspoon smoked paprika
⅛ teaspoon cayenne pepper
½ teaspoon sea salt
1 cup raw cashews, soaked overnight or in hot water for at least 1 hour
½ cup water
½ teaspoon sea salt

1. In a small saucepan, whisk all ingredients together. Simmer over low heat until thickened and reduced, about 10 minutes. Store in an airtight container in the refrigerator for up to 1 week.

Buttery Marinara Sauce

Prep time: 5 minutes | Cook time: 5 minutes | Makes for 1½ pounds pasta

2 (28-ounce / 794-g) cans diced tomatoes
2 medium yellow onions, peeled and halved
4 medium garlic cloves, peeled
and minced
1 stick butter, cut into chunks
1 teaspoon dried oregano
½ teaspoon ground black pepper
¼ teaspoon table salt

1. Stir all the ingredients in cooking pot. Assemble pressure lid, making sure the pressure release valve is in the Seal position. 2. Select Pressure and set to high (HI). Set time to 5 minutes. 3. Quick release pressure by moving the pressure release valve to the Vent position. Fish out and discard the onion halves (or pieces, if they've come apart). Either use an immersion blender in the pot to purée the mixture into a sauce; or pour the mixture into a large blender, cover, and blend until smooth.

Baked Potato

Prep time: 1 minute | Cook time: 15 minutes | Serves 4 to 6

1 cup water
4 to 6 medium Russet or Idaho potatoes, rinsed, scrubbed, with skins pierced
Optional Toppings:
Butter
Sour Cream
Chives
Bacon

1. Add the reversible rack and water to Ninja Foodi pressure cooker. Arrange the pierced potatoes on the rack. 2. Assemble pressure lid, making sure the pressure release valve is in the Seal position. Select Pressure and set to high (HI). Set time to 15 minutes. Press Start. Let pressure release naturally for 10 minutes; quick-release any remaining pressure. 3. Using tongs, carefully transfer the potatoes to a plate, slice open, top as you wish, and serve!

My Favorite Salt Substitute Blend

Prep time: 2 minutes | Cook time: 0 minutes | Makes about ½ cup

¼ cup nutritional yeast
2 tablespoons dried parsley
2 tablespoons tomato powder (can substitute carrot powder)
1 tablespoon granulated garlic
1½ teaspoons dry ground lemon peel
1 teaspoon onion powder
1 teaspoon ground celery seed
1 teaspoon paprika
1 teaspoon dried basil
1 teaspoon dried thyme
1 teaspoon dried marjoram
¾ teaspoon mustard powder

1. Blend the nutritional yeast, parsley, tomato powder, granulated garlic, lemon peel, onion powder, celery seed, paprika, basil, thyme, marjoram and mustard powder together in a small food processor, small blender or spice grinder. 2. Store in an airtight container for up to 4 months.

Garlic Marinara Sauce

Prep time: 5 minutes | Cook time: 25 minutes | Serves 4 to 6

½ cup extra-virgin olive oil
1 very large Spanish (or yellow) onion, diced
30 cloves garlic, 6 minced, 24 sliced into slivers
1 (28-ounce / 794-g) can crushed tomatoes
1 (28-ounce / 794-g) can whole peeled tomatoes
2 cups vegetable or garlic broth
½ cup dry red wine
1 tablespoon Italian seasoning
1 tablespoon oregano
1 tablespoon parsley
1½ teaspoons granulated sugar
1 to 2 tablespoons seasoned salt
2 teaspoons black pepper
1 bunch fresh basil leaves, rinsed
1 (6-ounce / 170-g) can tomato paste

1. Add oil to the Ninja Foodi pressure cooker, select Sauté and set to high (HI). 2. Add the onion and sauté until slightly translucent, about 3 minutes. Add the garlic and sauté for 5 minutes longer, until lightly browned. 3. Pour in the crushed and peeled tomatoes, followed by the broth, wine, Italian seasoning, oregano, parsley, sugar, seasoned salt, and black pepper and stir to combine. Top with the basil leaves but do not stir them in. 4. Assemble pressure lid, making sure the pressure release valve is in the Seal position. Select Pressure and set to high (HI). Set time to 10 minutes. Quick release pressure by moving the pressure release valve to the Vent position. 5. Remove the lid and use a potato masher to lightly crush the plum tomatoes to the desired chunkiness. Stir in the tomato paste, and let stand for 10 to 20 minutes longer, until slightly thickened.

Pressure Cooker Date Syrup

Prep time: 2 minutes | Cook time: 35 minutes | Makes about 1 cup

2 cups water
2 cups chopped dates

1. Add the water and dates to cooking pot. Assemble pressure lid, making sure the pressure release valve is in the Seal position. Select Pressure and set to high (HI). Set time to 20 minutes. 2. When pressure cooking is complete, allow pressure to natural release. Place a strainer over a large bowl and pour the mixture in. Use a potato masher and carefully mash the liquid out of the date pieces. 3. Rinse out the stainless steel liner and add the liquid back into it. Place the liner in your pressure cooker. Select Sauté and set on high (HI) and—without the lid on—let the date syrup reduce by half. This will take about 15 minutes. 4. Store in the fridge. It will last for about 2 weeks.

Peach Freezer Jam

Prep time: 15 minutes | Cook time: 1 minute | Makes 4 pints

6 cups chopped peaches, peeled and pitted
4 cups sugar
1 (1¾-ounce / 50-g) packet pectin
1 tablespoon lemon juice

1. In a large bowl, mash chopped peaches with a potato masher. Places mashed peaches inside cooking pot. 2. Pour sugar over peaches and let sit 2 to 3 minutes until the juices have been released. 3. Mix in pectin and lemon juice. 4. Assemble pressure lid, making sure the pressure release valve is in the Seal position. 5. Select Pressure and set to high (HI). Set time to 1 minute. 6. When pressure cooking is complete, allow pressure to natural release. 7. Spoon into pint-sized canning jars, leaving 1 inch of space between jam and lid. 8. Let cool and then refrigerate or freeze.

DIY Cajun Seasoning Blend

Prep time: 2 minutes | Cook time: 0 minutes | Makes about 2½ tablespoons

2 teaspoons paprika
2 teaspoons dried thyme
2 teaspoons dried oregano or marjoram
1 teaspoon granulated garlic
½ teaspoon onion powder
1½ to 1 teaspoon cayenne pepper (depending on heat preference)
¼ teaspoon ground black pepper
¼ teaspoon allspice
⅛ teaspoon cloves

1. Mix the paprika, thyme, oregano, granulated garlic, onion powder, cayenne pepper, black pepper, allspice and cloves well. Store in a lidded container. You can also use a spice grinder to make it more like store-bought and to distribute the spices more evenly.

Chapter 8 Stews and Soups

Shrimp and White Bean Soup

Prep time: 15 minutes | Cook time: 35 minutes | Serves 4

2 tablespoons unsalted butter
2 stalks celery, finely chopped
1 medium sweet onion, peeled and finely chopped
1 medium green bell pepper, seeded and finely chopped
1 clove garlic, peeled and minced
½ teaspoon seafood seasoning
½ teaspoon dried thyme
½ teaspoon ground black pepper

1 bay leaf
1 cup dried cannellini beans, soaked overnight in water to cover and drained
4 cups chicken broth
1 pound (454 g) small peeled and deveined shrimp
1 cup frozen or fresh corn kernels
¼ teaspoon hot sauce

1. Melt butter to the Ninja Foodi pressure cooker, select Sauté and set to medium (MD). Add celery, onion, and green pepper and cook until just tender, about 5 minutes. Add garlic, seafood seasoning, thyme, black pepper, and bay leaf and cook until garlic is fragrant, about 1 minute. 2. Add beans and broth to pot. Assemble pressure lid, making sure the pressure release valve is in the Seal position. Select Pressure and set to high (HI). Set time to 30 minutes. 3. When pressure cooking is complete, allow pressure to natural release, about 15 minutes. Open lid, remove bay leaf, and stir in shrimp and corn. Select Sauté, set to low (LO), and simmer until shrimp are opaque and curled into C shapes, about 5 to 8 minutes. Drizzle with hot sauce before serving.

Ethiopian Cabbage Stew

Prep time: 5 minutes | Cook time: 10 minutes | Serves 4

2 tablespoons extra-virgin olive oil (optional)
1 small yellow onion, sliced
1 teaspoon freshly grated ginger
½ teaspoon ground turmeric
¼ teaspoon fenugreek seeds
⅓ cup vegetable broth
3 large carrots, cut into ¾-inch

slices (about 2 cups)
1 pound (454 g) gold potatoes, diced into 1-inch cubes (2 to 3 cups)
½ head cabbage, shredded
1 teaspoon sea salt
½ teaspoon freshly ground black pepper

1. Select Sauté, set to medium (MD), and heat the oil, if using, in the inner pot until hot. (Otherwise, you can dry sauté in the hot pot or add a bit of water in the bottom of the pot.) Add the onion and sauté until softened and golden, 3 to 5 minutes. Add the ginger, turmeric, and fenugreek, and sauté 1 minute more. Add the vegetable broth to deglaze the pan, scraping up any bits that may be stuck to the bottom. Add the carrots, potatoes, cabbage, salt, and pepper. 2. Assemble pressure lid, making sure the pressure release valve is in the Seal position. Select Pressure and set to high (HI). Set time to 3 minutes. 3. Quick release pressure by moving the

pressure release valve to the Vent position. Carefully remove the lid and make sure the vegetables are tender. If not, lock the lid and pressure cook for 1 minute more. 4. Stir and adjust any seasonings to taste. Serve immediately.

Split Pea Soup with Ham

Prep time: 10 minutes | Cook time: 20 minutes | Serves 8

4 tablespoons unsalted butter
1 medium yellow onion, peeled and finely diced
2 stalks celery, finely diced
2 cups diced ham steak
2 cloves garlic, peeled and minced

1 pound (454 g) dried green split peas
6 cups ham stock or chicken stock
1 bay leaf
½ teaspoon salt
½ teaspoon ground black pepper

1. Melt butter in the Ninja Foodi pressure cooker, select Sauté and set to medium (MD). Add onion, celery, and ham. Sauté about 3 minutes. Add garlic and cook until fragrant, about 30 seconds. Press the Cancel button. 2. Add peas, stock, bay leaf, salt, and pepper to pot. Assemble pressure lid, making sure the pressure release valve is in the Seal position. Select Pressure and set to high (HI). Set time to 20 minutes. Press Start. Quick release pressure by moving the pressure release valve to the Vent position. Open lid, and discard bay leaf. 3. Purée one-third of the soup in a blender, then return to the pot and stir well. Serve hot.

Green Pea and Mint Bisque

Prep time: 20 minutes | Cook time: 10 minutes | Serves 6

¼ cup unsalted butter
1 stalk celery, finely chopped
1 medium leek, white and light green parts only, finely chopped
1 clove garlic, peeled and minced
1 tablespoon minced fresh mint leaves

½ teaspoon dried thyme
⅛ teaspoon ground nutmeg
3 cups vegetable broth or chicken stock
1 pound (454 g) frozen green peas
½ cup heavy cream

1. Melt butter in the Ninja Foodi pressure cooker, select Sauté and set to medium (MD). Add celery and leek and cook until tender, about 5 minutes. Add garlic, mint, thyme, and nutmeg and cook until fragrant, about 1 minute. 2. Add broth and peas and stir well. Assemble pressure lid, making sure the pressure release valve is in the Seal position. Select Pressure and set to high (HI). Set time to 5 minutes. 3. When pressure cooking is complete, allow pressure to natural release, about 15 minutes. Remove lid and stir well. Use an immersion blender, or work in batches with a blender, to purée soup until smooth. 4. Add cream to pot and mix well. Let stand on the Keep Warm setting to warm cream, about 5 minutes. Serve hot.

Wonton Soup

Prep time: 35 minutes | Cook time: 11 minutes | Serves 8

8 ounces (227 g) ground pork
1 teaspoon plus ¼ cup cornstarch, divided
¼ cup soy sauce, divided
2 scallions, thinly sliced, divided
¼ teaspoon toasted sesame oil
1¼ teaspoons minced garlic, divided
1¼ teaspoons minced fresh

ginger, divided
20 wonton skins
5 cups chicken broth
2 baby bok choy, chopped
1 medium carrot, peeled and thinly sliced
6 ounces (170 g) shiitake mushrooms, stemmed and sliced
⅓ cup water

1. In a large bowl combine pork, 1 teaspoon cornstarch, 1 teaspoon soy sauce, 1 tablespoon sliced scallion, sesame oil, ¼ teaspoon garlic, and ¼ teaspoon ginger. Mix well. 2. Place wonton skins on a work surface, then divide pork mixture among skins. Dampen a finger with water and run along one side of wonton, then fold and press to seal. Cover filled wontons with a kitchen towel and set aside. 3. Add broth, bok choy, carrot, mushrooms, and remaining soy sauce, garlic, and ginger to the cooking pot. Assemble pressure lid, making sure the pressure release valve is in the Seal position. Select Pressure and set to high (HI). Set time to 5 minutes. 4. Quick release pressure by moving the pressure release valve to the Vent position. Select Sauté, set to medium (MD), and drop in prepared wontons. Cook, stirring occasionally, until wontons float, about 5 minutes. 5. In a small bowl combine water and remaining ¼ cup cornstarch. Mix until smooth, then stir into pot and cook, stirring constantly, until soup starts to thicken, about 1 minute. Top with remaining scallions and serve hot.

Cheeseburger Soup

Prep time: 10 minutes | Cook time: 17 minutes | Serves 4

1 tablespoon olive oil
1 pound (454 g) ground beef
1 medium yellow onion, peeled and diced
1 small green bell pepper, seeded and diced
1 medium carrot, peeled and shredded
1 (15-ounce / 425-g) can diced tomatoes, including juice

2 teaspoons yellow mustard
1 teaspoon smoked paprika
1 teaspoon garlic powder
½ teaspoon salt
4 cups beef broth
2 cups shredded iceberg lettuce
1 cup shredded Cheddar cheese, divided
½ cup diced dill pickles

1. Select Sauté, set to medium (MD), and heat the oil 30 seconds. Add beef, onion, and green pepper to the pot. Sauté 5 minutes until beef begins to brown. Add carrot and heat for an additional minute. 2. Add tomatoes with juice, mustard, paprika, garlic powder, salt, and beef broth to pot. Assemble pressure lid, making sure the pressure release valve is in the Seal position. 3. Select Pressure and set to high (HI). Set time to 7 minutes. Quick release pressure by moving the pressure release valve to the Vent position. 4. Stir in lettuce and ½ cup cheese and simmer 3 minutes. 5. Ladle soup into four bowls and garnish with diced dill pickles and remaining cheese. Serve warm.

Beefy Cabbage and Bean Stew

Prep time: 30 minutes | Cook time: 10 minutes | Serves 6

Prep: 30 min. • Cook: 5 min. • Makes: 6 servings

½ pound (227 g) 90% lean ground beef
3 cups shredded cabbage or angel hair coleslaw mix
1 (16-ounce / 454-g) can red beans, rinsed and drained
1 (14½-ounce / 411-g) can diced tomatoes, undrained
1 (8-ounce / 227-g) can tomato

sauce
¾ cup water
¾ cup salsa or picante sauce
1 medium green pepper, chopped
1 small onion, chopped
3 garlic cloves, minced
1 teaspoon ground cumin
½ teaspoon pepper

1. Select Sauté and set to medium (MD). Cook beef until no longer pink, 6 to 8 minutes, breaking into crumbles; drain. Return beef to cooker. 2. Stir in the remaining ingredients. Assemble pressure lid, making sure the pressure release valve is in the Seal position. Select Pressure and set to high (HI). Set time to 3 minutes. Quick release pressure by moving the pressure release valve to the Vent position.

Creamy Spinach Soup

Prep time: 20 minutes | Cook time: 18 minutes | Serves 4 to 6

2 tablespoons grass-fed butter, ghee or avocado oil
1 yellow onion, peeled and diced
5 fresh cloves garlic, finely minced
2 large celery ribs, thickly sliced
1 pound (454 g) frozen organic spinach, thawed and moisture squeezed out
2 organic russet potatoes, peeled and cubed

1 teaspoon sea salt
1 teaspoon dried thyme
1 teaspoon dried dill
¼ teaspoon ground allspice
4 cups chicken or vegetable stock
8 ounces (227 g) sour cream, plus more for garnish
1 cup shredded cheddar cheese
Extra-virgin olive oil, for garnish (optional)

1. Add your healthy fat of choice to the Ninja Foodi pressure cooker, select Sauté and set to medium (MD). Once the fat has melted, add the onion and sauté for 7 minutes, stirring occasionally, then add the garlic and continue to sauté for 1 minute, stirring occasionally. Add the celery, spinach, potatoes, salt, thyme, dill, allspice and stock, then give the mixture a stir. 2. Assemble pressure lid, making sure the pressure release valve is in the Seal position. Select Pressure and set to high (HI). Set time to 9 minutes. 3. Quick release pressure by moving the pressure release valve to the Vent position. 4. In batches, ladle the soup into a blender, taking care to fill the blender only about halfway (hot liquids will expand in the blender, so please use caution). Blend on a low setting just until puréed and combined. Return the puréed soup to the pot, select Sauté, set to low (LO), and bring to a boil and give it a few stirs. Add the sour cream and cheese and stir until fully combined. 5. Serve immediately. Garnish with a dollop of sour cream or a drizzle of quality extra-virgin olive oil (if using).

Triple Mushroom Stew

Prep time: 10 minutes | Cook time: 20 minutes | Serves 4

2 tablespoons olive oil
1½ cups portabella mushroom caps, sliced
1½ cups cremini mushrooms, sliced
1 cup oyster mushrooms, sliced
1 tablespoon fresh thyme
¼ cup balsamic vinegar
2 cloves garlic, crushed and

minced
¼ cup shallots, minced
1 cup celery, chopped
2 tablespoons flour
4 cups vegetable stock
½ teaspoon salt
1 teaspoon coarse ground black pepper
¼ cup fresh parsley, chopped

1. Select Sauté, set to medium (MD) and add 1 tablespoon of olive oil. 2. Working in batches if necessary, add the mushrooms to the cooker and season with the fresh thyme and balsamic vinegar. Sauté the mushrooms for 3 to 4 minutes until they are softened and the balsamic vinegar has reduced. 3. Using a slotted spoon, remove the mushrooms from the cooker and set aside. 4. Add the remaining olive oil to the cooker while remaining on the Sauté setting. 5. Add the garlic, shallot and celery. Sauté the mixture for 5 minutes. 6. Add the mushrooms back into the cooker, along with the flour, and stir. 7. Next, add in the vegetable stock and season with salt and black pepper, as desired. 8. Assemble pressure lid, making sure the pressure release valve is in the Seal position. Select Pressure and set to high (HI). Set time to 10 minutes. 9. Quick release pressure by moving the pressure release valve to the Vent position. 10. Carefully remove the cover and let any remaining steam dissipate. 11. Serve garnished with fresh parsley.

Beef and Roots Soup

Prep time: 10 minutes | Cook time: 51 minutes | Serves 6

2 tablespoons butter
1 medium yellow onion, chopped
1½ pounds (680 g) beef bottom round, cut into 1-inch pieces
2 medium garlic cloves, peeled and minced
1½ quarts beef or chicken broth
⅓ cup raw long-grain brown

rice
1 medium rutabaga, peeled and diced
2 medium carrots, thinly sliced
2 teaspoons dried oregano
2 teaspoons dried thyme
¼ teaspoon table salt
Ground black pepper, for garnish

1. Select Sauté, set to medium (MD). 2. Melt the butter in the cooker. Add the onion and cook, stirring often, until softened, about 4 minutes. Add the beef and garlic; continue cooking, stirring once in a while, until all the pieces of beef have lost their raw, red color, about 4 minutes. 3. Pour in the broth and scrape up every speck of browned stuff on the pot's bottom. Stir in the rice. Assemble pressure lid, making sure the pressure release valve is in the Seal position. 4. Select Pressure and set to high (HI). Set time to 30 minutes. 5. Quick release pressure by moving the pressure release valve to the Vent position. Stir in the rutabaga, carrots, oregano, thyme, and salt. Lock the lid back onto the pot. 6. Select Pressure and set to high (HI). Set time to 6 minutes. 7. When pressure cooking is complete, allow pressure to natural release, about 30 minutes. Stir well before serving. Garnish the bowls with lots of ground black pepper.

Cauliflower and White Cheddar Soup

Prep time: 5 minutes | Cook time: 22 minutes | Serves 4 to 6

¼ cup (½ stick) butter
6 cups trimmed cauliflower florets
1 teaspoon table salt
½ teaspoon ground dried ginger

¼ teaspoon baking soda
3 cups vegetable broth
2 ounces (57 g) white Cheddar cheese, shredded
¼ cup heavy cream

1. Melt butter in the Ninja Foodi pressure cooker, select Sauté and set to medium (MD). 2. Add the cauliflower and stir well until the florets are coated in butter. Stir in the salt, dried ginger, and baking soda. Turn off the Sauté function, then pour in the broth and stir well. Assemble pressure lid, making sure the pressure release valve is in the Seal position. 3. Select Pressure and set to high (HI). Set time to 12 minutes. 4. Quick release pressure by moving the pressure release valve to the Vent position. Unlatch the lid and open the pot. Use an immersion blender to purée the soup right in the cooker. Or transfer about half the contents of the cooker to a large blender, cover but remove the center knob in the blender's lid, cover with a kitchen towel, and blend until smooth. Then transfer this purée to a large bowl and purée the rest of the soup before returning it all to the pot. 5. Select Sauté and set on low (LO). 6. Add the cheese and cream. Stir until quite steamy but not yet boiling, less than 1 minute. Turn off the Sauté function, remove the hot insert from the machine, set the lid askew over it, and set aside for 5 minutes to blend the flavors.

Turkey Meatball Soup with White Beans and Kale

Prep time: 10 minutes | Cook time: 29 minutes | Serves 6

1 pound (454 g) lean ground turkey
½ cup Italian-seasoned dried bread crumbs
1 large egg white
2 tablespoons olive oil
1 medium yellow onion, chopped
2 ounces (57 g) hard salami,

chopped
2 medium garlic cloves, peeled and minced
4 cups chopped stemmed kale
5 cups chicken broth
1 (15-ounce / 425-g) can white beans, drained and rinsed
1 teaspoon dried oregano
1 teaspoon dried thyme

1. Mix the ground turkey, bread crumbs, and egg white in a large bowl until uniform. Use cleaned and dried hands to form the mixture into 16 balls, each made from about 2 tablespoons of the ground turkey mélange. 2. Select Sauté button and set on medium (MD). 3. Warm the oil in cooker for a minute or two. Add the onion, salami, and garlic; cook, stirring often, until the onion begins to soften, about 4 minutes. Stir in the kale; continue cooking, stirring more frequently, until the greens wilt, about 3 minutes. 4. Stir in the broth, turn off the Sauté function, and scrape up the browned bits on the pot's bottom. Stir in the beans, oregano, and thyme. Add the meatballs and lock the lid onto the pot. 5. Select Pressure and set to high (HI). Set time to 19 minutes. 6. Quick release pressure by moving the pressure release valve to the Vent position. Unlatch the lid and open the pot. Stir gently (to preserve the meatballs) before serving.

Ground Turkey Stew with Black-Eyed Peas

Prep time: 10 minutes | Cook time: 15 minutes | Serves 4

1 large jarred roasted red bell pepper
6 sun-dried tomatoes packed in oil
¼ cup dry but light red wine
1 tablespoon mild paprika
½ teaspoon ground cinnamon
½ teaspoon table salt
¼ teaspoon red pepper flakes
2 tablespoons butter

1 pound (454 g) lean ground turkey
1 (15-ounce / 425-g) can black-eyed peas, drained and rinsed
1 (14-ounce / 397-g) can diced tomatoes
½ cup chicken broth
2 tablespoons loosely packed fresh dill fronds, finely chopped

1. Put the roasted pepper, sun-dried tomatoes, wine, paprika, cinnamon, salt, and red pepper flakes in a food processor. Cover and pulse to create a coarse but thin sauce, stopping the machine at least once to scrape down the inside. 2. Select Sauté button and set on medium (MD). 3. Melt the butter in the cooker. Crumble in the ground turkey and cook, stirring often to break up any clumps, until lightly browned, about 4 minutes. Scrape every bit of the red pepper paste into the cooker and cook, stirring all the while, for 1 minute. 4. Turn off the Sauté function. Stir in the black-eyed peas, tomatoes, broth, and dill until uniform. Assemble pressure lid, making sure the pressure release valve is in the Seal position. 5. Select Pressure and set to high (HI). Set time to 5 minutes. 6. Quick release pressure by moving the pressure release valve to the Vent position. Stir well before serving.

Beer Cheese Soup

Prep time: 20 minutes | Cook time: 5 minutes | Serves 8

3 tablespoons unsalted butter
2 medium carrots, peeled and chopped
2 stalks celery, chopped
1 medium onion, peeled and chopped
1 clove garlic, peeled and minced
1 teaspoon dried mustard
½ teaspoon smoked paprika

¼ cup all-purpose flour
1 (12-ounce / 340-g) bottle lager beer or ale
4 cups chicken broth
½ cup heavy cream
2 cups shredded sharp Cheddar cheese
1 cup shredded smoked Gouda cheese

1. Melt butter in the Ninja Foodi pressure cooker, select Sauté and set to medium (MD). Add carrots, celery, and onion. Cook, stirring often, until softened, about 5 minutes. Add garlic and cook until fragrant, about 30 seconds, then add mustard and paprika and stir well. 2. Add flour and stir well to combine, then cook for 1 minute. Slowly stir in beer, scraping the bottom of pot well, then add broth. 3. Assemble pressure lid, making sure the pressure release valve is in the Seal position. Select Pressure and set to high (HI). Set time to 5 minutes. Press Start. When pressure cooking is complete, allow pressure to natural release, about 15 minutes. Open lid and purée mixture with an immersion blender. Stir in cream, then stir in cheese 1 cup at a time, whisking each addition until completely melted before adding another. Serve hot.

Basic Beef Stew

Prep time: 10 minutes | Cook time: 45 minutes | Serves 4

1½ pounds (680 g) beef stew meat
¼ cup all-purpose flour
2 tablespoons vegetable oil
6 cups low-sodium beef broth
1 large onion, cut into 8 wedges
8 carrots, cut into 1-inch pieces

4 potatoes, scrubbed or peeled, cut into 1-inch chunks
3 celery stalks, cut into 1-inch pieces
½ teaspoon fine sea salt
¼ teaspoon ground black pepper

1. In a medium mixing bowl, toss the stew meat with the flour until coated. 2. Select Sauté and adjust the heat to High. Add the oil to the inner cooking pot. Add about half of the meat to the oil and brown (the longer you brown the meat, the darker your sauce will be). 3. Transfer the browned beef to a plate and repeat with the remaining meat. Add the broth and onion and return the first batch of beef to the pot. 4. Assemble pressure lid, making sure the pressure release valve is in the Seal position. Select Pressure and set to high (HI). Set time to 30 minutes. Press Start. Quick release pressure by moving the pressure release valve to the Vent position. 5. Unlock and remove the lid. Add the carrots, potatoes, celery, salt, and pepper. 6. Bring to pressure again and cook for 8 minutes. Press Start. Quick release pressure again. Unlock and remove the lid.

Potato, Bacon, and Apple Chowder

Prep time: 15 minutes | Cook time: 22 minutes | Serves 6

2 tablespoons butter
2 thick-cut strips of bacon, chopped
1 medium yellow onion, chopped
1 medium russet potato, peeled and cut into 1-inch pieces
3 medium tart green apples

½ teaspoon caraway seeds
½ teaspoon dried thyme
½ teaspoon table salt
½ teaspoon ground black pepper
1 quart vegetable broth
½ cup heavy cream
2 teaspoons cornstarch

1. Select Sauté button and set on medium (MD). 2. Melt the butter in the cooker. Add the bacon pieces and cook, stirring often, until well browned, about 3 minutes. Add the onion and continue cooking, stirring more often, until the onion begins to soften, about 3 minutes. 3. Stir in the potatoes, apples, caraway seeds, thyme, salt, and pepper. Pour in the broth and scrape up every speck of browned stuff on the pot's bottom. Assemble pressure lid, making sure the pressure release valve is in the Seal position. 4. Select Pressure and set to high (HI). Set time to 7 minutes. 5. Quick release pressure by moving the pressure release valve to the Vent position. 6. Unlatch the lid and open the pot. Whisk the cream and cornstarch in a small bowl until smooth. 7. Select Sauté button and set on medium (MD). 8. Bring the soup to a low simmer, stirring constantly. Add the cream slurry and continue cooking, stirring constantly, until thickened, about 1 minute. Remove the hot insert from the pot to stop any cooking. Serve warm.

Curried Lentil and Kale Soup

Prep time: 10 minutes | Cook time: 15 minutes | Serves 4

1½ cups red lentils
1 tablespoon coconut oil
2 cloves garlic, crushed and minced
1 tablespoon fresh grated ginger
1 cup sweet yellow onion, sliced
2 cups kale, chopped

2 tablespoons red curry paste
2 cups vegetable broth
2 cups unsweetened coconut milk
½ cup cashews, chopped
1 tablespoon fresh lemongrass, chopped (optional)

1. Begin by picking though, rinsing and thoroughly draining the lentils. Set aside. 2. Add the coconut oil to the Ninja Foodi pressure cooker, select Sauté and set to medium (MD). 3. Once the oil is hot, add in the garlic, ginger, onion and kale. Sauté the vegetable mixture for 3 minutes. 4. Add in the red curry paste and sauté for an additional 1 to 2 minutes. 5. Next, add in the lentils, vegetable broth, and coconut milk. 6. Assemble pressure lid, making sure the pressure release valve is in the Seal position. Select Pressure and set to high (HI). Set time to 10 minutes. 7. Quick release pressure by moving the pressure release valve to the Vent position. 9. Carefully open the lid and ladle the soup into serving bowls, 10. Garnish with chopped cashews and lemongrass before serving.

White Bean and Broccoli Soup

Prep time: 10 minutes | Cook time: 18 minutes | Serves 4

1½ tablespoons olive oil
1 small yellow onion, diced
3 garlic cloves, minced
¼ to ½ teaspoon crushed red pepper flakes, to taste
¼ cup dry white wine (such as Pinot Grigio or Sauvignon Blanc)
1 pound (454 g) broccoli, cut into florets and stems thinly sliced
1¾ cups cooked cannellini beans or 1 (15-ounce / 425-g) can cannellini beans, drained and rinsed
6 sprigs fresh thyme
½ cup loosely packed fresh basil leaves, roughly chopped
2½ cups low-sodium vegetable broth
1½ teaspoons kosher salt, plus

more to taste
Freshly cracked black pepper
Almond Crumble (omit for a nut-free option):
¼ cup raw almonds
1½ tablespoons nutritional yeast
¼ teaspoon kosher salt
¼ teaspoon extra-virgin olive oil
For Finishing:
1 teaspoon reduced-sodium tamari or soy sauce
1 teaspoon Dijon or whole-grain mustard
¼ cup nutritional yeast
1 cup canned lite or reduced-fat coconut milk (optional)
Kosher salt and freshly cracked black pepper
2 tablespoons finely slivered fresh basil, for garnish

1. Select Sauté, set to medium (MD), and let the pot heat up for a few minutes before adding the olive oil. Once the oil is hot, add the onion and cook until the onion has softened, about 4 minutes. Add the garlic and pepper flakes and cook for 1 minute, tossing frequently to prevent sticking. 2. Pour in the wine to deglaze the pot, using a wooden spoon to scrape up any browned bits on the bottom of the pot. Simmer until the liquid has mostly evaporated and the smell of alcohol has dissipated, about 3 minutes. 3. Add

the broccoli florets and stems and cook for 1 to 2 minutes. Select the Cancel setting. 4. Add the cannellini beans, thyme sprigs, the chopped basil, vegetable broth, salt, and black pepper to taste. Stir to combine all of the ingredients. 5. Assemble pressure lid, making sure the pressure release valve is in the Seal position. Select Pressure and set to high (HI). Set time to 5 minutes. 6. Meanwhile, make the almond crumble: In a food processor, combine the almonds, nutritional yeast, salt, and extra-virgin olive oil and pulse repeatedly for about 30 seconds, or until the mixture has a fine, crumbly texture. Don't overpulse or you'll end up with almond butter. 7. Let pressure release naturally for 5 minutes; quick-release any remaining pressure. 8. Open the pot and discard the thyme sprigs. To finish the soup, stir in the tamari, mustard, nutritional yeast, and coconut milk (if using). Using an immersion blender, purée for a few minutes until you have a thick and creamy soup. Taste the soup for seasonings and add salt and black pepper as needed. 9. Garnish each bowl with a few spoons of almond crumble and the slivered basil.

White Bean and Kale Soup

Prep time: 5 minutes | Cook time: 20 minutes | Serves 6

1 pound (454 g) dried white beans
2 stalks celery, chopped
1 medium yellow onion, peeled and diced
1 clove garlic, minced

3 cups chopped kale
1 teaspoon salt
½ teaspoon black pepper
6 cups vegetable broth
1 tablespoon olive oil

1. In a large bowl, soak beans overnight in water to cover. Drain and add to the cooking pot. 2. Add remaining ingredients to the pot. Assemble pressure lid, making sure the pressure release valve is in the Seal position. Select Pressure and set to high (HI). Set time to 20 minutes. Press Start. When pressure cooking is complete, allow pressure to natural release, about 20 minutes. 3. Remove lid and stir well. Serve hot.

Vegetable and Barley Stew

Prep time: 15 minutes | Cook time: 20 minutes | Serves 4 to 5

2 or 3 parsnips, peeled and chopped
2 cups chopped peeled sweet potato, russet potato, winter squash, or pumpkin
1 large yellow onion, chopped
1 cup pearl barley
1 (28-ounce / 794-g) can diced

tomatoes
4 cups water or unsalted vegetable broth
2 to 3 teaspoons dried mixed herbs or 1 teaspoon dried basil plus 1 teaspoon dried oregano
Salt
Freshly ground black pepper

1. In cooking pot, combine the parsnips, sweet potato, onion, barley, tomatoes with their juice, water, and herbs. Assemble pressure lid, making sure the pressure release valve is in the Seal position. Select Pressure and set to high (HI). Set time to 20 minutes. 2. Quick release pressure by moving the pressure release valve to the Vent position. 3. Taste and season with salt and pepper.

Curried Cauliflower Soup

Prep time: 10 minutes | Cook time: 26 minutes | Serves 4

2 teaspoons olive oil	1 large head cauliflower, broken
1 medium onion, chopped	into florets, core discarded
3 cloves garlic, minced	1 (13½-ounce / 383-g) can
1 tablespoon red curry paste	coconut milk
3 cups chicken stock	1 teaspoon coarse salt

1. Select Sauté button and set on medium (MD). Once hot, add the olive oil, then the onion. Cook, stirring occasionally, until the onion is soft, about 5 minutes. Add the garlic and red curry paste. Cook for about another minute, stirring frequently. 2. Add the chicken stock, taking care to scrape up any browned bits from the bottom of the pot. Add the cauliflower florets. 3. Assemble pressure lid, making sure the pressure release valve is in the Seal position. Select Pressure and set to high (HI). Set time to 20 minutes. 4. Let pressure release naturally for 10 minutes; quick-release any remaining pressure. Stir in the coconut milk and salt. Using an immersion blender, purée the soup until smooth. Serve immediately.

Thai Coconut-Chickpea Stew

Prep time: 10 minutes | Cook time: 3 minutes | Serves 4 to 5

8 ounces (227 g) mushrooms, sliced (about 3 cups)	coconut milk
3 cups cooked chickpeas (from 1 cup dried)	2 tablespoons tamari or soy sauce
1 red bell pepper, seeded and chopped	1 teaspoon Thai chili paste
1 (13½-ounce / 383-g) can	1 teaspoon ground ginger
	Salt

1. In cooking pot, combine the mushrooms, chickpeas, red bell pepper, coconut milk, tamari, chili paste, and ginger. Assemble pressure lid, making sure the pressure release valve is in the Seal position. Select Pressure and set to high (HI). Set time to 3 minutes. 2. Quick release pressure by moving the pressure release valve to the Vent position. 3. Once all the pressure has released, carefully unlock and remove the lid. Taste and season with salt.

Heirloom Tomato Basil Soup

Prep time: 10 minutes | Cook time: 15 minutes | Serves 4

1 tablespoon olive oil	¼ cup julienned fresh basil
1 small onion, peeled and diced	1 teaspoon sea salt
1 celery stalk, sliced	3 cups chicken broth
8 medium heirloom tomatoes, seeded and quartered	1 cup heavy cream
	1 teaspoon ground black pepper

1. Select Sauté, set to medium (MD), and heat the oil. Add the onion and celery and sauté for 3 to 5 minutes until the onions are translucent. Add the tomatoes. Continue to sauté for 3 minutes until tomatoes are tender and start to break down. Add basil, salt, and broth. Assemble pressure lid, making sure the pressure release valve

is in the Seal position. 2. Select Pressure and set to high (HI). Set time to 7 minutes. Quick release pressure by moving the pressure release valve to the Vent position. 3. Add heavy cream and pepper. In the pot, purée soup with an immersion blender, or use a stand blender and purée in batches. Ladle into bowls and serve warm.

French Dip Soup

Prep time: 30 minutes | Cook time: 30 minutes | Serves 6

3 tablespoons vegetable oil	½ teaspoon salt
1 pound (454 g) bottom round roast, cut into 3-inch pieces	½ teaspoon black pepper
3 medium yellow onions, peeled and sliced	½ cup sherry
	3 cups beef broth
4 cloves garlic, peeled and minced	1 teaspoon Worcestershire sauce
	1 bay leaf
1 teaspoon dried thyme	2 cups plain croutons
½ teaspoon dried oregano	1 cup shredded provolone cheese

1. Select Sauté, set to medium (MD), and heat oil. Add half the beef, leaving space between each piece to avoid steaming, browning for 3 minutes per side. Transfer beef to a plate and repeat with remaining beef. 2. To pot add onions and cook until tender, about 5 minutes. Add garlic, thyme, oregano, salt, and pepper and cook until fragrant, about 1 minute. Add sherry, scraping bottom of pot well, and cool until reduced by half, about 1 minute. 3. Add browned beef, broth, Worcestershire sauce, and bay leaf to pot and stir well. Assemble pressure lid, making sure the pressure release valve is in the Seal position. Select Pressure and set to high (HI). Set time to 30 minutes. 4. When pressure cooking is complete, allow pressure to natural release, about 20 minutes. Open lid and remove bay leaf. Remove beef from pot and shred with two forks. Return to pot and stir well. Serve hot with croutons and cheese for garnish.

Avgolemono Soup

Prep time: 2 minutes | Cook time: 10 minutes | Serves 4 to 6

6 cups chicken broth	Juice of 2 lemons
1 cup uncooked orzo	Topping:
3 large eggs	Crumbled feta cheese (optional)

1. Place the chicken broth and orzo in the cooking pot. 2. Assemble pressure lid, making sure the pressure release valve is in the Seal position. Select Pressure and set to high (HI). Set time to 5 minutes. While the broth and orzo are cooking, combine the eggs and lemon juice in a bowl and beat with a fork until totally combined. Set aside. 3. Quick release pressure by moving the pressure release valve to the Vent position. Then select Sauté and set to low (MD). 4. Whisking the entire time, slowly pour 1 cup of the cooked broth into the lemon-egg mixture to temper and stir until totally combined. 5. While still stirring, slowly pour the lemon-egg-broth mixture into the pot, stirring for a good 3 minutes, until the mixture looks creamy and there is no unincorporated egg visible anywhere. Serve topped with some crumbled feta, if desired.

Creamy Pumpkin White Chicken Chili

Prep time: 15 minutes | Cook time: 14 minutes | Serves 6

2 tablespoons avocado oil or extra-virgin olive oil
1 medium yellow onion, diced
2 jalapeño peppers, seeded and chopped
2 poblano peppers, diced
2 pounds (907 g) chicken breast
1 tablespoon chili powder
2 teaspoons paprika
2 teaspoons ground cumin
½ teaspoon cayenne pepper
1 teaspoon sea salt

1 (14½-ounce / 411-g) can diced tomatoes
1 (15-ounce / 425-g) can pure pumpkin purée
2 (4-ounce / 113-g) cans diced green chiles
1 cup chicken stock
8 ounces (227 g) softened cream cheese
Chopped fresh cilantro, for garnish

1. Select Sauté and set to medium (MD). Once hot, coat the bottom of the pot with the oil and add the onion. Cook for 2 to 3 minutes, then add the jalapeño and poblano peppers. Continue to sauté for another 2 to 3 minutes. Select Cancel. 2. Add the chicken, chili powder, paprika, cumin, cayenne, salt, diced tomatoes, pumpkin, diced green chiles and chicken stock and stir. 3. Assemble pressure lid, making sure the pressure release valve is in the Seal position. Select Pressure and set to high (HI). Set time to 8 minutes. 4. Quick release pressure by moving the pressure release valve to the Vent position. Transfer the chicken to a cutting board. Using a fork or knife, shred the chicken and place it back in the pot. 5. Stir in the cream cheese and allow it to melt into the chili. Serve hot with fresh cilantro and any other chili toppings.

All The Beans Soup

Prep time: 20 minutes | Cook time: 50 minutes | Serves 6

1 tablespoon mild oil (or dry sauté or add a little water/vegetable broth)
1 cup minced onion
½ cup minced bell pepper
2 teaspoons minced garlic
7 cups water
1 (16-ounce / 454-g) bag mixed soup beans with barley
2 stalks celery, diced
2 cups diced butternut squash

3 bay leaves
1 tablespoon dried thyme
1 teaspoon smoked paprika
½ teaspoon ground rosemary or ½ teaspoon regular dried
½ teaspoon liquid smoke (optional)
¼ cup nutritional yeast
Salt and pepper, to taste (I used 1½ teaspoons salt and ½ teaspoon black pepper)

1. Select Sauté, set to medium (MD), and heat the oil or broth. Add the onion and sauté until transparent, 5 minutes. Then add the bell pepper and garlic. Sauté until the bell peppers soften, 5 minutes. 2. Add the water, beans, celery, butternut squash, bay leaves, thyme and smoked paprika to the onion mixture and stir to combine. Assemble pressure lid, making sure the pressure release valve is in the Seal position. Select Pressure and set to high (HI). Set time to 40 minutes. 3. When pressure cooking is complete, allow pressure to natural release. Remove and discard the bay leaves. 4. Before serving, mix in the ground rosemary, liquid smoke and nutritional yeast and add salt and pepper to taste. I like to serve mine with a side of chipotle salt to add a little kick to it.

Lima Bean, Kale, and Sausage Soup

Prep time: 10 minutes | Cook time: 30 minutes | Serves 6 to 8

1 pound (454 g) dried lima beans
2 tablespoons olive oil
1 pound (454 g) spicy pork or turkey Italian sausage links, cut into 1-inch pieces
2 medium yellow onions,

chopped
1½ quarts chicken broth
4 fresh oregano sprigs
6 cups packed chopped stemmed kale leave
1 tablespoon fresh lemon juice

1. Pour the beans into a large bowl, fill the bowl with cool tap water, and set aside overnight, for at least 8 hours or up to 12 hours. 2. Select Sauté button and set on medium (MD). 3. Warm the oil in cooking pot for a minute or two. Add the sausage pieces and brown well, stirring occasionally, about 6 minutes. Transfer the pieces to a nearby bowl. 4. Add the onion and cook, stirring often, until softened, about 3 minutes. Pour in the broth and scrape up every speck of browned stuff on the pot's bottom. Turn off the Sauté function. Drain the beans in a colander set in the sink and add them to the pot along with all the sausage in the bowl and the oregano sprigs. Assemble pressure lid, making sure the pressure release valve is in the Seal position. 5. Select Pressure and set to high (HI). Set time to 15 minutes. 6. Quick release pressure by moving the pressure release valve to the Vent position. Find and discard the oregano sprigs, then stir in the kale. Lock the lid back onto the pot. 7. Select Pressure and set to high (HI). Set time to 5 minutes. 8. When pressure cooking is complete, allow pressure to natural release, about 35 minutes. Stir in the lemon juice before serving.

Manchester Stew

Prep time: 25 minutes | Cook time: 10 minutes | Serves 6

2 tablespoons olive oil
2 medium onions, chopped
2 garlic cloves, minced
1 teaspoon dried oregano
1 cup dry red wine
1 pound (454 g) small red potatoes, quartered
1 (16-ounce / 454-g) can kidney beans, rinsed and drained
½ pound (227 g) sliced fresh mushrooms

2 medium leeks (white portion only), sliced
1 cup fresh baby carrots
2½ cups water
1 (14½-ounce / 411-g) can no-salt-added diced tomatoes
1 teaspoon dried thyme
½ teaspoon salt
¼ teaspoon pepper
Fresh basil leaves

1. Select Sauté, set to medium (MD), and add oil. When oil is hot, cook and stir onions until crisp-tender, 2 to 3 minutes. Add garlic and oregano; cook and stir 1 minute longer. Stir in wine. Bring to a boil; cook until liquid is reduced by half, 3 to 4 minutes. Press Cancel. 2. Add potatoes, beans, mushrooms, leeks and carrots. Stir in water, tomatoes, thyme, salt and pepper. Assemble pressure lid, making sure the pressure release valve is in the Seal position. Select Pressure and set to high (HI). Set time to 3 minutes. Let pressure release naturally for 10 minutes; quick-release any remaining pressure. Top with basil leaves.

Black Bean and Kielbasa Soup

Prep time: 15 minutes | Cook time: 30 minutes | Serves 6 to 8

1 pound (454 g) dried black beans
1½ tablespoons vegetable, corn, or canola oil
2 medium green bell peppers, stemmed, cored, and chopped
1 large yellow onion, chopped
10 ounces (283 g) smoked kielbasa, cut into 1-inch pieces
2 tablespoons fresh lime juice

2 medium garlic cloves, peeled and minced
2 teaspoons ground cumin
2 teaspoons dried oregano
2 teaspoons dried thyme
1 teaspoon ground allspice
½ teaspoon ground black pepper
1½ quarts chicken broth

1. Pour the beans into a large bowl, fill it with cool tap water, and set aside to soak at room temperature overnight, for at least 8 hours or up to 12 hours. Drain the beans in a large colander set in the sink. 2. Select Sauté and set to medium (MD). 3. Warm the oil in cooking pot for a minute or two. Add the bell pepper and onion; cook, stirring often, until the onion begins to soften, about 4 minutes. Add the sausage and cook, stirring once in a while, just until lightly browned, about 3 minutes. 4. Stir in the garlic, cumin, oregano, thyme, allspice, and pepper until aromatic, just a few seconds. Pour in the broth and scrape up any browned bits on the pot's bottom. Turn off the Sauté function, stir in the drained beans, and lock the lid onto the pot. 5. Select Pressure and set to high (HI). Set time to 20 minutes. 6. Quick release pressure by moving the pressure release valve to the Vent position. 7. Unlatch the lid and open the pot. Stir in the lime juice and serve hot.

Vegan Root Vegetable Bisque

Prep time: 25 minutes | Cook time: 12 minutes | Serves 6

4 tablespoons olive oil
1 medium onion, peeled and finely chopped
1 medium parsnip, peeled and finely chopped
1 medium celery root or celeriac, peeled and finely chopped
1 medium carrot, peeled and chopped
2 cloves garlic, peeled and

minced
½ teaspoon dried thyme
½ teaspoon smoked paprika
1 cup peeled, seeded, and cubed butternut squash
1 small russet potato, peeled and cubed
6 cups vegetable stock
3 tablespoons chopped fresh flat-leaf parsley

1. Add oil to the Ninja Foodi pressure cooker, select Sauté and set to medium (MD). Add onion, parsnip, celery root, and carrot. Cook, stirring often, until tender, about 12 minutes. Add garlic, thyme and paprika and cook until fragrant, about 30 seconds. 2. Add squash, potato, and stock and stir well. Assemble pressure lid, making sure the pressure release valve is in the Seal position. Select Pressure and set to high (HI). Set time to 12 minutes. 3. When pressure cooking is complete, allow pressure to natural release, about 15 minutes. Remove lid and use an immersion blender, or work in batches in a blender, to purée soup until smooth. Serve hot with parsley for garnish.

Chicken Potpie Soup

Prep time: 15 minutes | Cook time: 15 minutes | Serves 6

3 tablespoons vegetable oil
2 stalks celery, chopped
1 medium onion, peeled and chopped
1 medium carrot, peeled and chopped
2 cloves garlic, peeled and minced
½ teaspoon salt
½ teaspoon ground black pepper

¼ teaspoon dried thyme
3 tablespoons all-purpose flour
3 cups chicken stock
3 cups shredded cooked chicken breast
½ cup heavy whipping cream
1 cup frozen peas
12 round butter crackers, such as Ritz

1. Add oil to the Ninja Foodi pressure cooker, select Sauté and set to medium (MD). Add celery, onion, and carrot and cook until tender, about 8 minutes. Add garlic, salt, pepper, and thyme and cook until fragrant, about 30 seconds. 2. Sprinkle flour over vegetables and cook, stirring well, until flour is completely moistened, about 1 minute. Slowly whisk in stock, making sure to scrape any bits off the bottom of the pot. Stir in chicken. Assemble pressure lid, making sure the pressure release valve is in the Seal position. Select Pressure and set to high (HI). Set time to 5 minutes. 3. Quick release pressure by moving the pressure release valve to the Vent position. Open lid, stir soup well, and stir in cream and peas. Let stand on the Keep Warm setting for 10 minutes, or until peas are hot and tender. Ladle into bowls and top each bowl with 2 crackers. Serve immediately.

Wisconsin Cheddar and Bratwurst Soup

Prep time: 5 minutes | Cook time: 15 minutes | Serves 8

4 tablespoons (½ stick) unsalted butter
1 (28-ounce / 794-g) bag frozen potatoes O'Brien
1 celery stalk, chopped (optional)
2 carrots, chopped
¼ cup all-purpose flour
2 (14-ounce / 397-g) cans low-

sodium chicken broth
1 tablespoon Dijon mustard
½ small head cabbage, shredded (optional)
1 pound (454 g) smoked sausage, cut into bite-size pieces
2 cups milk or half-and-half
2 cups shredded sharp Cheddar cheese

1. Melt butter in the Ninja Foodi pressure cooker, select Sauté and set to medium (MD). Add the potatoes, celery (if using), and carrots and sauté for 5 minutes. 2. Add the flour to the vegetables and stir constantly until the vegetables are coated. Slowly add the broth, stirring constantly to blend the roux into the broth. Add the mustard and stir to get out any lumps, for about 5 minutes. Add the cabbage (if using) and sausage. 3. Assemble pressure lid, making sure the pressure release valve is in the Seal position. Select Pressure and set to high (HI). Set time to 5 minutes. Press Start. Quick release pressure by moving the pressure release valve to the Vent position. 4. Stir the milk into the soup. Add the cheese and stir until it melts.

Eggroll Soup with Crispy Wontons

Prep time: 20 minutes | Cook time: 8 minutes | Serves 6

1 tablespoon vegetable oil
1 pound (454 g) ground pork
2 tablespoons hoisin sauce
1 medium yellow onion, peeled and sliced
3 cloves garlic, minced
1 tablespoon soy sauce
¼ teaspoon Chinese five-spice

powder
¼ teaspoon black pepper
3 cups chicken broth
1 (16-ounce / 454-g) bag coleslaw mix with carrots
2 cups fried wonton strips
2 scallions, thinly sliced

1. Add oil to the Ninja Foodi pressure cooker, select Sauté and set to medium (MD). Add pork and cook, crumbling well, until browned, about 10 minutes. Add hoisin sauce and stir to coat pork, then add onion and cook until tender, about 5 minutes. Add garlic, soy sauce, Chinese five-spice, and pepper and cook until fragrant, about 1 minute. 2. Add broth and coleslaw mix to pot and stir well. Assemble pressure lid, making sure the pressure release valve is in the Seal position. Select Pressure and set to high (HI). Set time to 8 minutes. 3. Quick release pressure by moving the pressure release valve to the Vent position. 4. Serve hot with wonton strips and scallions for garnish.

Irish Stew

Prep time: 20 minutes | Cook time: 40 minutes | Serves 4

2 tablespoons olive oil
2 pounds (907 g) boneless leg of lamb, fat trimmed, cut into 1-inch pieces
Salt and freshly ground black pepper
1 medium yellow onion, thinly sliced through the root end
½ cup Guinness or Murphy's

Irish stout
1½ cups store-bought beef broth, or homemade
3 medium carrots, peeled and cut into 1-inch-thick coins
1 large (16-ounce /454-g) russet potato, peeled and cut into ½-inch slices
2 tablespoons cornstarch

1. Select Sauté, set to high (HI), and heat the oil. Season the lamb all over with salt and pepper. Add 1 cup of the meat (or the chops, in batches) to the pot and cook, stirring occasionally, until browned, 8 minutes. Do not overcrowd the meat or it will simmer in its juices instead of browning. 2. Add the onion to the pot and cook, stirring occasionally, until the onion begins to brown, 5 minutes. Add the stout and cook for 1 minute, scraping up the browned bits on the bottom of the pot. 3. Add the remaining lamb, the broth, and the carrots and stir to combine. Place the potatoes on the top, but don't stir them into the lamb mixture. Assemble pressure lid, making sure the pressure release valve is in the Seal position. Select Pressure and set to high (HI). Set time to 25 minutes. Let pressure release naturally for 10 minutes; quick-release any remaining pressure. 4. Select Sauté and set to high (HI). Mix the cornstarch with 2 tablespoons water and gently stir the mixture into the stew. Simmer until bubbly, 1 minute. Season with salt and pepper. Serve.

Carrot Apple Soup

Prep time: 20 minutes | Cook time: 15 minutes | Serves 6

¼ cup unsalted butter
4 medium carrots, peeled and finely chopped
2 medium Granny Smith apples, cored and chopped
½ medium sweet onion, peeled and finely chopped
1 clove garlic, peeled and minced
1 teaspoon grated fresh ginger

½ teaspoon dried tarragon
⅛ teaspoon ground nutmeg
3 cups vegetable broth or chicken stock
¾ cup heavy cream
½ teaspoon salt
½ teaspoon ground black pepper
3 tablespoons chopped fresh chives

1. Melt butter in the Ninja Foodi pressure cooker, select Sauté and set to medium (MD). Add carrots and cook until tender, about 5 minutes. Add apples, onion, garlic, ginger, tarragon, and nutmeg and cook until fragrant, about 2 minutes. 2. Add broth and stir well. Assemble pressure lid, making sure the pressure release valve is in the Seal position. Select Pressure and set to high (HI). Set time to 10 minutes. 3. When pressure cooking is complete, allow pressure to natural release, about 15 minutes. Remove lid and stir well. Use an immersion blender, or work in batches with a blender, to purée soup until smooth. Stir in cream, salt, and pepper. Sprinkle with chives and serve hot.

Beef and Barley Soup

Prep time: 20 minutes | Cook time: 25 minutes | Serves 8

1 tablespoon vegetable oil
½ pound (227 g) 90% lean ground beef
½ medium yellow onion, peeled and chopped
1 medium carrot, peeled and chopped
1 stalk celery, chopped
1 medium green bell pepper, seeded and chopped
1 (15-ounce / 425-g) can diced tomatoes, undrained

1 large russet potato, peeled and cut into ½-inch cubes
½ cup medium pearled barley
2 cloves garlic, peeled and minced
½ teaspoon dried thyme
½ teaspoon ground black pepper
4 cups beef broth
2 cups water
1 (15-ounce / 425-g) can cut green beans, drained
½ teaspoon salt

1. Select Sauté, set to medium (MD), and heat the oil. Add beef and brown well, about 8 minutes. Add onion, carrot, celery, and bell pepper. Cook until just tender, about 5 minutes. Add tomatoes, potato, barley, garlic, thyme, black pepper, broth, and water. 2. Assemble pressure lid, making sure the pressure release valve is in the Seal position. Select Pressure and set to high (HI). Set time to 20 minutes. Press Start. When pressure cooking is complete, allow pressure to natural release, about 15 minutes. Open lid, stir soup, and add green beans and salt. Replace the lid, press the Keep Warm, and simmer for 5 minutes. Serve hot.

Shane's Fabulous Lentil Soup

Prep time: 10 minutes | Cook time: 10 minutes | Serves 4 to 6

2 cups chopped onion
2 carrots, chopped
2 bay leaves
2 sprigs fresh thyme
6 cups vegetable stock or water

1½ cups green or brown lentils, rinsed and picked over
½ cup red lentils, rinsed and picked over
1 medium potato, peeled if desired and diced
1 teaspoon salt
Freshly ground black pepper

1. Select Sauté and set to medium (MD). Add the onion and dry sauté for about 2 minutes, until no longer raw. Add a tablespoon of water if sticking occurs. Add the carrots and sauté for another minute. Add the bay leaves, thyme, stock, lentils, and potato. Stir well. 2. Assemble pressure lid, making sure the pressure release valve is in the Seal position. Select Pressure and set to high (HI). Set time to 6 minutes. When pressure cooking is complete, allow pressure to natural release. 3. Remove and discard the bay leaves and thyme stems with a pair of tongs. Add the salt and pepper to taste.

Rustic White Bean and Rosemary Stew

Prep time: 10 minutes | Cook time: 15 minutes | Serves 6

2 tablespoons olive oil
3 cloves garlic, crushed and minced
1 cup red onion, sliced
¼ cup dry white wine
2 cups stewed tomatoes, with liquid
4 cups potatoes, cubed

2 (15-ounce / 425-g) cans cannellini beans
½ teaspoon salt
1 teaspoon coarse ground black pepper
1 tablespoon fresh rosemary, chopped
4 cups vegetable stock
¼ cup chopped walnuts, for garnish

1. Select Sauté, set to medium (MD), and heat the olive oil in the cooking pot. 2. Add the garlic and red onion to the cooker. 3. Sauté the garlic and red onion for 2 minutes before adding the white wine. Continue cooking for an additional 3 minutes. 4. Next, add in the remaining ingredients, except for the walnuts. 5. Assemble pressure lid, making sure the pressure release valve is in the Seal position. Select Pressure and set to high (HI). Set time to 8 minutes. 6. Quick release pressure by moving the pressure release valve to the Vent position. 7. Garnish each bowl with chopped walnuts before serving.

Buffalo Chicken Chowder

Prep time: 10 minutes | Cook time: 15 minutes | Serves 4

2 tablespoons olive or avocado oil
1 white or yellow onion, chopped
1⅓ pounds (603 g) chicken breast
1 cup diced celery
1 cup diced carrot

1½ cups diced Yukon gold potato
5 cups chicken stock
¾ cup buffalo hot sauce
⅔ cup full-fat canned coconut milk or half-and-half
¼ cup fresh cilantro, for garnish (optional)

1. Select Sauté and set to medium (MD). Coat the bottom of the pot with the oil once hot, add the onion and sauté for 2 to 3 minutes. Select Cancel. 2. Place the chicken in the pot first. Then add the celery, carrot, potato, chicken stock and buffalo sauce on top of the chicken. 3. Assemble pressure lid, making sure the pressure release valve is in the Seal position. Select Pressure and set to high (HI). Set time to 12 minutes. 4. Quick release pressure by moving the pressure release valve to the Vent position. 5. Add the coconut milk. Top with the fresh cilantro (if using) and serve.

Chapter 9 Vegetables and Sides

Creamy or Crispy Parmesan Polenta

Prep time: 5 minutes | Cook time: 26 minutes | Serves 4

2 tablespoons olive oil
2 medium garlic cloves, thinly sliced
4 cups store-bought chicken or vegetable broth, or homemade, warmed

1 bay leaf
Salt and freshly ground black pepper
1 cup polenta (not quick-cooking)
½ cup grated Parmesan cheese

1. Place the oil in the pot, select Sauté, and set to Medium. When the oil is hot, add the garlic and cook, stirring frequently, until fragrant, 30 seconds. Add the broth, bay leaf, and ½ teaspoon salt. When the liquid comes to a simmer, gradually whisk in the polenta. 2. Assemble pressure lid, making sure the pressure release valve is in the Seal position.Select Pressure and set to low (LO). Set time to 9 minutes. 3. Let pressure release naturally for 10 minutes; quick-release any remaining pressure. It will look watery at first, but will come together and thicken as it stands. Whisk in the cheese and season with salt and pepper. Discard the bay leaf before serving. 4. For solid polenta to pan-fry or broil, transfer the polenta to a storage container and refrigerate, uncovered, until solid, at least 2 hours. Cut into squares and pan-fry in a nonstick sauté pan with a few tablespoons of olive oil over medium heat until golden brown, about 5 minutes per side. To broil, spread squares of polenta on a foil-lined baking sheet, drizzle with oil, sprinkle with a little Parmesan cheese, and broil 4 inches from the broiler element until the cheese is bubbly, 6 minutes.

Broccoli Salad

Prep time: 5 minutes | Cook time: 0 minutes | Serves 2 to 4

½ cup chicken stock
1 pound (454 g) broccoli florets
1 onion, sliced
1 tablespoon lemon juice
1 teaspoon oregano

1 teaspoon garlic powder
3 tablespoons raisins
2 tablespoons crushed walnuts
1 teaspoon olive oil
1 tablespoon kosher salt

1. Pour the stock into the cooking pot and insert a steamer basket. 2. Put the broccoli in the basket. Assemble pressure lid, making sure the pressure release valve is in the Seal position. 3. Select Pressure and set to high (HI). Set time to 0 minutes. 4. Prepare the bowl with very cold water. 5. Quick release pressure by moving the pressure release valve to the Vent position. 6. Immediately transfer the broccoli to the bowl with cold water to keep bright green color. 7. Transfer the chilled broccoli to a serving bowl. 8. Add the onion, raisins, crushed walnuts and season with lemon juice, oregano, garlic powder, salt and oil. Gently stir to combine. 9. Serve.

Roasted Grape Tomatoes and Asparagus

Prep time: 5 minutes | Cook time: 12 minutes | Serves 6
2 cups grape tomatoes
1 bunch asparagus, trimmed
2 tablespoons olive oil
3 garlic cloves, minced
½ teaspoon kosher salt

1. Preheat the pressure cooker to 380ºF(193ºC). 2. In a large bowl, combine all of the ingredients, tossing until the vegetables are well coated with oil. 3. Pour the vegetable mixture into the cooking pot and spread into a single layer. Close crisping lid. Select Roast and set time to 12 minutes.

Marinara Pepperoni Mushroom Pizza

Prep time: 5 minutes | Cook time: 18 minutes | Serves 4
4 large portobello mushrooms, stems removed
4 teaspoons olive oil
1 cup marinara sauce
1 cup shredded Mozzarella cheese
10 slices sugar-free pepperoni

1. Preheat the pressure cooker to 375ºF (191ºC). 2. Brush each mushroom cap with the olive oil, one teaspoon for each cap. 3. Put in cooking pot. Close crisping lid. Select Bake and set time to 8 minutes. 4. Take out of the pot and divide the marinara sauce, Mozzarella cheese and pepperoni evenly among the caps. 5. Bake for another 10 minutes until browned. 6. Serve hot.

Blueberry Dijon Sprouted Wheatberry Salad

Prep time: 10 minutes | Cook time: 25 minutes | Serves 4

1½ cups wheat berries, soaked overnight
4 cups water
¼ cup walnut oil
¼ cup apple cider vinegar
1 tablespoon Dijon mustard

½ teaspoon salt
½ teaspoon black pepper
½ cup red onion, minced
1 cup fresh blueberries
½ cup sliced almonds

1. Drain the excess water off the soaked wheat berries and place them in the cooking pot. 2. Add in the water and stir. 3. Select Pressure and set to high (HI). Set time to 25 minutes. 4. When pressure cooking is complete, allow pressure to natural release. 5. While releasing pressure, combine the walnut oil, apple cider vinegar, Dijon mustard, salt and black pepper. Whisk together until thoroughly combined. 6. Remove the cooked wheat berries from the cooker. Add the dressing and stir. 7. Cover and place in the refrigerator for at least 1 hour to chill. 8. Remove the wheat berries from the cooker and fluff with a fork. 10. Add the blueberries and almonds and stir gently before serving.

Green Pea and Cauliflower Curry

Prep time: 5 minutes | Cook time: 5 minutes | Serves 4

1 (1-inch) piece fresh ginger, peeled and minced (optional)
1 tablespoon coconut oil or olive oil
1 head cauliflower, chopped
1 (28-ounce / 794-g) can crushed tomatoes

2 cups frozen peas
1 cup water
2 tablespoons tomato paste
1 tablespoon curry powder
Salt
Freshly ground black pepper

1. Select Sauté and set to medium (MD). Add the ginger (if using) and coconut oil and cook for 2 to 3 minutes, stirring occasionally, until the ginger is softened. 2. Add the cauliflower, tomatoes, peas, water, tomato paste, and curry powder and stir to combine. Cancel Sauté. 3. Assemble pressure lid, making sure the pressure release valve is in the Seal position. Select Pressure and set to low (LO). Set time to 1 to 2 minutes. 4. Quick release pressure by moving the pressure release valve to the Vent position. 5. Taste and season with salt and pepper.

Orange Juice Beets

Prep time: 5 minutes | Cook time: 10 minutes | Serves 6

1 cup water
6 medium beets, ends trimmed
Juice of 1 medium orange

2 teaspoons unsalted butter
1 teaspoon salt

1. Add the reversible rack and water to Ninja Foodi pressure cooker. Add beets on the rack. Assemble pressure lid, making sure the pressure release valve is in the Seal position. 2. Select Pressure and set to high (HI). Set time to 10 minutes. Quick release pressure by moving the pressure release valve to the Vent position. 3. Let beets rest 5 minutes. Once cool, peel off their outer skin with your hands. Cut beets into quarters and transfer to a serving dish. 4. Add orange juice, butter, and salt to dish. Toss and serve warm.

Candied Carrots

Prep time: 2 minutes | Cook time: 2 minutes | Serves 4 to 6

1 (1-pound / 454-g) bag baby carrots
1 cup water
3 tablespoons vegan butter

3 tablespoons packed light brown sugar
½ to 1 teaspoon salt

1. Add the reversible rack and water to Ninja Foodi pressure cooker. Put the carrots on the rack. Assemble pressure lid, making sure the pressure release valve is in the Seal position. Select Pressure and set to high (HI). Set time to 2 minutes. 2. Quick release pressure by moving the pressure release valve to the Vent position. 3. Carefully remove the lid and add the butter, letting it melt into the carrots for 1 minute or so. 4. Add the brown sugar and salt. Stir, stir, stir until the carrots are coated. Taste and add a touch more salt, if you'd like.

Maple-Balsamic Parsnips

Prep time: 5 minutes | Cook time: 6 minutes | Serves 4

2 or 3 parsnips, peeled and chopped
1 garlic clove, minced
2 tablespoons balsamic vinegar
1 tablespoon pure maple syrup

1 tablespoon olive oil
½ teaspoon dried thyme leaves or ¼ teaspoon ground thyme
Pinch salt

1. In a heat-proof dish that fits inside your pressure cooker's cooking pot, combine the parsnips, garlic, vinegar, maple syrup, olive oil, thyme, and salt. 2. Add the reversible rack and water to Ninja Foodi pressure cooker. Lower the dish onto the rack. Assemble pressure lid, making sure the pressure release valve is in the Seal position. Select Pressure and set to high (HI). Set time to 6 minutes. 3. When pressure cooking is complete, allow pressure to natural release, about 10 minutes. 4. Once all the pressure has released, carefully unlock and remove the lid. Using oven mitts, lift out the dish and serve.

Potatoes, Bacon and Cheese

Prep time: 10 minutes | Cook time: 7 minutes | Serves 4 to 6

3 tablespoons water
2 pounds (907 g) red potatoes, quartered
3 bacon strips, cut into small pieces
1 teaspoon garlic powder

2 teaspoons dried parsley
1 teaspoon kosher salt
⅓ cup ranch dressing
5 ounces (142 g) Cheddar cheese, shredded

1. In the cooking pot, combine the water, potatoes, and bacon. 2. Season with garlic powder, parsley, and salt. Stir well. 3. Assemble pressure lid, making sure the pressure release valve is in the Seal position. Select Pressure and set to high (HI). Set time to 7 minutes. 4. Quick release pressure by moving the pressure release valve to the Vent position. 5. Add the ranch dressing and cheese. Mix well. Serve warm.

Cranberry-Orange Sauce

Prep time: 5 minutes | Cook time: 1 minute | Serves 8

4 cups fresh cranberries
½ cup canned crushed pineapple
Juice from 1 orange
2 teaspoons orange zest

½ cup pure maple syrup
¼ teaspoon cinnamon
Pinch of salt
2 tablespoons sugar

1. Add all ingredients to cooking pot. Assemble pressure lid, making sure the pressure release valve is in the Seal position. 2. Select Pressure and set to high (HI). Set time to 1 minute. When pressure cooking is complete, allow pressure to natural release. 3. Stir ingredients in the pot and smash any unpopped cranberries with the back of a wooden spoon. Transfer sauce to a serving dish and serve warm.

Saucy Mushroom Lettuce Cups

Prep time: 5 minutes | Cook time: 12 minutes | Serves 4

1 tablespoon vegetable oil
¼ cup shallots, minced
2 tablespoon cooking sherry
4 cups cremini mushrooms, quartered
½ cup water chestnuts, chopped
¼ cup low-sodium soy sauce
¼ cup vegetable broth
¼ cup fresh basil
8 butter lettuce leaves

1. Add oil in the cooking pot, select Sauté, and set to medium (MD). 2. Once the oil is hot, add in the shallots and sauté for 3 minutes. 3. Next, add in the cooking sherry and sauté for an additional 2 minutes. 4. Add the remaining ingredients, except for the lettuce leaves, to the cooker. 5. Assemble pressure lid, making sure the pressure release valve is in the Seal position. Select Pressure and set to high (HI). Set time to 4 minutes. 6. Quick release pressure by moving the pressure release valve to the Vent position.. 7. Select Sauté, set to medium (MD), and cook the mushroom mixture, stirring frequently, until the sauce thickens. 8. Press Cancel and let the mushrooms cool for several minutes. 9. Spoon equal amounts of the mushroom mixture into lettuce leaves and serve.

Maple-Cranberry Brussels Sprouts

Prep time: 10 minutes | Cook time: 10 minutes | Serves 4
1 tablespoon olive oil
¼ cup shallots, minced
4 cups Brussels sprouts, halved
1 cup orange juice
¼ cup cranberry juice
2 tablespoons maple syrup
¼ cup dried cranberries, chopped
¼ cup walnuts, chopped

1. Add olive oil in cooking pot, select Sauté, and set to medium (MD). 2. Once the oil is hot, add in the shallots and sauté them for 3 minutes. 3. Next, combine the orange juice, cranberry juice and maple syrup. Whisk together until well blended. 4. Add the sauce and the brussels sprouts to the cooker. 5. Select Pressure and set to high (HI). Set time to 4 minutes. 6. Quick release pressure by moving the pressure release valve to the Vent position.. 7. Use a slotted spoon to remove the brussels sprouts from the cooker and transfer them to a serving plate or bowl. 8. Turn the cooker to the Sauté setting and cook the remaining sauce for 3 to 5 minutes, or until it thickens slightly and reduces. 9. Pour the sauce over the brussels sprouts and toss to coat. 10. Garnish the brussels sprouts with dried cranberries and walnuts before serving.

Frijoles (Mexican-Style Pinto Beans)

Prep time: 10 minutes | Cook time: 60 minutes | Makes about 7 cups
1 pound (454 g) dried pinto beans (about 2½ cups)
1 tablespoon olive oil
1 medium yellow onion, diced
1 red bell pepper, diced
2 teaspoons kosher salt, plus more to taste
Freshly cracked black pepper
2 jalapeño peppers, diced
4 garlic cloves, minced
4 cups low-sodium vegetable broth
1 tablespoon chili powder
2 teaspoons ground cumin
1½ teaspoons dried oregano
1½ teaspoons smoked paprika
¼ to ½ teaspoon cayenne pepper (optional for spicy), to taste
2 bay leaves
1 (14½-ounce / 411-g) can crushed fire-roasted tomatoes
½ cup fresh cilantro, roughly chopped
Optional Garnishes:
Chopped tomatoes and/or avocado
Shredded vegan Cheddar cheese

1. Place the beans in a large bowl and cover with a generous amount of cold water. Soak for 15 minutes. Drain the beans in a colander and rinse with fresh water. 2. Select Sauté, set to medium (MD), and let the pot heat up for a few minutes before adding the olive oil. Once the oil is hot, add the onion and bell pepper. Season with a pinch each of salt and black pepper and cook for 4 to 5 minutes, stirring occasionally. Add the jalapeños and garlic and cook for 1 minute, stirring frequently to prevent burning. 3. Add the soaked and drained pinto beans, vegetable broth, chili powder, cumin, oregano, smoked paprika, cayenne (if using), bay leaves, 2 teaspoons salt, and black pepper to taste. Stir well to combine. Top the mixture with the crushed tomatoes but do not stir, allowing the tomatoes to sit on top. 4. Assemble pressure lid, making sure the pressure release valve is in the Seal position. Select Pressure and set to high (HI). Set time to 50 minutes. 5. When pressure cooking is complete, allow pressure to natural release. 6. Open the pot, stir the beans, and discard the bay leaves. Add the cilantro and taste for seasonings, adding more salt as needed. Garnish the beans as desired.

All-American Pulled Vegetables

Prep time: 15 minutes | Cook time: 20 minutes | Serves 6

2½ cups water
¾ cup green lentils
1 medium sweet potato, peeled and shredded
2 cups cored and shredded green cabbage
2 cups cored and shredded red cabbage
3 medium carrots, shredded
1 (10-ounce / 283-g) can Rotel tomatoes
1 small red onion, halved and thinly sliced into half-moons
¾ cup unsweetened apple juice
2 tablespoons Worcestershire sauce
2 tablespoons Dijon mustard
2 tablespoons dark brown sugar
2 tablespoons mild smoked paprika
1 tablespoon standard chile powder

1. Mix the water and lentils in cooking pot. Assemble pressure lid, making sure the pressure release valve is in the Seal position. 2. Select Pressure and set to high (HI). Set time to 15 minutes. 3. Quick release pressure by moving the pressure release valve to the Vent position. Drain the contents of the hot insert through a fine-mesh sieve such as a chinois or a colander lined with cheesecloth, either set in the sink. Cool a few minutes, then put the lentils in a food processor and process until smooth, stopping the machine and scraping down the inside at least once. 4. Do not clean the insert; set it back in the machine. Stir the sweet potato, red cabbage, green cabbage, carrots, Rotel tomatoes, onion, apple juice, Worcestershire sauce, mustard, brown sugar, smoked paprika, and chile powder into the pot. Lock the lid back on the cooker. 5. Select Pressure and set to high (HI). Set time to 5 minutes. 6. Quick release pressure again. Scrape the lentil purée into the pot; stir well until uniform. Set the lid askew over the pot for 5 to 10 minutes to blend the flavors and allow the vegetables to continue to absorb the liquid.

Creamy Corn

Prep time: 5 minutes | Cook time: 20 minutes | Serves 4 to 6

1 cup raw cashews, soaked in water overnight, drained, and rinsed well
1 cup vegetable stock
2 tablespoons freshly squeezed lemon juice
1 tablespoon sugar
1 teaspoon salt, plus more for seasoning
½ teaspoon vegetable oil
20 ounces (567 g) frozen sweet corn
¾ cup nondairy milk
1 tablespoon vegan butter
¼ teaspoon smoked paprika
Freshly ground black pepper

1. In a blender or food processor, combine the cashews, stock, lemon juice, sugar, salt, and oil. Blend until smooth. Pour the cashew mixture into the cooking pot. Add the corn, milk, butter, and paprika. Season to taste with salt and pepper. Select Pressure and set to low (LO). Set time to 20 minutes. Cover the cooker with a tempered glass lid. 2. When the cook time is complete, carefully remove the lid and stir the creamed corn. If there's too much liquid, select Sauté, set to medium (MD), and cook for 1 to 2 minutes to reduce it (be careful of spatter!).

The Best Damn Ratatouille

Prep time: 20 minutes | Cook time: 35 minutes | Serves 8

1 pound (454 g) eggplant, cut into ¾-inch cubes
1 tablespoon kosher salt, plus more to taste
¼ cup olive oil
1 large sweet onion, diced
8 garlic cloves, chopped
2 medium summer squash or zucchini, cut into pieces roughly the same size as the eggplant
2 medium red or yellow bell peppers, cut into pieces roughly the same size as the eggplant
½ to 1 teaspoon crushed red pepper flakes, to taste
½ teaspoon freshly cracked
black pepper
1 cup fresh basil leaves
2 tablespoons capers, drained
1 bay leaf
6 sprigs fresh thyme
1 pound (454 g) heirloom or Campari tomatoes, roughly chopped, or 1 (14½-ounce / 411-g) can diced San Marzano tomatoes
2 tablespoons tomato paste
½ tablespoon high-quality balsamic vinegar
½ cup fresh Italian flat-leaf parsley, finely chopped

1. Place the eggplant cubes on a cutting board or plate and sprinkle with 1 tablespoon salt. Toss to evenly coat, then place the eggplant in a colander to drain. 2. Select Sauté, set to medium (MD), and let the pot heat up for a few minutes before adding the oil. Once the oil is hot, add the onion. Cook until the onion is soft and almost translucent, 4 to 5 minutes. Add the garlic, squash, and a pinch of salt and cook until the vegetables are slightly softened, about 3 minutes. 3. Add the bell peppers, pepper flakes, black pepper, and ½ cup of the basil (leaves kept whole). Cook for 4 minutes, tossing occasionally. Transfer the vegetable mixture to a bowl and set aside. 4. Add the remaining 2 tablespoons olive oil to the cooking pot, followed by the drained eggplant. Stir gently and frequently to prevent the eggplant from sticking to the bottom of the pot. Cook until the eggplant is soft and starting to turn golden, 4 to 5 minutes. Press Cancel. 5. Return the vegetable mixture to the pot, along with the capers, bay leaf, and thyme sprigs. Stir all of the ingredients to combine. Top the mixture with the tomatoes and tomato paste, but do not stir, allowing the tomatoes and tomato paste to sit on top. 6. Assemble pressure lid, making sure the pressure release valve is in the Seal position. Select Pressure and set to high (HI). Set time to 9 minutes. 7. While the ratatouille is cooking, make a chiffonade of the remaining ½ cup basil by stacking the leaves on top of one another, rolling them up, and slicing thinly into strips. 8. Quick release pressure by moving the pressure release valve to the Vent position. 9. Open the pot and check the ratatouille—it should be a bit soupy and the vegetables should be very tender. Discard the thyme sprigs and bay leaf. 10. Select Sauté, set to medium (MD), and bring the ratatouille to a boil to reduce the liquid and thicken the sauce. This should take 5 to 8 minutes. 11. Press Cancel and stir in the vinegar, parsley, and sliced basil. Taste for salt and adjust accordingly. Use a slotted spoon to transfer the ratatouille to a serving platter.

Eggplant Spread

Prep time: 10 minutes | Cook time: 11 minutes | Serves 4 to 6

4 tablespoons olive oil
2 pounds (907 g) eggplant, sliced
4 cloves garlic, sliced
1 teaspoon kosher salt
1 cup water
1 lemon, juiced
1 tablespoon tahini
1 teaspoon extra-virgin olive oil
¼ cup black olives, pitted and sliced
2 sprigs of thyme

1. Select Sauté, set to medium (MD), and heat the oil. 2. Put the eggplant in the pot and sauté for 3 minutes on both sides. 3. Add the garlic and cook for 1 to 2 minutes more, until fragrant. 4. Sprinkle with salt and pour in the water. 5. Assemble pressure lid, making sure the pressure release valve is in the Seal position. Select Pressure and set to high (HI). Set time to 6 minutes. 6. Let pressure release naturally for 5 minutes; quick-release any remaining pressure. 7. Place the mixture in a blender or food processor; add the lemon juice and tahini. Blend until the texture is smooth. 8. Transfer to a serving bowl and drizzle with extra-virgin olive oil. 9. Serve with olives and thyme.

Garlicky Braised Kale

Prep time: 5 minutes | Cook time: 5 minutes | Serves 4

1 large bunch kale (about 10 ounces / 283 g)
2 tablespoons extra-virgin olive oil
6 cloves garlic, thinly sliced
crosswise
½ cup vegetable broth
¼ teaspoon sea salt
Freshly ground black pepper, to taste

1. Remove and discard the middle stems from the kale, and roughly chop the leafy parts. Rinse and drain the kale. 2. Select Sauté, set to low (LO), and heat the oil in the cooking pot. Add the garlic and sauté for about 2 minutes until tender and golden, taking care not to burn it. Transfer the garlic and oil to a small bowl and set aside. 3. Add the broth to the pot. Place the kale on top and sprinkle with salt and pepper. Assemble pressure lid, making sure the pressure release valve is in the Seal position. Select Pressure and set to low (LO). Set time to 3 minutes. 4. Quick release pressure by moving the pressure release valve to the Vent position. Return the garlic and oil to the pot, and toss to combine. Serve immediately.

Carrots and Turnips

Prep time: 15 minutes | Cook time: 10 minutes | Serves 2 to 4

1 tablespoon olive oil
1 small onion, chopped
3 medium carrots, sliced
2 medium turnips, peeled and sliced

1 teaspoon ground cumin
1 teaspoon lemon juice
Salt and ground black pepper, to taste
1 cup water

1. Select Sauté, set to medium (MD), and heat the oil. 2. Add the onion and sauté for 2 minutes until fragrant. 3. Add the carrots, turnips, cumin, and lemon juice. Sauté for 1 minute more. 4. Season with salt and pepper, stir well. 5. Pour in the water. 6. Assemble pressure lid, making sure the pressure release valve is in the Seal position. 7. Select Pressure and set to high (HI). Set time to 7 minutes. 8. Quick release pressure by moving the pressure release valve to the Vent position. 9. Taste for seasoning. Serve.

Burgundy Mushrooms

Prep time: 5 minutes | Cook time: 30 minutes | Serves 8

½ cup ghee
3 cloves garlic, halved
16 ounces (454 g) whole white mushrooms
16 ounces (454 g) whole baby bella mushrooms
1½ cups dry red wine

1 teaspoon Worcestershire sauce
1 teaspoon dried thyme
1 tablespoon Dijon mustard
1 teaspoon ground celery seed
½ teaspoon ground black pepper
3 cups beef broth
2 slices bacon

1. Select Sauté and set to medium (MD). Add ghee and melt. Add garlic and mushrooms and toss to coat with butter. Stir-fry for 3 minutes until mushrooms start to get tender. Add red wine. Set the cooker to low (LO), and simmer for 5 minutes. 2. Place remaining ingredients into cooking pot. Assemble pressure lid, making sure the pressure release valve is in the Seal position. 3. Select Pressure and set to high (HI). Set time to 20 minutes. Press Start. When pressure cooking is complete, allow pressure to natural release. Discard bacon and garlic. 4. Using a slotted spoon, remove mushrooms and transfer to a serving bowl. Serve warm.

Garlicky Kale and Potatoes

Prep time: 5 minutes | Cook time: 10 minutes | Serves 4
½ cup vegetable broth
3 cloves garlic, minced
2 medium russet potatoes, diced, or other favorite mashing potato
4 cups loosely packed chopped

kale
1 tablespoon almond or other plant-based milk
Salt, to taste (optional)
Ground black pepper, to taste (optional)

1. Select Sauté, set to low (LO), and heat vegetable broth and garlic in the cooking pot for 3 minutes. Add the potatoes. Place reversible rack over the potatoes and set a steamer basket on top. Add the kale to the steamer basket. 2. Assemble pressure lid, making sure the pressure release valve is in the Seal position. Select Pressure and set to low (LO). Set time to 7 minutes. Quick release pressure by

moving the pressure release valve to the Vent position. 3. Remove the cover and pull the steam basket with the kale out of the pot with tongs or silicone gloves. Set aside. Add the almond milk, salt, and pepper to the potatoes, and mash with a hand masher. If there's too much liquid, select Sauté, set to low (LO), and mash until the liquid is absorbed. Transfer the cooked kale into the pot and stir to combine.

Lightened-Up Mashed Potatoes and Gravy

Prep time: 10 minutes | Cook time: 10 minutes | Serves 6
2 pounds (907 g) Yukon gold potatoes
1 yellow onion, chopped
4 ounces (113 g) cremini mushrooms, chopped (about 1 cup)
2 cloves garlic, minced
2 tablespoons soy sauce or

tamari
Fine sea salt and freshly ground black pepper
1 cup water
1 pound (454 g) cauliflower, cut into florets
2 tablespoons chopped fresh chives

1. Cut the potatoes into 1-inch chunks, reserving one cut-up potato for the gravy. 2. Combine the onion, mushrooms, the reserved cut-up potato, the garlic, soy sauce, ¼ teaspoon salt, several grinds of black pepper, and the water in the cooking pot. Arrange reversible rack on top of the mushroom mixture, and place the cauliflower florets and the remaining potatoes on the rack. Assemble pressure lid, making sure the pressure release valve is in the Seal position. Select Pressure and set to high (HI). Set time to 10 minutes. 3. Let pressure release naturally for 10 minutes; quick-release any remaining pressure. 4. Transfer the cauliflower and potatoes to a large bowl. Use a potato masher to mash them, then season generously with salt and pepper to taste. (Add a little more water if you want a thinner consistency.) Stir in the chives. 5. Use an immersion blender to blend the gravy directly in the bottom of the pot. Alternatively, you can pour the mixture into a blender and blend until smooth. Taste and adjust the seasonings. 6. Serve the mash immediately with the gravy on top. Store leftovers in an airtight container in the fridge for 5 days.

"Sour Cream" Mashed Potatoes

Prep time: 10 minutes | Cook time: 4 minutes | Serves 4
1½ pounds (680 g) russet potatoes, peeled and sliced into ¾-inch rounds
½ cup unsweetened nondairy milk

½ cup vegan sour cream
¾ teaspoon fine sea salt, plus more as needed
¼ teaspoon freshly ground black pepper, plus more as needed

1. Add the reversible rack and 1 cup water to Ninja Foodi pressure cooker. Add the potatoes on the rack. 2. Assemble pressure lid, making sure the pressure release valve is in the Seal position. Select Steam and set to high (HI). Set time to 4 minutes. 3. Quick release pressure by moving the pressure release valve to the Vent position. Open the pot and, wearing heat-resistant mitts, lift out the rack. Lift out the inner pot and discard the water. 4. Return the potatoes to the still-warm inner pot. Add the nondairy milk, sour cream, salt, and pepper, then use a potato masher to mash the potatoes to your desired texture. Taste for seasoning and add more salt and pepper, if needed. 5. Spoon the mashed potatoes into a serving bowl and serve warm.

Caramelized Eggplant with Harissa Yogurt

Prep time: 10 minutes | Cook time: 15 minutes | Serves 2

1 medium eggplant (about ¾ pound / 340 g), cut crosswise into ½-inch-thick slices and quartered
2 tablespoons vegetable oil
Kosher salt and freshly ground
black pepper, to taste
½ cup plain yogurt (not Greek)
2 tablespoons harissa paste
1 garlic clove, grated
2 teaspoons honey

1. Preheat the pressure cooker to 400°F (204°C). In a bowl, toss together the eggplant and oil, season with salt and pepper, and toss to coat evenly. Transfer to the cooking pot. Close crisping lid. Select Roast and set time to 15 minutes, shaking every 5 minutes. 2. Meanwhile, in a small bowl, whisk together the yogurt, harissa, and garlic, then spread onto a serving plate. 3. Pile the warm eggplant over the yogurt and drizzle with the honey just before serving.

Easy Potato Croquettes

Prep time: 15 minutes | Cook time: 15 minutes | Serves 10

¼ cup nutritional yeast
2 cups boiled potatoes, mashed
1 flax egg
1 tablespoon flour
2 tablespoons chopped chives
Salt and ground black pepper, to taste
2 tablespoons vegetable oil
¼ cup bread crumbs

1. Preheat the pressure cooker to 400°F (204°C). 2. In a bowl, combine the nutritional yeast, potatoes, flax egg, flour, and chives. Sprinkle with salt and pepper as desired. 3. In a separate bowl, mix the vegetable oil and bread crumbs to achieve a crumbly consistency. 4. Shape the potato mixture into small balls and dip each one into the bread crumb mixture. 5. Put the croquettes in the cook & crisp basket. Close crisping lid. Select Air Crisp and set time to 15 minutes. 6. Serve immediately.

Tofu Bites

Prep time: 15 minutes | Cook time: 30 minutes | Serves 4

1 packaged firm tofu, cubed and pressed to remove excess water
1 tablespoon soy sauce
1 tablespoon ketchup
1 tablespoon maple syrup
½ teaspoon vinegar
1 teaspoon liquid smoke
1 teaspoon hot sauce
2 tablespoons sesame seeds
1 teaspoon garlic powder
Salt and ground black pepper, to taste
Cooking spray

1. Combine all the ingredients to coat the tofu completely and allow the marinade to absorb for half an hour. 2. Preheat the pressure cooker to 375°F (191°C). Spritz a baking dish with cooking spray. 3. Transfer the tofu to the baking dish, and put into cooking pot. Close crisping lid. Select Bake and set time to 30 minutes, flipping halfway through. 5. Serve immediately.

Scalloped Potatoes

Prep time: 5 minutes | Cook time: 20 minutes | Serves 4
2 cup sliced frozen potatoes, thawed
3 cloves garlic, minced
Pinch salt
Freshly ground black pepper, to taste
¾ cup heavy cream

1. Preheat the pressure cooker to 380°F (193°C). 2. Toss the potatoes with the garlic, salt, and black pepper in cooking pot until evenly coated. Pour the heavy cream over the top. 3. Close crisping lid. Select Bake and set time to 15 minutes, or until the potatoes are tender and top is golden brown. Check for doneness and bake for another 5 minutes as needed. 4. Serve hot.

Cabbage Wedges with Caraway Butter

Prep time: 30 minutes | Cook time: 35 to 40 minutes | Serves 6
1 tablespoon caraway seeds
½ cup (1 stick) unsalted butter, at room temperature
½ teaspoon grated lemon zest
1 small head green or red
cabbage, cut into 6 wedges
1 tablespoon avocado oil
½ teaspoon sea salt
¼ teaspoon freshly ground black pepper

1. Place the caraway seeds in a small dry skillet over medium-high heat. Toast the seeds for 2 to 3 minutes, then remove them from the heat and let cool. Lightly crush the seeds using a mortar and pestle or with the back of a knife. 2. Place the butter in a small bowl and stir in the crushed caraway seeds and lemon zest. Form the butter into a log and wrap it in parchment paper or plastic wrap. Refrigerate for at least 1 hour or freeze for 20 minutes. 3. Brush or spray the cabbage wedges with the avocado oil, and sprinkle with the salt and pepper. 4. Preheat the pressure cooker to 375°F (191°C). Place the cabbage in a single layer in the cooking pot. Close crisping lid. Select Roast and set time to 35 to 40 minutes, flipping after 20 minutes. Plate the cabbage and dot with caraway butter. Tent with foil for 5 minutes to melt the butter, and serve.

Indian Eggplant Bharta

Prep time: 15 minutes | Cook time: 20 minutes | Serves 4
1 medium eggplant
2 tablespoons vegetable oil
½ cup finely minced onion
½ cup finely chopped fresh tomato
2 tablespoons fresh lemon juice
2 tablespoons chopped fresh cilantro
½ teaspoon kosher salt
⅛ teaspoon cayenne pepper

1. Preheat the pressure cooker to 400°F (204°C). Rub the eggplant all over with the vegetable oil. Place the eggplant in the cooking pot. Close crisping lid. Select Roast and set time to 20 minutes, or until the eggplant skin is blistered and charred. 2. Transfer the eggplant to a resealable plastic bag, seal, and set aside for 15 to 20 minutes (the eggplant will finish cooking in the residual heat trapped in the bag). 3. Transfer the eggplant to a large bowl. Peel off and discard the charred skin. Roughly mash the eggplant flesh. Add the onion, tomato, lemon juice, cilantro, salt, and cayenne. Stir to combine.

Cauliflower with Lime Juice

Prep time: 10 minutes | Cook time: 7 minutes | Serves 4

2 cups chopped cauliflower florets
2 tablespoons coconut oil, melted

2 teaspoons chili powder
½ teaspoon garlic powder
1 medium lime
2 tablespoons chopped cilantro

1. Preheat the pressure cooker to 350ºF (177ºC). In a large bowl, toss cauliflower with coconut oil. Sprinkle with chili powder and garlic powder. Place seasoned cauliflower into the cooking pot. 2. Close crisping lid. Select Roast and set time to 7 minutes. 3. Cauliflower will be tender and begin to turn golden at the edges. Place into a serving bowl. 4. Cut the lime into quarters and squeeze juice over cauliflower. Garnish with cilantro.

Chiles Rellenos with Red Chile Sauce

Prep time: 20 minutes | Cook time: 20 minutes | Serves 2

Peppers:
2 poblano peppers, rinsed and dried
⅔ cup thawed frozen or drained canned corn kernels
1 scallion, sliced
2 tablespoons chopped fresh cilantro
½ teaspoon kosher salt
¼ teaspoon black pepper
⅔ cup grated Monterey Jack cheese
Sauce:
3 tablespoons extra-virgin olive oil

½ cup finely chopped yellow onion
2 teaspoons minced garlic
1 (6-ounce / 170-g) can tomato paste
2 tablespoons ancho chile powder
1 teaspoon dried oregano
1 teaspoon ground cumin
½ teaspoon kosher salt
2 cups chicken broth
2 tablespoons fresh lemon juice
Mexican crema or sour cream, for serving

1. For the peppers: Preheat the pressure cooker to 400ºF (204ºC). Place the peppers in the cooking pot. Close crisping lid. Select Roast and set time to 10 minutes, turning halfway through. Transfer the peppers to a resealable plastic bag, seal, and set aside to steam for 5 minutes. Peel the peppers and discard the skins. Cut a slit down the center of each pepper, starting at the stem and continuing to the tip. Remove the seeds, being careful not to tear the chile. 2. In a medium bowl, combine the corn, scallion, cilantro, salt, black pepper, and cheese; set aside. 3. Meanwhile, for the sauce: In a large skillet, heat the olive oil over medium-high heat. Add the onion and cook, stirring, until tender, about 5 minutes. Add the garlic and cook, stirring, for 30 seconds. Stir in the tomato paste, chile powder, oregano, and cumin, and salt. Cook, stirring, for 1 minute. Whisk in the broth and lemon juice. Bring to a simmer and cook, stirring occasionally, while the stuffed peppers finish cooking. 4. Cut a slit down the center of each poblano pepper, starting at the stem and continuing to the tip. Remove the seeds, being careful not to tear the chile. 5. Carefully stuff each pepper with half the corn mixture. Place the stuffed peppers in cooking pot. Roast for 10 minutes, or until the cheese has melted. 6. Transfer the stuffed peppers to a serving platter and drizzle with the sauce and some crema.

Garlic Herb Radishes

Prep time: 10 minutes | Cook time: 10 minutes | Serves 4
1 pound (454 g) radishes
2 tablespoons unsalted butter, melted
½ teaspoon garlic powder

½ teaspoon dried parsley
¼ teaspoon dried oregano
¼ teaspoon ground black pepper

1. Preheat the pressure cooker to 350ºF (177ºC). Remove roots from radishes and cut into quarters. 2. In a small bowl, add butter and seasonings. Toss the radishes in the herb butter and place into the cooking pot. 3. Close crisping lid. Select Roast and set time to 10 minutes, tossing halfway through. 5. Serve.

Tomato with Tofu

Prep time: 5 minutes | Cook time: 4 minutes | Serves 4
14 ounces (397 g) firm tofu, cubed
1 cup diced tomatoes
2 tablespoons jarred banana pepper rings

½ cup vegetable or chicken broth
2 teaspoons Italian seasoning
1 tablespoon olive oil

1. In the cooking pot, combine the tofu, tomatoes, banana pepper rings, and broth. 2. Season with Italian seasoning and oil. Mix well. 3. Assemble pressure lid, making sure the pressure release valve is in the Seal position. Select Pressure and set to high (HI). Set time to 4 minutes. 4. Quick release pressure by moving the pressure release valve to the Vent position. 5. Serve.

Loaded Mashed Cauliflower

Prep time: 10 minutes | Cook time: 10 minutes | Serves 6
½ pound (227 g) bacon
1 cup water
2 medium heads cauliflower, cut into florets and core removed
1½ cups shredded sharp cheddar

cheese, divided
4 tablespoons unsalted butter (at room temperature)
½ cup heavy cream
2 green onions, chopped

1. Select Sauté button and set on medium (MD). Once hot, add the bacon. Cook until the bacon is browned and crispy, then remove it with a slotted spoon and place on paper towels to drain any excess fat. Press Cancel. Discard the drippings and wipe the pot clean. 2. Add the reversible rack and water to Ninja Foodi pressure cooker. Place the cauliflower on the rack. 3. Assemble pressure lid, making sure the pressure release valve is in the Seal position. Select Pressure and set to high (HI). Set time to 4 minutes. 4. Quick release pressure by moving the pressure release valve to the Vent position. Carefully transfer the cauliflower to a large bowl and mash until very smooth. Add 1 cup of the shredded cheese plus the butter and cream, stirring to combine. 5. Place the cauliflower mixture into a 7 x 11–inch baking dish. Sprinkle the remaining ½ cup of cheese on top, the broil until the cheese is melted, about 5 minutes. Crumble the bacon and sprinkle over the top along with the green onions.

Spicy Potato Bites with Avocado Dip

Prep time: 10 minutes | Cook time: 8 minutes | Serves 4

4 to 6 medium russet potatoes, scrubbed and cut in large uniform cubes (4 to 5 cups)
1 avocado, peeled and pitted
2 tablespoons freshly squeezed lime juice
2 teaspoons onion powder, divided
1 teaspoon garlic powder,
divided
Pinch salt
1 to 2 tablespoons water, if needed
1 tablespoon olive oil
½ teaspoon smoked paprika
¼ teaspoon ground chipotle pepper

1. Put the potatoes in a steaming basket. 2. Put reversible rack in cooking pot, pour in a cup or two of water, and set the steaming basket on top. Assemble pressure lid, making sure the pressure release valve is in the Seal position. Select Pressure and set to high (HI). Set time to 6 minutes. 3. When pressure cooking is complete, allow pressure to natural release, about 10 minutes. 4. In a blender, combine the avocado, lime juice, 1 teaspoon of onion powder, ½ teaspoon of garlic powder, and the salt. Purée, adding the water if needed to achieve your preferred consistency. Transfer to a serving bowl. 5. Once all the pressure has released, carefully unlock and remove the lid. Using oven mitts, lift the steaming basket out of the pot. 6. Put the empty pot back into the pressure cooker, select Sauté, and set to medium (MD). Return the potatoes to the pot and add the olive oil, remaining 1 teaspoon of onion powder, remaining ½ teaspoon of garlic powder, paprika, and chipotle pepper. Cook for about 2 minutes, stirring occasionally, until any liquid has evaporated. Serve the potatoes with the avocado dipping sauce.

Creamy Mushroom Risotto

Prep time: 15 minutes | Cook time: 15 minutes | Serves 6 to 8

4 tablespoons grass-fed butter or ghee, divided
1 medium yellow onion, diced
1½ pounds (680 g) mushrooms, woody ends removed, thinly sliced
5 cloves garlic, finely chopped
½ cup dry white wine
1 cup uncooked Arborio or other short-grain white rice
1 large celery rib with leaves, thinly sliced
1 teaspoon sea salt
2 cups chicken or vegetable stock
¼ cup heavy cream
½ cup shredded Parmesan cheese, plus more for garnish
¼ cup finely chopped fresh flat-leaf parsley, plus more for garnish
1 teaspoon finely chopped fresh thyme leaves

1. Add 2 tablespoons healthy fat of your choice to the Ninja Foodi pressure cooker, select Sauté and set to medium (MD). Once the fat has melted, add the onion and mushrooms and sauté, stirring occasionally, for 7 minutes, or until caramelized. Then, add the garlic and sauté for 1 minute, stirring occasionally. 2. Add the wine and deglaze the pot, scraping up any browned bits with a wooden spoon. Add the rice, then give everything a stir to combine, stirring for 1 minute. Press Keep Warm. 3. Add the celery, salt and stock, then give everything a quick stir. 4. Assemble pressure lid, making sure the pressure release valve is in the Seal position. Select Pressure and set to high (HI). Set time to 6 minutes. 5. Let pressure release naturally for 10 minutes; quick-release any remaining pressure. 6. Add the cream, the remaining 2 tablespoons of your healthy fat, and the Parmesan, parsley and thyme, then quickly stir until the cream and Parmesan are fully mixed in. Allow the mixture to rest for 10 minutes. 7. Serve immediately, garnished with shredded Parmesan and chopped fresh flat-leaf parsley.

Gorgonzola Mushrooms with Horseradish Mayo

Prep time: 15 minutes | Cook time: 10 minutes | Serves 5

½ cup bread crumbs
2 cloves garlic, pressed
2 tablespoons chopped fresh coriander
⅓ teaspoon kosher salt
½ teaspoon crushed red pepper flakes
1½ tablespoons olive oil
20 medium mushrooms, stems removed
½ cup grated Gorgonzola cheese
¼ cup low-fat mayonnaise
1 teaspoon prepared horseradish, well-drained
1 tablespoon finely chopped fresh parsley

1. Preheat the pressure cooker to 380ºF (193ºC). 2. Combine the bread crumbs together with the garlic, coriander, salt, red pepper, and olive oil. 3. Take equal-sized amounts of the bread crumb mixture and use them to stuff the mushroom caps. Add the grated Gorgonzola on top of each. 4. Put the mushrooms in acooking pot. 5. Close crisping lid. Select Roast and set time to 10 minutes. 6. In the meantime, prepare the horseradish mayo. Mix the mayonnaise, horseradish and parsley. 7. When the mushrooms are ready, serve with the mayo.

Creamy Mushroom Curry with Brown Basmati Rice Pilaf

Prep time: 20 minutes | Cook time: 27 minutes | Serves 2

Brown Basmati Rice Pilaf:
1 cup brown basmati rice
1½ cups water
1 cardamom pod
1 cinnamon stick
½ teaspoon cumin seeds
¼ teaspoon ground turmeric
¼ teaspoon salt
Creamy Mushroom Curry:
1½ cups sliced mushrooms
1 cup cubed potatoes, cauliflower florets, carrots,
sweet potato or combination
½ cup unsweetened nondairy milk
¼ cup unsweetened plain vegan yogurt or cashew cream
1 teaspoon grated ginger
½ teaspoon minced garlic
½ teaspoon salt
½ teaspoon garam masala
¼ teaspoon ground turmeric
¼ teaspoon ground coriander
⅛ teaspoon chili powder

Make the Rice Pilaf: 1. Combine the rice, water, cardamom pod, cinnamon stick, cumin seeds, turmeric and salt in cooking pot. Make the Mushroom Curry: 2. Get a Pyrex dish that fits your pressure cooker, then mix the mushrooms, potatoes, milk, yogurt, ginger, garlic, salt, garam masala, turmeric, coriander and chili powder in it. Cover with foil. 3. Lower the pan on reversible rack in the cooker. Assemble pressure lid, making sure the pressure release valve is in the Seal position. 4. Select Pressure and set to high (HI). Set time to 27 minutes. 5. When pressure cooking is complete, allow pressure to natural release. Carefully lift the pan. Remove and discard the cardamom pod and cinnamon stick from the rice.

Vegetable Dish

Prep time: 15 minutes | Cook time: 14 minutes | Serves 4

1 tablespoon extra-virgin olive oil
1 red onion, sliced
2 red bell peppers, sliced thinly
2 green bell pepper, sliced thinly
1 yellow bell peppers, sliced thinly
2 tomatoes, chopped
Salt and ground black pepper, to taste
2 cloves garlic, chopped
1 bunch parsley, finely chopped

1. Select Sauté, set to medium (MD), and heat the oil. 2. Add the onion and sauté for 3 minutes. 3. Add the bell peppers, stir and sauté for another 5 minutes. 4. Add the tomatoes and sprinkle with salt and pepper. Mix well. Assemble pressure lid, making sure the pressure release valve is in the Seal position. 5. Assemble pressure lid, making sure the pressure release valve is in the Seal position. Select Pressure and set to high (HI). Set time to 6 minutes. 6. Quick release pressure by moving the pressure release valve to the Vent position. 7. Transfer the veggies to a serving bowl and add the garlic and parsley. Stir well. 8. Serve.

Brussels Sprouts and Pomegranate

Prep time: 10 minutes | Cook time: 4 minutes | Serves 2 to 4

1 cup water
1 pound (454 g) Brussels sprouts, trimmed and cut into half
Salt and ground black pepper, to taste
¼ cup pine nuts, toasted
1 pomegranate, seeds separated
1 teaspoon olive oil

1. Add the reversible rack and water to Ninja Foodi pressure cooker. 2. Place the Brussels sprouts on the rack. 3. Assemble pressure lid, making sure the pressure release valve is in the Seal position. Select Pressure and set to high (HI). Set time to 4 minutes. 4. Quick release pressure by moving the pressure release valve to the Vent position. 5. Transfer the sprouts to a serving plate. 6. Season with salt, pepper and pine nuts. Add the pomegranate seeds and stir. 7. Drizzle with oil and stir well. Serve.

Cauliflower Patties

Prep time: 5 minutes | Cook time: 10 minutes | Serves 4

1½ cups water
1 cauliflower head, chopped
1 cup ground almonds
1 cup vegan cheese, shredded
Salt and ground black pepper, to taste
2 tablespoons olive oil

1. Add the reversible rack and water to Ninja Foodi pressure cooker. 2. Put the cauliflower on the rack. 3. Assemble pressure lid, making sure the pressure release valve is in the Seal position. Select Pressure and set to high (HI). Set time to 5 minutes. 4. Quick release pressure by moving the pressure release valve to the Vent position. 5. Place the cauliflower in a food processor and ground it. 6. Add the almonds and cheese. Season with salt and pepper. Mix well. 7. Shape the mixture into oval patties, each ½ inch thick. 8. Carefully pour the water out of the pot and completely dry the pot before replacing it. 9. Select Sauté, set to medium (MD), and heat the oil. 10. Add the patties and cook on both sides until golden. You may have to do it in two batches. 11. Serve.

Sesame-Ginger Broccoli

Prep time: 10 minutes | Cook time: 15 minutes | Serves 4

3 tablespoons toasted sesame oil
2 teaspoons sesame seeds
1 tablespoon chili-garlic sauce
2 teaspoons minced fresh ginger
½ teaspoon kosher salt
½ teaspoon black pepper
1 (16-ounce / 454-g) package frozen broccoli florets (do not thaw)

1. In a large bowl, combine the sesame oil, sesame seeds, chili-garlic sauce, ginger, salt, and pepper. Stir until well combined. Add the broccoli and toss until well coated. 2. Preheat the pressure cooker to 325°F (163°C). Arrange the broccoli in the cooking pot. Close crisping lid. Select Roast and set time to 15 minutes, gently tossing halfway through the cooking time.

Butternut Squash Croquettes

Prep time: 5 minutes | Cook time: 17 minutes | Serves 4

⅓ butternut squash, peeled and grated
⅓ cup all-purpose flour
2 eggs, whisked
4 cloves garlic, minced
1½ tablespoons olive oil
1 teaspoon fine sea salt
⅓ teaspoon freshly ground black pepper, or more to taste
⅓ teaspoon dried sage
A pinch of ground allspice

1. Preheat the pressure cooker to 345°F (174°C). Line the cook & crisp basket with parchment paper. 2. In a mixing bowl, stir together all the ingredients until well combined. 3. Make the squash croquettes: Use a small cookie scoop to drop tablespoonfuls of the squash mixture onto a lightly floured surface and shape into balls with your hands. Transfer them to the basket. 4. Close crisping lid. Select Air Crisp and set time to 17 minutes. 5. Serve warm.

Garlic-Parmesan Crispy Baby Potatoes

Prep time: 10 minutes | Cook time: 15 minutes | Serves 4

Oil, for spraying
1 pound (454 g) baby potatoes
½ cup grated Parmesan cheese, divided
3 tablespoons olive oil
2 teaspoons granulated garlic
½ teaspoon onion powder
½ teaspoon salt
¼ teaspoon freshly ground black pepper
¼ teaspoon paprika
2 tablespoons chopped fresh parsley, for garnish

1. Preheat the pressure cooker to 400°F (204°C). Line cook & crisp basket with parchment and spray lightly with oil. 2. Rinse the potatoes, pat dry with paper towels, and place in a large bowl. 3. In a small bowl, mix together ¼ cup of Parmesan cheese, the olive oil, garlic, onion powder, salt, black pepper, and paprika. Pour the mixture over the potatoes and toss to coat. 4. Transfer the potatoes to the prepared basket and spread them out in an even layer, taking care to keep them from touching. 5. Close crisping lid. Select Air Crisp and set time to 15 minutes, stirring after 7 to 8 minutes. 6. Sprinkle with the parsley and the remaining Parmesan cheese and serve.

Crispy Lemon Artichoke Hearts

Prep time: 10 minutes | Cook time: 15 minutes | Serves 2

1 (15-ounce / 425-g) can artichoke hearts in water, drained
1 egg
1 tablespoon water
¼ cup whole wheat bread crumbs
¼ teaspoon salt
¼ teaspoon paprika
½ lemon

1. Preheat the pressure cooker to 380°F(193°C). 2. In a medium shallow bowl, beat together the egg and water until frothy. 3. In a separate medium shallow bowl, mix together the bread crumbs, salt, and paprika. 4. Dip each artichoke heart into the egg mixture, then into the bread crumb mixture, coating the outside with the crumbs. Place the artichokes hearts in a single layer of the cook & crisp basket. 5. Close crisping lid. Select Air Crisp and set time to 15 minutes. 6. Remove the artichokes from the basket, and squeeze fresh lemon juice over the top before serving.

Creamed Spinach

Prep time: 10 minutes | Cook time: 15 minutes | Serves 4

Vegetable oil spray
1 (10-ounce / 283-g) package frozen spinach, thawed and squeezed dry
½ cup chopped onion
2 cloves garlic, minced
4 ounces (113 g) cream cheese, diced
½ teaspoon ground nutmeg
1 teaspoon kosher salt
1 teaspoon black pepper
½ cup grated Parmesan cheese

1. Preheat the pressure cooker to 350ºF (177ºC). Spray cooking pot with vegetable oil spray. 2. In a medium bowl, combine the spinach, onion, garlic, cream cheese, nutmeg, salt, and pepper. Transfer to the pot. 3. Close crisping lid. Select Bake and set time to 10 minutes. Open and stir to thoroughly combine the cream cheese and spinach. 4. Sprinkle the Parmesan cheese on top. Bake at 400ºF (204ºC) for 5 minutes, or until the cheese has melted and browned.

Spicy Roasted Bok Choy

Prep time: 10 minutes | Cook time: 7 to 10 minutes | Serves 4

2 tablespoons olive oil
2 tablespoons reduced-sodium coconut aminos
2 teaspoons sesame oil
2 teaspoons chili-garlic sauce
2 cloves garlic, minced
1 head (about 1 pound / 454 g) bok choy, sliced lengthwise into quarters
2 teaspoons black sesame seeds

1. Preheat the pressure cooker to 400°F (204°C). 2. In a large bowl, combine the olive oil, coconut aminos, sesame oil, chili-garlic sauce, and garlic. Add the bok choy and toss, massaging the leaves with your hands if necessary, until thoroughly coated. 3. Arrange the bok choy in the cooking pot. Close crisping lid. Select Roast and set time to 7 to 10 minutes, shaking halfway through. 4. Let cool for a few minutes before coarsely chopping. Serve sprinkled with the sesame seeds.

Lemon-Garlic Mushrooms

Prep time: 10 minutes | Cook time: 10 to 15 minutes | Serves 6

12 ounces (340 g) sliced mushrooms
1 tablespoon avocado oil
Sea salt and freshly ground black pepper, to taste
3 tablespoons unsalted butter
1 teaspoon minced garlic
1 teaspoon freshly squeezed lemon juice
½ teaspoon red pepper flakes
2 tablespoons chopped fresh parsley

1. Preheat the pressure cooker to 375ºF (191ºC). Place the mushrooms in a medium bowl and toss with the oil. Season to taste with salt and pepper. 2. Place the mushrooms in a single layer in the cooking pot. Close crisping lid. Select Roast and set time to 10 to 15 minutes. 3. While the mushrooms cook, melt the butter in a small pot or skillet over medium-low heat. Stir in the garlic and cook for 30 seconds. Remove the pot from the heat and stir in the lemon juice and red pepper flakes. 4. Toss the mushrooms with the lemon-garlic butter and garnish with the parsley before serving.

Burger Bun for One

Prep time: 2 minutes | Cook time: 5 minutes | Serves 1

2 tablespoons salted butter, melted
¼ cup blanched finely ground almond flour
¼ teaspoon baking powder
⅛ teaspoon apple cider vinegar
1 large egg, whisked

1. Preheat the pressure cooker to 350ºF (177ºC). Pour butter into an ungreased ramekin. Add flour, baking powder, and vinegar to ramekin and stir until combined. Add egg and stir until batter is mostly smooth. 2. Place ramekin into cooking pot. Close crisping lid. Select Bake and set time to 5 minutes. When done, the center will be firm and the top slightly browned. Let cool, about 5 minutes, then remove from ramekin and slice in half. Serve.

Mediterranean Zucchini Boats

Prep time: 5 minutes | Cook time: 10 minutes | Serves 4

1 large zucchini, ends removed, halved lengthwise
6 grape tomatoes, quartered
¼ teaspoon salt
¼ cup feta cheese
1 tablespoon balsamic vinegar
1 tablespoon olive oil

1. Preheat the pressure cooker to 350ºF (177ºC). Use a spoon to scoop out 2 tablespoons from center of each zucchini half, making just enough space to fill with tomatoes and feta. 2. Place tomatoes evenly in centers of zucchini halves and sprinkle with salt. Place into cooking pot. Close crisping lid. Select Roast and set time to 10 minutes. When done, zucchini will be tender. 3. Transfer boats to a serving tray and sprinkle with feta, then drizzle with vinegar and olive oil. Serve warm.

Green Peas with Mint

Prep time: 5 minutes | Cook time: 5 minutes | Serves 4

1 cup shredded lettuce
1 (10-ounce / 283-g) package
frozen green peas, thawed

1 tablespoon fresh mint,
shredded
1 teaspoon melted butter

1. Preheat the pressure cooker to 360°F (182°C). Lay the shredded lettuce in the cooking pot. 2. Toss together the peas, mint, and melted butter and spoon over the lettuce. 3. Close crisping lid. Select Bake and set time to 5 minutes, until peas are warm and lettuce wilts.

Asian Tofu Salad

Prep time: 25 minutes | Cook time: 15 minutes | Serves 2

Tofu:
1 tablespoon soy sauce
1 tablespoon vegetable oil
1 teaspoon minced fresh ginger
1 teaspoon minced garlic
8 ounces (227 g) extra-firm tofu,
drained and cubed
Salad:
¼ cup rice vinegar

1 tablespoon sugar
1 teaspoon salt
1 teaspoon black pepper
¼ cup sliced scallions
1 cup julienned cucumber
1 cup julienned red onion
1 cup julienned carrots
6 butter lettuce leaves

1. For the tofu: In a small bowl, whisk together the soy sauce, vegetable oil, ginger, and garlic. Add the tofu and mix gently. Let stand at room temperature for 10 minutes. 2. Preheat the pressure cooker to 400°F (204°C). Arrange the tofu in a single layer in the cooking pot. Close crisping lid. Select Roast and set time to 15 minutes, shaking halfway through. 3. Meanwhile, for the salad: In a large bowl, whisk together the vinegar, sugar, salt, pepper, and scallions. Add the cucumber, onion, and carrots and toss to combine. Set aside to marinate while the tofu cooks. 4. To serve, arrange three lettuce leaves on each of two plates. Pile the marinated vegetables (and marinade) on the lettuce. Divide the tofu between the plates and serve.

Tingly Chili-Roasted Broccoli

Prep time: 5 minutes | Cook time: 10 minutes | Serves 2

12 ounces (340 g) broccoli
florets
2 tablespoons Asian hot chili oil
1 teaspoon ground Sichuan
peppercorns (or black pepper)

2 garlic cloves, finely chopped
1 (2-inch) piece fresh ginger,
peeled and finely chopped
Kosher salt and freshly ground
black pepper, to taste

1. Preheat the pressure cooker to 375°F (191°C). In a bowl, toss together the broccoli, chili oil, Sichuan peppercorns, garlic, ginger, and salt and black pepper to taste. 2. Transfer to the cooking pot. Close crisping lid. Select Roast and set time to 10 minutes, shaking halfway through. Serve warm.

Bacon-Wrapped Asparagus

Prep time: 10 minutes | Cook time: 10 minutes | Serves 4

8 slices reduced-sodium bacon,
cut in half
16 thick (about 1 pound / 454

g) asparagus spears, trimmed of
woody ends

1. Preheat the pressure cooker to 350°F (177°C). 2. Wrap a half piece of bacon around the center of each stalk of asparagus. 3. Working in batches, if necessary, arrange seam-side down in a single layer in the cooking pot. Close crisping lid. Select Bake and set time to 10 minutes until the bacon is crisp and the stalks are tender.

Fried Asparagus

Prep time: 5 minutes | Cook time: 12 minutes | Serves 4

1 tablespoon olive oil
1 pound (454 g) asparagus
spears, ends trimmed
¼ teaspoon salt

¼ teaspoon ground black pepper
1 tablespoon salted butter,
melted

1. Preheat the pressure cooker to 375°F (191°C). In a large bowl, drizzle olive oil over asparagus spears and sprinkle with salt and pepper. 2. Place spears into cook & crisp basket. Close crisping lid. Select Air Crisp and set time to 12 minutes, shaking halfway through. Asparagus will be lightly browned and tender when done. 3. Transfer to a large dish and drizzle with butter. Serve warm.

Blackened Zucchini with Kimchi-Herb Sauce

Prep time: 10 minutes | Cook time: 15 minutes | Serves 2

2 medium zucchini, ends
trimmed (about 6 ounces / 170 g
each)
2 tablespoons olive oil
½ cup kimchi, finely chopped
¼ cup finely chopped fresh
cilantro
¼ cup finely chopped fresh

flat-leaf parsley, plus more for
garnish
2 tablespoons rice vinegar
2 teaspoons Asian chili-garlic
sauce
1 teaspoon grated fresh ginger
Kosher salt and freshly ground
black pepper, to taste

1. Preheat the pressure cooker to 400°F (204°C). Brush the zucchini with half of the olive oil, place in the cooking pot. Close crisping lid. Select Roast and set time to 15 minutes, turning halfway through. 2. Meanwhile, in a small bowl, combine the remaining 1 tablespoon olive oil, the kimchi, cilantro, parsley, vinegar, chili-garlic sauce, and ginger. 3. Once the zucchini is finished cooking, transfer it to a colander and let it cool for 5 minutes. Using your fingers, pinch and break the zucchini into bite-size pieces, letting them fall back into the colander. Season the zucchini with salt and pepper, toss to combine, then let sit a further 5 minutes to allow some of its liquid to drain. Pile the zucchini atop the kimchi sauce on a plate and sprinkle with more parsley to serve.

Grits Casserole

Prep time: 5 minutes | Cook time: 28 to 30 minutes | Serves 4

10 fresh asparagus spears, cut into 1-inch pieces
2 cups cooked grits, cooled to room temperature
1 egg, beaten
2 teaspoons Worcestershire sauce

½ teaspoon garlic powder
¼ teaspoon salt
2 slices provolone cheese (about 1½ ounces / 43 g)
Oil for misting or cooking spray

1. Preheat the pressure cooker to 390°F (199°C). Mist asparagus spears with oil and place into cooking pot. Close crisping lid. Select Roast and set time to 5 minutes, until crisp-tender. 2. In a medium bowl, mix together the grits, egg, Worcestershire, garlic powder, and salt. 3. Spoon half of grits mixture into cooking pot and top with asparagus. 4. Tear cheese slices into pieces and layer evenly on top of asparagus. 5. Top with remaining grits. 6. Close crisping lid. Select Bake, set temperature to 360°F (182°C), and set time to 23 to 25 minutes. The casserole will rise a little as it cooks. When done, the top will have browned lightly with just a hint of crispiness.

Green Tomato Salad

Prep time: 10 minutes | Cook time: 8 to 10 minutes | Serves 4

4 green tomatoes
½ teaspoon salt
1 large egg, lightly beaten
½ cup peanut flour
1 tablespoon Creole seasoning
1 (5-ounce / 142-g) bag arugula
Buttermilk Dressing:
1 cup mayonnaise

½ cup sour cream
2 teaspoons fresh lemon juice
2 tablespoons finely chopped fresh parsley
1 teaspoon dried dill
1 teaspoon dried chives
½ teaspoon salt
½ teaspoon garlic powder
½ teaspoon onion powder

1. Preheat the pressure cooker to 400°F (204°C). 2. Slice the tomatoes into ½-inch slices and sprinkle with the salt. Let sit for 5 to 10 minutes. 3. Place the egg in a small shallow bowl. In another small shallow bowl, combine the peanut flour and Creole seasoning. Dip each tomato slice into the egg wash, then dip into the peanut flour mixture, turning to coat evenly. 4. Working in batches if necessary, arrange the tomato slices in a single layer in cook & crisp basket and spray both sides lightly with olive oil. Close crisping lid. Select Air Crisp and set time to 8 to 10 minutes. 5. To make the buttermilk dressing: In a small bowl, whisk together the mayonnaise, sour cream, lemon juice, parsley, dill, chives, salt, garlic powder, and onion powder. 6. Serve the tomato slices on top of a bed of the arugula with the dressing on the side.

Zesty Fried Asparagus

Prep time: 3 minutes | Cook time: 10 minutes | Serves 4

Oil, for spraying
10 to 12 spears asparagus, trimmed
2 tablespoons olive oil
1 tablespoon granulated garlic

1 teaspoon chili powder
½ teaspoon ground cumin
¼ teaspoon salt

1. Preheat the pressure cooker to 390°F (199°C). Line the cook & crisp basket with parchment and spray lightly with oil. 2. If the asparagus are too long to fit easily in the basket, cut them in half. 3. Place the asparagus, olive oil, garlic, chili powder, cumin, and salt in a zip-top plastic bag, seal, and toss until evenly coated. 4. Place the asparagus in the prepared basket. 5. Close crisping lid. Select Air Crisp and set time to 10 minutes, flipping halfway through, or until bright green and firm but tender.

Chapter 10 Desserts

Cherry Pie

Prep time: 15 minutes | Cook time: 35 minutes | Serves 6

All-purpose flour, for dusting	cherry pie filling
2 refrigerated piecrusts, at room temperature	1 egg
	1 tablespoon water
1 (12.5-ounce / 354-g) can	1 tablespoon sugar

1. Dust a work surface with flour and place the piecrust on it. Roll out the piecrust. Invert a shallow baking pan, or your own pie pan that fits inside the cooking pot, on top of the dough. Trim the dough around the pan, making your cut ½ inch wider than the pan itself. 2. Repeat with the second piecrust but make the cut the same size as or slightly smaller than the pan. 3. Put the larger crust in the bottom of the baking pan. Don't stretch the dough. Gently press it into the pan. 4. Spoon in enough cherry pie filling to fill the crust. Do not overfill. 5. Using a knife or pizza cutter, cut the second piecrust into 1-inch-wide strips. Weave the strips in a lattice pattern over the top of the cherry pie filling. 6. Preheat the pressure cooker to 325°F (163°C). 7. In a small bowl, whisk the egg and water. Gently brush the egg wash over the top of the pie. Sprinkle with the sugar and cover the pie with aluminum foil. 8. Place the pie into cooking pot. 9. Close crisping lid. Select Bake and set time to 35 minutes. 10. After 30 minutes, remove the foil and resume cooking for 3 to 5 minutes more. The finished pie should have a flaky golden brown crust and bubbling pie filling. 11. When the cooking is complete, serve warm.

Chocolate Chip-Pecan Biscotti

Prep time: 15 minutes | Cook time: 20 to 22 minutes | Serves 10

1¼ cups finely ground blanched almond flour	1 teaspoon pure vanilla extract
¾ teaspoon baking powder	⅓ cup chopped pecans
½ teaspoon xanthan gum	¼ cup stevia-sweetened chocolate chips, such as Lily's Sweets brand
¼ teaspoon sea salt	
3 tablespoons unsalted butter, at room temperature	Melted stevia-sweetened chocolate chips and chopped pecans, for topping (optional)
⅓ cup Swerve	
1 large egg, beaten	

1. In a large bowl, combine the almond flour, baking powder, xanthan gum, and salt. 2. Preheat the pressure cooker to 325°F (163°C). Line the cooking pot with parchment paper. 3. In the bowl of a stand mixer, beat together the butter and Swerve. Add the beaten egg and vanilla, and beat for about 3 minutes. 4. Add the almond flour mixture to the butter-and-egg mixture; beat until just combined. 5. Stir in the pecans and chocolate chips. 6. Transfer the dough to the pot, and press it into the bottom. 7. Close crisping lid. Select Bake and set time to 12 minutes. Let cool for 15 minutes. Using a sharp knife, cut the cookie into thin strips, then return the strips to the pot with the bottom sides facing up. 8. Bake at 300°F (149°C) for 8 to 10 minutes. 9. Let cool completely on a wire rack. If desired, dip one side of each biscotti piece into melted chocolate chips, and top with chopped pecans.

Pecan and Cherry Stuffed Apples

Prep time: 10 minutes | Cook time: 20 minutes | Serves 4

4 apples (about 1¼ pounds / 567 g)	3 tablespoons brown sugar
	¼ teaspoon allspice
¼ cup chopped pecans	Pinch salt
⅓ cup dried tart cherries	Ice cream, for serving
1 tablespoon melted butter	

1. Cut off top ½ inch from each apple; reserve tops. With a melon baller, core through stem ends without breaking through the bottom. (Do not trim bases.) 2. Preheat the pressure cooker to 350°F (177°C). Combine pecans, cherries, butter, brown sugar, allspice, and a pinch of salt. Stuff mixture into the hollow centers of the apples. Cover with apple tops. Put in the cooking pot, using tongs. Close crisping lid. Select Bake and set time to 20 to 25 minutes, or just until tender. 3. Serve warm with ice cream.

Pears with Honey-Lemon Ricotta

Prep time: 10 minutes | Cook time: 8 minutes | Serves 4

2 large Bartlett pears	½ cup whole-milk ricotta cheese
3 tablespoons butter, melted	1 tablespoon honey, plus additional for drizzling
3 tablespoons brown sugar	
½ teaspoon ground ginger	1 teaspoon pure almond extract
¼ teaspoon ground cardamom	1 teaspoon pure lemon extract

1. Preheat the pressure cooker to 375°F (191°C). Peel each pear and cut in half lengthwise. Use a melon baller to scoop out the core. Place the pear halves in a medium bowl, add the melted butter, and toss. Add the brown sugar, ginger, and cardamom; toss to coat. 2. Place the pear halves, cut side down, in the cooking pot. Close crisping lid. Select Bake and set time to 8 to 10 minutes, or until the pears are lightly browned and tender, but not mushy. 3. Meanwhile, in a medium bowl, combine the ricotta, honey, and almond and lemon extracts. Beat with an electric mixer on medium speed until the mixture is light and fluffy, about 1 minute. 4. To serve, divide the ricotta mixture among four small shallow bowls. Place a pear half, cut side up, on top of the cheese. Drizzle with additional honey and serve.

Ricotta Lemon Poppy Seed Cake

Prep time: 10 minutes | Cook time: 55 minutes | Serves 4

Unsalted butter, at room temperature	¼ cup coconut oil, melted
1 cup almond flour	2 tablespoons poppy seeds
½ cup sugar	1 teaspoon baking powder
3 large eggs	1 teaspoon pure lemon extract
¼ cup heavy cream	Grated zest and juice of 1
¼ cup full-fat ricotta cheese	lemon, plus more zest for garnish

1. Preheat the pressure cooker to 325ºF (163ºC). Generously butter cooking pot. Line the bottom of the pot with parchment paper cut to fit. 2. In a large bowl, combine the almond flour, sugar, eggs, cream, ricotta, coconut oil, poppy seeds, baking powder, lemon extract, lemon zest, and lemon juice. Beat with a hand mixer on medium speed until well blended and fluffy. 3. Pour the batter into the pot. Close crisping lid. Select Bake and set time to 55 minutes. 4. Let the cake cool before slicing. 5. Top with additional lemon zest, slice and serve.

Simple Apple Turnovers

Prep time: 10 minutes | Cook time: 10 minutes | Serves 4

1 apple, peeled, quartered, and thinly sliced	1 tablespoon granulated sugar
½ teaspoons pumpkin pie spice	Pinch of kosher salt
Juice of ½ lemon	6 sheets phyllo dough

1. Preheat the pressure cooker to 330ºF (166ºC). 2. In a medium bowl, combine the apple, pumpkin pie spice, lemon juice, granulated sugar, and kosher salt. 3. Cut the phyllo dough sheets into 4 equal pieces and place individual tablespoons of apple filling in the center of each piece, then fold in both sides and roll from front to back. 4. Spray the cooking pot with nonstick cooking spray, then place the turnovers in the pot. Close crisping lid. Select Bake and set time to 10 minutes or until golden brown. 5. Allow to cool on a wire rack for 10 minutes before serving.

Mini Peanut Butter Tarts

Prep time: 25 minutes | Cook time: 12 to 15 minutes | Serves 8

1 cup pecans	4 ounces (113 g) cream cheese
1 cup finely ground blanched almond flour	½ cup sugar-free peanut butter
2 tablespoons unsalted butter, at room temperature	1 teaspoon pure vanilla extract
½ cup plus 2 tablespoons Swerve, divided	⅛ teaspoon sea salt
½ cup heavy (whipping) cream	½ cup stevia-sweetened chocolate chips
2 tablespoons mascarpone cheese	1 tablespoon coconut oil
	¼ cup chopped peanuts or pecans

1. Place the pecans in the bowl of a food processor; process until they are finely ground. 2. Transfer the ground pecans to a medium bowl and stir in the almond flour. Add the butter and 2 tablespoons of Swerve, and stir until the mixture becomes wet and crumbly. 3. Divide the mixture among 8 silicone muffin cups, pressing the crust firmly with your fingers into the bottom and part way up the sides of each cup. 4. Preheat the pressure cooker to 300ºF (149ºC). Arrange the muffin cups in the cooking pot. Close crisping lid. Select Bake and set time to 12 to 15 minutes. Remove and set them aside to cool. 5. In the bowl of a stand mixer, combine the heavy cream and mascarpone cheese. Beat until peaks form. Transfer to a large bowl. 6. In the same stand mixer bowl, combine the cream cheese, peanut butter, remaining ½ cup of Swerve, vanilla, and salt. Beat at medium-high speed until smooth. 7. Reduce the speed to low and add the heavy cream mixture back a spoonful at a time, beating after each addition. 8. Spoon the peanut butter mixture over the crusts, and freeze the tarts for 30 minutes. 9. Place the chocolate chips and coconut oil in the top of a double boiler over high heat. Stir until melted, then remove from the heat. 10. Drizzle the melted chocolate over the peanut butter tarts. Top with the chopped nuts and freeze the tarts for another 15 minutes, until set. 11. Store the peanut butter tarts in an airtight container in the refrigerator for up to 1 week or in the freezer for up to 1 month.

Cinnamon Cupcakes with Cream Cheese Frosting

Prep time: 10 minutes | Cook time: 20 to 25 minutes | Serves 6

½ cup plus 2 tablespoons almond flour	½ teaspoon vanilla extract
2 tablespoons low-carb vanilla protein powder	2 tablespoons heavy cream
⅛ teaspoon salt	Cream Cheese Frosting:
1 teaspoon baking powder	4 ounces (113 g) cream cheese, softened
¼ teaspoon ground cinnamon	2 tablespoons unsalted butter, softened
¼ cup unsalted butter	½ teaspoon vanilla extract
¼ cup Swerve	2 tablespoons powdered Swerve
2 eggs	1 to 2 tablespoons heavy cream

1. Preheat the pressure cooker to 320ºF (160ºC). Lightly coat 6 silicone muffin cups with oil and set aside. 2. In a medium bowl, combine the almond flour, protein powder, salt, baking powder, and cinnamon; set aside. 3. In a stand mixer fitted with a paddle attachment, beat the butter and Swerve until creamy. Add the eggs, vanilla, and heavy cream, and beat again until thoroughly combined. Add half the flour mixture at a time to the butter mixture, mixing after each addition, until you have a smooth, creamy batter. 4. Divide the batter evenly among the muffin cups, filling each one about three-fourths full. Arrange the muffin cups in the cooking pot. Close crisping lid. Select Bake and set time to 20 to 25 minutes, or until a toothpick inserted into the center of a cupcake comes out clean. Transfer the cupcakes to a rack and let cool completely. 5. To make the cream cheese frosting: In a stand mixer fitted with a paddle attachment, beat the cream cheese, butter, and vanilla until fluffy. Add the Swerve and mix again until thoroughly combined. With the mixer running, add the heavy cream a tablespoon at a time until the frosting is smooth and creamy. Frost the cupcakes as desired.

Pumpkin Pudding with Vanilla Wafers

Prep time: 10 minutes | Cook time: 12 to 17 minutes | Serves 4

1 cup canned no-salt-added pumpkin purée (not pumpkin pie filling)
¼ cup packed brown sugar
3 tablespoons all-purpose flour
1 egg, whisked
2 tablespoons milk

1 tablespoon unsalted butter, melted
1 teaspoon pure vanilla extract
4 low-fat vanilla wafers, crumbled
Nonstick cooking spray

1. Preheat the pressure cooker to 350°F (177°C). Coat cooking pot with nonstick cooking spray. Set aside. 2. Mix the pumpkin purée, brown sugar, flour, whisked egg, milk, melted butter, and vanilla in a medium bowl and whisk to combine. Transfer the mixture to the pot. 3. Close crisping lid. Select Bake and set time to 12 to 17 minutes until set. 4. Allow to cool on wire rack. 5. Divide the pudding into four bowls and serve with the vanilla wafers sprinkled on top.

Strawberry Shortcake

Prep time: 10 minutes | Cook time: 25 minutes | Serves 6

2 tablespoons coconut oil
1 cup blanched finely ground almond flour
2 large eggs, whisked
½ cup granular erythritol
1 teaspoon baking powder

1 teaspoon vanilla extract
2 cups sugar-free whipped cream
6 medium fresh strawberries, hulled and sliced

1. Preheat the pressure cooker to 300°F (149°C). In a large bowl, combine coconut oil, flour, eggs, erythritol, baking powder, and vanilla. Pour batter into cooking pot. 2. Close crisping lid. Select Bake and set time to 25 minutes. When done, shortcake should be golden and a toothpick inserted in the middle will come out clean. 3. Let cool 1 hour. 4. Once cooled, top cake with whipped cream and strawberries to serve.

Apple Wedges with Apricots

Prep time: 5 minutes | Cook time: 15 to 18 minutes | Serves 4

4 large apples, peeled and sliced into 8 wedges
2 tablespoons olive oil

½ cup dried apricots, chopped
1 to 2 tablespoons sugar
½ teaspoon ground cinnamon

1. Preheat the pressure cooker to 350°F (180°C). 2. Toss the apple wedges with the olive oil in a mixing bowl until well coated. 3. Place the apple wedges in the cooking pot. Close crisping lid. Select Bake and set time to 12 to 15 minutes. 4. Sprinkle with the dried apricots and bake for another 3 minutes. 5. Meanwhile, thoroughly combine the sugar and cinnamon in a small bowl. 6. Remove the apple wedges from the pot to a plate. Serve sprinkled with the sugar mixture.

Pumpkin Cookie with Cream Cheese Frosting

Prep time: 10 minutes | Cook time: 7 minutes | Serves 6

½ cup blanched finely ground almond flour
½ cup powdered erythritol, divided
2 tablespoons butter, softened
1 large egg
½ teaspoon unflavored gelatin
½ teaspoon baking powder
½ teaspoon vanilla extract

½ teaspoon pumpkin pie spice
2 tablespoons pure pumpkin purée
½ teaspoon ground cinnamon, divided
¼ cup low-carb, sugar-free chocolate chips
3 ounces (85 g) full-fat cream cheese, softened

1. Preheat the pressure cooker to 300°F (149°C). In a large bowl, mix almond flour and ¼ cup erythritol. Stir in butter, egg, and gelatin until combined. 2. Stir in baking powder, vanilla, pumpkin pie spice, pumpkin purée, and ¼ teaspoon cinnamon, then fold in chocolate chips. 3. Pour batter into cooking pot. 4. Close crisping lid. Select Bake and set time to 7 minutes. 5. When fully cooked, the top will be golden brown and a toothpick inserted in center will come out clean. Let cool at least 20 minutes. 6. To make the frosting: mix cream cheese, remaining ¼ teaspoon cinnamon, and remaining ¼ cup erythritol in a large bowl. Using an electric mixer, beat until it becomes fluffy. Spread onto the cooled cookie. Garnish with additional cinnamon if desired.

Lemon Poppy Seed Macaroons

Prep time: 10 minutes | Cook time: 14 minutes | Makes 1 dozen cookies

2 large egg whites, room temperature
⅓ cup Swerve confectioners'-style sweetener or equivalent amount of powdered sweetener
2 tablespoons grated lemon zest, plus more for garnish if desired
2 teaspoons poppy seeds
1 teaspoon lemon extract

¼ teaspoon fine sea salt
2 cups unsweetened shredded coconut
Lemon Icing:
¼ cup Swerve confectioners'-style sweetener or equivalent amount of powdered sweetener
1 tablespoon lemon juice

1. Preheat the pressure cooker to 325°F (163°C). Line cooking pot with parchment paper. 2. Place the egg whites in a medium-sized bowl and use a hand mixer on high to beat the whites until stiff peaks form. Add the sweetener, lemon zest, poppy seeds, lemon extract, and salt. Mix on low until combined. Gently fold in the coconut with a rubber spatula. 3. Use a 1-inch cookie scoop to place the cookies on the parchment, spacing them about ¼ inch apart. Close crisping lid. Select Bake and set time to 12 to 14 minutes, until the cookies are golden and a toothpick inserted into the center comes out clean. 4. While the cookies bake, make the lemon icing: Place the sweetener in a small bowl. Add the lemon juice and stir well. If the icing is too thin, add a little more sweetener. If the icing is too thick, add a little more lemon juice. 5. Remove the cookies from the pot and allow to cool for about 10 minutes, then drizzle with the icing. Garnish with lemon zest, if desired.

Gluten-Free Spice Cookies

Prep time: 10 minutes | Cook time: 12 minutes | Serves 4

4 tablespoons (½ stick) unsalted butter, at room temperature
2 tablespoons agave nectar
1 large egg
2 tablespoons water
2½ cups almond flour
½ cup sugar

2 teaspoons ground ginger
1 teaspoon ground cinnamon
½ teaspoon freshly grated nutmeg
1 teaspoon baking soda
¼ teaspoon kosher salt

1. Preheat the pressure cooker to 325ºF (163ºC). Line the bottom of the cooking pot with parchment paper cut to fit. 2. In a large bowl using a hand mixer, beat together the butter, agave, egg, and water on medium speed until light and fluffy. 3. Add the almond flour, sugar, ginger, cinnamon, nutmeg, baking soda, and salt. Beat on low speed until well combined. 4. Roll the dough into 2-tablespoon balls and arrange them on the parchment paper in the pot. Close crisping lid. Select Bake and set time to 12 minutes, or until the tops of cookies are lightly browned. 5. Transfer to a wire rack and let cool completely.

Apple Hand Pies

Prep time: 15 minutes | Cook time: 25 minutes | Serves 8

2 apples, cored and diced
¼ cup honey
1 teaspoon ground cinnamon
1 teaspoon vanilla extract
⅛ teaspoon ground nutmeg

2 teaspoons cornstarch
1 teaspoon water
4 refrigerated piecrusts
Cooking oil spray

1. Preheat the pressure cooker to 400ºF (204ºC). 2. In a metal bowl that fits into the cook & crisp basket, stir together the apples, honey, cinnamon, vanilla, and nutmeg. 3. In a small bowl, whisk the cornstarch and water until the cornstarch dissolves. 4. Place the metal bowl with the apples into the basket. 5. Close crisping lid. Select Air Crisp and set time to 5 minutes. 6. After 2 minutes, stir the apples. Resume cooking for 2 minutes. 7. Remove the bowl and stir the cornstarch mixture into the apples. Reinsert the metal bowl into the basket and resume cooking for about 30 seconds until the sauce thickens slightly. 8. When the cooking is complete, refrigerate the apples while you prepare the piecrust. 9. Cut each piecrust into 2 (4-inch) circles. You should have 8 circles of crust. 10. Lay the piecrusts on a work surface. Divide the apple filling among the piecrusts, mounding the mixture in the center of each round. 11. Fold each piecrust over so the top layer of crust is about an inch short of the bottom layer. (The edges should not meet.) Use the back of a fork to seal the edges. 12. Preheat the pressure cooker to 400ºF (204ºC). 13. Spray the basket with cooking oil, line the basket with parchment paper, and spray it with cooking oil. Working in batches, place the hand pies into the basket in a single layer. 14. Close crisping lid. Select Air Crisp and set time to 10 minutes. 15. When the cooking is complete, let the hand pies cool for 5 minutes before removing from the basket. 16. Repeat steps 13, 14, and 15 with the remaining pies.

5-Ingredient Brownies

Prep time: 10 minutes | Cook time: 25 minutes | Serves 6

Vegetable oil
½ cup (1 stick) unsalted butter
½ cup chocolate chips

3 large eggs
½ cup sugar
1 teaspoon pure vanilla extract

1. Preheat the pressure cooker to 350ºF (177ºC). Generously grease cooking pot with vegetable oil. 2. In a microwave-safe bowl, combine the butter and chocolate chips. Microwave on high for 1 minute. Stir very well. 3. In a medium bowl, combine the eggs, sugar, and vanilla. Whisk until light and frothy. While whisking continuously, slowly pour in the melted chocolate in a thin stream and whisk until everything is incorporated. 4. Pour the batter into the pot. Close crisping lid. Select Bake and set time to 25 minutes, or until a toothpick inserted into the center comes out clean. 5. Let cool for 30 minutes before cutting into squares.

Shortcut Spiced Apple Butter

Prep time: 5 minutes | Cook time: 1 hour | Makes 1¼ cups

Cooking spray
2 cups store-bought unsweetened applesauce
⅔ cup packed light brown sugar

3 tablespoons fresh lemon juice
½ teaspoon kosher salt
¼ teaspoon ground cinnamon
⅛ teaspoon ground allspice

1. Preheat the pressure cooker to 340ºF (171ºC). Spray cooking pot with cooking spray. Whisk together all the ingredients in a bowl until smooth, then pour into the greased pot. Close crisping lid. Select Bake and set time to 1 hour. 2. Stir to combine the caramelized bits at the edge with the rest, then let cool completely to thicken. Scrape the apple butter into a jar and store in the refrigerator for up to 2 weeks.

Apple Fries

Prep time: 10 minutes | Cook time: 7 minutes | Serves 8

Oil, for spraying
1 cup all-purpose flour
3 large eggs, beaten
1 cup graham cracker crumbs
¼ cup sugar

1 teaspoon ground cinnamon
3 large Gala apples, peeled, cored, and cut into wedges
1 cup caramel sauce, warmed

1. Preheat the pressure cooker to 380ºF (193ºC). Line cook & crisp basket with parchment and spray lightly with oil. 2. Place the flour and beaten eggs in separate bowls and set aside. In another bowl, mix together the graham cracker crumbs, sugar, and cinnamon. 3. Working one at a time, coat the apple wedges in the flour, dip in the egg, and dredge in the graham cracker mix until evenly coated. 4. Place the apples in the prepared basket, taking care not to overlap, and spray lightly with oil. 5. Close crisping lid. Select Air Crisp and set time to 7 minutes, flipping and spraying with oil after 5 minutes. 6. Drizzle the caramel sauce over the top and serve.

Vanilla Pound Cake

Prep time: 10 minutes | Cook time: 25 minutes | Serves 6

1 cup blanched finely ground almond flour	1 teaspoon baking powder
¼ cup salted butter, melted	½ cup full-fat sour cream
½ cup granular erythritol	1 ounce (28 g) full-fat cream cheese, softened
1 teaspoon vanilla extract	2 large eggs

1. Preheat the pressure cooker to 300ºF (149ºC). In a large bowl, mix almond flour, butter, and erythritol. 2. Add in vanilla, baking powder, sour cream, and cream cheese and mix until well combined. Add eggs and mix. 3. Pour batter into cooking pot. 4. Close crisping lid. Select Bake and set time to 25 minutes. 5. When the cake is done, a toothpick inserted in center will come out clean. The center should not feel wet. Allow it to cool completely, or the cake will crumble when moved.

Dark Brownies

Prep time: 10 minutes | Cook time: 11 to 13 minutes | Serves 4

1 egg	¼ cup cocoa
½ cup granulated sugar	Cooking spray
¼ teaspoon salt	Optional:
½ teaspoon vanilla	Vanilla ice cream
¼ cup butter, melted	Caramel sauce
¼ cup flour, plus 2 tablespoons	Whipped cream

1. Preheat the pressure cooker to 330ºF (166ºC). Beat together egg, sugar, salt, and vanilla until light. 2. Add melted butter and mix well. 3. Stir in flour and cocoa. 4. Spray cooking pot lightly with cooking spray. 5. Spread batter in pot. Close crisping lid. Select Bake and set time to 11 to 13 minutes. Cool and cut into 4 large squares or 16 small brownie bites.

Air Fryer Apple Fritters

Prep time: 30 minutes | Cook time: 7 to 8 minutes | Serves 6

1 cup chopped, peeled Granny Smith apple	2 tablespoons milk
½ cup granulated sugar	2 tablespoons butter, melted
1 teaspoon ground cinnamon	1 large egg, beaten
1 cup all-purpose flour	Cooking spray
1 teaspoon baking powder	¼ cup confectioners' sugar (optional)
1 teaspoon salt	

1. Mix together the apple, granulated sugar, and cinnamon in a small bowl. Allow to sit for 30 minutes. 2. Combine the flour, baking powder, and salt in a medium bowl. Add the milk, butter, and egg and stir to incorporate. 3. Pour the apple mixture into the bowl of flour mixture and stir with a spatula until a dough forms. 4. Make the fritters: On a clean work surface, divide the dough into 12 equal portions and shape into 1-inch balls. Flatten them into patties with your hands. 5. Preheat the pressure cooker to 350ºF (177ºC).

Line the cook & crisp basket with parchment paper and spray it with cooking spray. 6. Transfer the apple fritters onto the parchment paper, evenly spaced but not too close together. Spray the fritters with cooking spray. 7. Close crisping lid. Select Air Crisp and set time to 7 to 8 minutes until lightly browned, flipping halfway through the cooking time. 8. Serve with the confectioners' sugar sprinkled on top, if desired.

Pumpkin-Spice Bread Pudding

Prep time: 15 minutes | Cook time: 35 minutes | Serves 6

Bread Pudding:	baguette or crusty country bread
¾ cup heavy whipping cream	4 tablespoons (½ stick) unsalted
½ cup canned pumpkin	butter, melted
⅓ cup whole milk	Sauce:
⅓ cup sugar	⅓ cup pure maple syrup
1 large egg plus 1 yolk	1 tablespoon unsalted butter
½ teaspoon pumpkin pie spice	½ cup heavy whipping cream
⅛ teaspoon kosher salt	½ teaspoon pure vanilla extract
4 cups 1-inch cubed day-old	

1. For the bread pudding: In a medium bowl, combine the cream, pumpkin, milk, sugar, egg and yolk, pumpkin pie spice, and salt. Whisk until well combined. 2. In a large bowl, toss the bread cubes with the melted butter. Add the pumpkin mixture and gently toss until the ingredients are well combined. 3. Preheat the pressure cooker to 350ºF (177ºC). Transfer the mixture to cooking pot. Close crisping lid. Select Bake and set time to 35 minutes, or until custard is set in the middle. 4. Meanwhile, for the sauce: In a small saucepan, combine the syrup and butter. Heat over medium heat, stirring, until the butter melts. Stir in the cream and simmer, stirring often, until the sauce has thickened, about 15 minutes. Stir in the vanilla. Remove the pudding from the pot. 5. Let the pudding stand for 10 minutes before serving with the warm sauce.

Roasted Honey Pears

Prep time: 7 minutes | Cook time: 18 to 23 minutes | Serves 4

2 large Bosc pears, halved lengthwise and seeded	½ teaspoon ground cinnamon
3 tablespoons honey	¼ cup walnuts, chopped
1 tablespoon unsalted butter	¼ cup part-skim ricotta cheese, divided

1. Preheat the pressure cooker to 350ºF (177ºC). 2. In cooking pot, place the pears cut-side up. 3. In a small microwave-safe bowl, melt the honey, butter, and cinnamon. Brush this mixture over the cut sides of the pears. Pour 3 tablespoons of water around the pears in the pot. 4. Close crisping lid. Select Roast and set time to 23 minutes. 5. After about 18 minutes, check the pears. They should be tender when pierced with a fork and slightly crisp on the edges. If not, resume cooking. 6. When the cooking is complete, baste the pears once with the liquid in the pan. Carefully remove the pears from the pan and place on a serving plate. Drizzle each with some liquid from the pan, sprinkle the walnuts on top, and serve with a spoonful of ricotta cheese.

Chocolate Cake

Prep time: 10 minutes | Cook time: 20 to 23 minutes | Serves 8

½ cup sugar
¼ cup flour, plus 3 tablespoons
3 tablespoons cocoa
½ teaspoon baking powder
½ teaspoon baking soda

¼ teaspoon salt
1 egg
2 tablespoons oil
½ cup milk
½ teaspoon vanilla extract

1. Preheat the pressure cooker to 330ºF (166ºC). 2. Grease and flour cooking pot. 3. In a medium bowl, stir together the sugar, flour, cocoa, baking powder, baking soda, and salt. 4. Add all other ingredients and beat with a wire whisk until smooth. 5. Pour batter into pot. Close crisping lid. Select Bake and set time to 20 to 23 minutes, until toothpick inserted in center comes out clean or with crumbs clinging to it.

Cardamom Custard

Prep time: 10 minutes | Cook time: 25 minutes | Serves 2

1 cup whole milk
1 large egg
2 tablespoons plus 1 teaspoon sugar

¼ teaspoon vanilla bean paste or pure vanilla extract
¼ teaspoon ground cardamom, plus more for sprinkling

1. In a medium bowl, beat together the milk, egg, sugar, vanilla, and cardamom. 2. Preheat the pressure cooker to 350ºF (177ºC). Place two 8-ounce (227-g) ramekins in the cooking pot. Divide the mixture between the ramekins. Sprinkle lightly with cardamom. Cover each ramekin tightly with aluminum foil. Close crisping lid. Select Bake and set time to 25 minutes, or until a toothpick inserted in the center comes out clean. 3. Let the custards cool on a wire rack for 5 to 10 minutes. 4. Serve warm, or refrigerate until cold and serve chilled.

Rhubarb and Strawberry Crumble

Prep time: 10 minutes | Cook time: 12 to 17 minutes | Serves 6

1½ cups sliced fresh strawberries
¾ cup sliced rhubarb
⅓ cup granulated sugar
⅔ cup quick-cooking oatmeal
½ cup whole-wheat pastry flour,

or all-purpose flour
¼ cup packed light brown sugar
½ teaspoon ground cinnamon
3 tablespoons unsalted butter, melted

1. Preheat the pressure cooker to 375ºF (191ºC). 2. In cooking pot, combine the strawberries, rhubarb, and granulated sugar. 3. In a medium bowl, stir together the oatmeal, flour, brown sugar, and cinnamon. Stir the melted butter into this mixture until crumbly. Sprinkle the crumble mixture over the fruit. 4. Close crisping lid. Select Bake and set time to 17 minutes. 5. After about 12 minutes, check the crumble. If the fruit is bubbling and the topping is golden brown, it is done. If not, resume cooking. 6. When the cooking is complete, serve warm.

Chocolate Croissants

Prep time: 5 minutes | Cook time: 24 minutes | Serves 8

1 sheet frozen puff pastry, thawed
⅓ cup chocolate-hazelnut

spread
1 large egg, beaten

1. On a lightly floured surface, roll puff pastry into a 14-inch square. Cut pastry into quarters to form 4 squares. Cut each square diagonally to form 8 triangles. 2. Spread 2 teaspoons chocolate-hazelnut spread on each triangle; from wider end, roll up pastry. Brush egg on top of each roll. 3. Preheat the pressure cooker to 375ºF (191ºC). Transfer the rolls in cook & crisp basket, 3 or 4 at a time. Close crisping lid. Select Air Crisp and set time to 8 minutes, or until pastry is golden brown. 4. Cool on a wire rack; serve while warm or at room temperature.

Baked Apples and Walnuts

Prep time: 6 minutes | Cook time: 20 minutes | Serves 4

4 small Granny Smith apples
⅓ cup chopped walnuts
¼ cup light brown sugar
2 tablespoons butter, melted

1 teaspoon ground cinnamon
½ teaspoon ground nutmeg
½ cup water, or apple juice

1. Cut off the top third of the apples. Spoon out the core and some of the flesh and discard. Place the apples in cooking pot. 2. Preheat the pressure cooker to 350ºF (177ºC). 3. In a small bowl, stir together the walnuts, brown sugar, melted butter, cinnamon, and nutmeg. Spoon this mixture into the centers of the hollowed-out apples. 4. Pour the water into pot. 5. Close crisping lid. Select Bake and set time to 20 minutes. 6. When the cooking is complete, the apples should be bubbly and fork-tender.

Blackberry Cobbler

Prep time: 15 minutes | Cook time: 25 to 30 minutes | Serves 6

3 cups fresh or frozen blackberries
1¾ cups sugar, divided
1 teaspoon vanilla extract

8 tablespoons (1 stick) butter, melted
1 cup self-rising flour
1 to 2 tablespoons oil

1. In a medium bowl, stir together the blackberries, 1 cup of sugar, and vanilla. 2. In another medium bowl, stir together the melted butter, remaining ¾ cup of sugar, and flour until a dough forms. 3. Preheat the pressure cooker to 350ºF (177ºC). Spritz cooking pot with oil. Add the blackberry mixture. Crumble the flour mixture over the fruit. Cover the pot with aluminum foil. 4. Close crisping lid. Select Bake and set time to 20 to 25 minutes until the filling is thickened. 5. Remove the foil and cook for 5 minutes more. Let sit for 5 minutes before serving.

Pretzels

Prep time: 10 minutes | Cook time: 10 minutes | Serves 6

1½ cups shredded Mozzarella cheese
1 cup blanched finely ground almond flour
2 tablespoons salted butter, melted, divided

¼ cup granular erythritol, divided
1 teaspoon ground cinnamon

1. Place Mozzarella, flour, 1 tablespoon butter, and 2 tablespoons erythritol in a large microwave-safe bowl. Microwave on high 45 seconds, then stir with a fork until a smooth dough ball forms. 2. Separate dough into six equal sections. Gently roll each section into a 12-inch rope, then fold into a pretzel shape. 3. Preheat the pressure cooker to 370°F (188°C). Place pretzels into cooking pot. Close crisping lid. Select Bake and set time to 8 minutes, turning halfway through. 4. In a small bowl, combine remaining butter, remaining erythritol, and cinnamon. Brush ½ mixture on both sides of pretzels. 5. Place pretzels back into pot and bake an additional 2 minutes. 6. Transfer pretzels to a large plate. Brush on both sides with remaining butter mixture, then let cool 5 minutes before serving.

Chapter 11 Snacks and Appetizers

Baked Spanakopita Dip

Prep time: 10 minutes | Cook time: 15 minutes | Serves 2

Olive oil cooking spray
3 tablespoons olive oil, divided
2 tablespoons minced white onion
2 garlic cloves, minced
4 cups fresh spinach
4 ounces (113 g) cream cheese, softened
4 ounces (113 g) feta cheese,

divided
Zest of 1 lemon
¼ teaspoon ground nutmeg
1 teaspoon dried dill
½ teaspoon salt
Pita chips, carrot sticks, or sliced bread for serving (optional)

1. Preheat the pressure cooker to 360°F(182°C). Coat the inside of a 6-inch ramekin with olive oil cooking spray. 2. In a large skillet over medium heat, heat 1 tablespoon of the olive oil. Add the onion, then cook for 1 minute. 3. Add in the garlic and cook, stirring for 1 minute more. 4. Reduce the heat to low and mix in the spinach and water. Let this cook for 2 to 3 minutes, or until the spinach has wilted. Remove the skillet from the heat. 5. In a medium bowl, combine the cream cheese, 2 ounces (57 g) of the feta, and the remaining 2 tablespoons of olive oil, along with the lemon zest, nutmeg, dill, and salt. Mix until just combined. 6. Add the vegetables to the cheese base and stir until combined. 7. Pour the dip mixture into the prepared ramekin and top with the remaining 2 ounces (57 g) of feta cheese. 8. Place the dip into the cooking pot. Close crisping lid. Select Bake and set time to 10 minutes, or until heated through and bubbling. 9. Serve with pita chips, carrot sticks, or sliced bread.

Grilled Ham and Cheese on Raisin Bread

Prep time: 5 minutes | Cook time: 10 minutes | Serves 1

2 slices raisin bread
2 tablespoons butter, softened
2 teaspoons honey mustard
3 slices thinly sliced honey ham

(about 3 ounces / 85 g)
4 slices Muenster cheese (about 3 ounces / 85 g)
2 toothpicks

1. Preheat the pressure cooker to 370°F (188°C). 2. Spread the softened butter on one side of both slices of raisin bread and place the bread, buttered side down on the counter. Spread the honey mustard on the other side of each slice of bread. Layer 2 slices of cheese, the ham and the remaining 2 slices of cheese on one slice of bread and top with the other slice of bread. Remember to leave the buttered side of the bread on the outside. 3. Transfer the sandwich to the cooking pot and secure the sandwich with toothpicks. 4. Close crisping lid. Select Bake and set time to 10 minutes, flipping halfway through. Cut the sandwich in half and enjoy!

Tangy Fried Pickle Spears

Prep time: 5 minutes | Cook time: 15 minutes | Serves 6

2 jars sweet and sour pickle spears, patted dry
2 medium-sized eggs
⅓ cup milk
1 teaspoon garlic powder

1 teaspoon sea salt
½ teaspoon shallot powder
⅓ teaspoon chili powder
⅓ cup all-purpose flour
Cooking spray

1. Preheat the pressure cooker to 385°F (196°C). Spritz the cook & crisp basket with cooking spray. 2. In a bowl, beat together the eggs with milk. In another bowl, combine garlic powder, sea salt, shallot powder, chili powder and all-purpose flour until well blended. 3. One by one, roll the pickle spears in the powder mixture, then dredge them in the egg mixture. Dip them in the powder mixture a second time for additional coating. 4. Arrange the coated pickles in the prepared basket. Close crisping lid. Select Air Crisp and set time to 15 minutes until golden and crispy, shaking halfway through. 5. Transfer to a plate and let cool for 5 minutes before serving.

Shrimp Pirogues

Prep time: 15 minutes | Cook time: 4 to 5 minutes | Serves 8

12 ounces (340 g) small, peeled, and deveined raw shrimp
3 ounces (85 g) cream cheese, room temperature
2 tablespoons plain yogurt
1 teaspoon lemon juice

1 teaspoon dried dill weed, crushed
Salt, to taste
4 small hothouse cucumbers, each approximately 6 inches long

1. Preheat the pressure cooker to 390°F (199°C). 2. Place shrimp in cook & crisp basket in single layer and Close crisping lid. Select Air Crisp and set time to 4 to 5 minutes. Watch carefully because shrimp cooks quickly, and overcooking makes it tough. 3. Chop shrimp into small pieces, no larger than ½ inch. Refrigerate while mixing the remaining ingredients. 4. With a fork, mash and whip the cream cheese until smooth. 5. Stir in the yogurt and beat until smooth. Stir in lemon juice, dill weed, and chopped shrimp. 6. Taste for seasoning. If needed, add ¼ to ½ teaspoon salt to suit your taste. 7. Store in refrigerator until serving time. 8. When ready to serve, wash and dry cucumbers and split them lengthwise. Scoop out the seeds and turn cucumbers upside down on paper towels to drain for 10 minutes. 9. Just before filling, wipe centers of cucumbers dry. Spoon the shrimp mixture into the pirogues and cut in half crosswise. Serve immediately.

Crunchy Tex-Mex Tortilla Chips

Prep time: 5 minutes | Cook time: 5 minutes | Serves 4

Olive oil
½ teaspoon salt
½ teaspoon ground cumin
½ teaspoon chili powder
½ teaspoon paprika
Pinch cayenne pepper
8 (6-inch) corn tortillas, each cut into 6 wedges

1. Preheat the pressure cooker to 375°F (191°C). Spray cook & crisp basket lightly with olive oil. 2. In a small bowl, combine the salt, cumin, chili powder, paprika, and cayenne pepper. 3. Place the tortilla wedges in the cook & crisp basket in a single layer. Spray the tortillas lightly with oil and sprinkle with some of the seasoning mixture. 4. Close crisping lid. Select Air Crisp and set time to 4 to 6 minutes, shaking halfway through. Watch the chips closely so they do not burn.

Rumaki

Prep time: 30 minutes | Cook time: 10 to 12 minutes per batch | Makes about 24 rumaki

10 ounces (283 g) raw chicken livers
1 can sliced water chestnuts, drained
¼ cup low-sodium teriyaki sauce
12 slices turkey bacon

1. Cut livers into 1½-inch pieces, trimming out tough veins as you slice. 2. Place livers, water chestnuts, and teriyaki sauce in small container with lid. If needed, add another tablespoon of teriyaki sauce to make sure livers are covered. Refrigerate for 1 hour. 3. When ready to cook, cut bacon slices in half crosswise. Preheat the pressure cooker to 390°F (199°C). 4. Wrap 1 piece of liver and 1 slice of water chestnut in each bacon strip. Secure with toothpick. 5. When you have wrapped half of the livers, place them in the cooking pot in a single layer. 6. Close crisping lid. Select Roast and set time to 10 to 12 minutes. 7. While first batch cooks, wrap the remaining livers. Repeat step 6 to cook your second batch.

Cinnamon Apple Chips

Prep time: 5 minutes | Cook time: 7 to 8 hours | Serves 4

4 medium apples, any type, cored and cut into ⅓-inch-thick slices (thin slices yield crunchy
chips)
¼ teaspoon ground cinnamon
¼ teaspoon ground nutmeg

1. Place the apple slices in a large bowl. Sprinkle the cinnamon and nutmeg onto the apple slices and toss to coat. 2. Preheat the pressure cooker to 135°F (57°C). 3. Place the apple chips into cook & crisp basket. It is okay to stack them. 4. Close crisping lid. Select Dehydrate and set time to 7 or 8 hours. 5. When the cooking is complete, cool the apple chips. Serve or store at room temperature in an airtight container for up to 1 week.

Cheese Drops

Prep time: 15 minutes | Cook time: 10 minutes per batch | Serves 8

¾ cup all-purpose flour
½ teaspoon kosher salt
¼ teaspoon cayenne pepper
¼ teaspoon smoked paprika
¼ teaspoon black pepper
Dash garlic powder (optional)
¼ cup butter, softened
1 cup shredded sharp Cheddar cheese, at room temperature
Olive oil spray

1. In a small bowl, combine the flour, salt, cayenne, paprika, pepper, and garlic powder, if using. 2. Using a food processor, cream the butter and cheese until smooth. Gently add the seasoned flour and process until the dough is well combined, smooth, and no longer sticky. (Or make the dough in a stand mixer fitted with the paddle attachment: Cream the butter and cheese on medium speed until smooth, then add the seasoned flour and beat at low speed until smooth.) 3. Divide the dough into 32 equal-size pieces. On a lightly floured surface, roll each piece into a small ball. 4. Preheat the pressure cooker to 325°F (163°C). Spray thecooking pot with oil spray. Arrange 16 cheese drops in the pot. Close crisping lid. Select Bake and set time to 10 minutes, or until drops are just starting to brown. Transfer to a wire rack. Repeat with remaining dough, checking for doneness at 8 minutes. 5. Cool the cheese drops completely on the wire rack.

Classic Spring Rolls

Prep time: 10 minutes | Cook time: 9 minutes | Makes 16 spring rolls

4 teaspoons toasted sesame oil
6 medium garlic cloves, minced or pressed
1 tablespoon grated peeled fresh ginger
2 cups thinly sliced shiitake mushrooms
4 cups chopped green cabbage
1 cup grated carrot
½ teaspoon sea salt
16 rice paper wrappers
Cooking oil spray (sunflower, safflower, or refined coconut)
Gluten-free sweet and sour sauce or Thai sweet chili sauce, for serving (optional)

1. Place a wok or sauté pan over medium heat until hot. 2. Add the sesame oil, garlic, ginger, mushrooms, cabbage, carrot, and salt. Cook for 3 to 4 minutes, stirring often, until the cabbage is lightly wilted. Remove the pan from the heat. 3. Gently run a rice paper under water. Lay it on a flat nonabsorbent surface. Place about ¼ cup of the cabbage filling in the middle. Once the wrapper is soft enough to roll, fold the bottom up over the filling, fold in the sides, and roll the wrapper all the way up. (Basically, make a tiny burrito.) 4. Repeat step 3 to make the remaining spring rolls until you have the number of spring rolls you want to cook right now. Refrigerate any leftover filling in an airtight container for about 1 week. 5. Preheat the pressure cooker to 390°F (199°C). 6. Spray the cook & crisp basket with cooking oil. Place the spring rolls into the basket, leaving a little room between them so they don't stick to each other. Spray the top of each spring roll with cooking oil. 7. Close crisping lid. Select Air Crisp and set time to 9 minutes. 8. When the cooking is complete, the egg rolls should be crisp-ish and lightly browned. Serve immediately, plain or with a sauce of choice.

Greek Yogurt Deviled Eggs

Prep time: 15 minutes | Cook time: 15 minutes | Serves 4

4 eggs
¼ cup nonfat plain Greek yogurt
1 teaspoon chopped fresh dill
⅛ teaspoon salt
⅛ teaspoon paprika
⅛ teaspoon garlic powder
Chopped fresh parsley, for garnish

1. Preheat the pressure cooker to 260°F(127°C). 2. Place the eggs in a single layer in the cooking pot. Close crisping lid. Select Bake and set time to 15 minutes. 3. Quickly remove the eggs from the pot and place them into a cold water bath. Let the eggs cool in the water for 10 minutes before removing and peeling them. 4. After peeling the eggs, cut them in half. 5. Spoon the yolk into a small bowl. Add the yogurt, dill, salt, paprika, and garlic powder and mix until smooth. 6. Spoon or pipe the yolk mixture into the halved egg whites. Serve with a sprinkle of fresh parsley on top.

Lemon-Pepper Chicken Drumsticks

Prep time: 30 minutes | Cook time: 30 minutes | Serves 2

2 teaspoons freshly ground coarse black pepper
1 teaspoon baking powder
½ teaspoon garlic powder
4 chicken drumsticks (4 ounces / 113 g each)
Kosher salt, to taste
1 lemon

1. In a small bowl, stir together the pepper, baking powder, and garlic powder. Place the drumsticks on a plate and sprinkle evenly with the baking powder mixture, turning the drumsticks so they're well coated. Let the drumsticks stand in the refrigerator for at least 1 hour or up to overnight. 2. Preheat the pressure cooker to 375°F (191°C). Sprinkle the drumsticks with salt, then transfer them to the cooking pot, standing them bone-end up and leaning against the wall of the pot. Close crisping lid. Select Roast and set time to 30 minutes. 3. Transfer the drumsticks to a serving platter and finely grate the zest of the lemon over them while they're hot. Cut the lemon into wedges and serve with the warm drumsticks.

Crispy Cauliflower in Buffalo Sauce

Prep time: 5 minutes | Cook time: 14 to 16 minutes | Serves 4

3 tablespoons butter, melted
3 tablespoons buffalo hot sauce
1 egg white
1 cup panko bread crumbs
Salt and black pepper to taste
½ head cauliflower, cut into florets
Cooking spray

1. Preheat the pressure cooker to .340°F (171°C) 2. In a bowl, whisk butter, buffalo sauce, and egg white. In a separate bowl, mix bread crumbs with salt and black pepper. Toss the florets in the buffalo mixture and roll them in the bread crumbs to coat. Spritz with cooking spray and transfer to cook & crisp basket. 3. Close crisping lid. Select Air Crisp and set time to 14 to 16 minutes, shaking twice. Serve hot.

Roasted Mushrooms with Garlic

Prep time: 3 minutes | Cook time: 22 to 27 minutes | Serves 4

16 garlic cloves, peeled
2 teaspoons olive oil, divided
16 button mushrooms
½ teaspoon dried marjoram
⅛ teaspoon freshly ground black pepper
1 tablespoon white wine or low-sodium vegetable broth

1. Preheat the pressure cooker to 350°F (177°C). In cooking pot, mix the garlic with 1 teaspoon of olive oil. Close crisping lid. Select Roast and set time to 12 minutes. 2. Add the mushrooms, marjoram, and pepper. Stir to coat. Drizzle with the remaining 1 teaspoon of olive oil and the white wine. 3. Roast for 10 to 15 minutes more, or until the mushrooms and garlic cloves are tender. Serve.

Spicy Tortilla Chips

Prep time: 5 minutes | Cook time: 8 to 12 minutes | Serves 4

½ teaspoon ground cumin
½ teaspoon paprika
½ teaspoon chili powder
½ teaspoon salt
Pinch cayenne pepper
8 (6-inch) corn tortillas, each cut into 6 wedges
Cooking spray

1. Preheat the pressure cooker to 375°F (191°C). Lightly spritz the cook & crisp basket with cooking spray. 2. Stir together the cumin, paprika, chili powder, salt, and pepper in a small bowl. 3. Working in batches, arrange the tortilla wedges in the basket in a single layer. Lightly mist them with cooking spray. Sprinkle some seasoning mixture on top of the tortilla wedges. 4. Close crisping lid. Select Air Crisp and set time to 4 to 6 minutes, shaking halfway through. 5. Repeat with the remaining tortilla wedges and seasoning mixture. 6. Let the tortilla chips cool for 5 minutes and serve.

Root Veggie Chips with Herb Salt

Prep time: 10 minutes | Cook time: 8 minutes | Serves 2

1 parsnip, washed
1 small beet, washed
1 small turnip, washed
½ small sweet potato, washed
1 teaspoon olive oil
Cooking spray
Herb Salt:
¼ teaspoon kosher salt
2 teaspoons finely chopped fresh parsley

1. Preheat the pressure cooker to 360°F (182°C). 2. Peel and thinly slice the parsnip, beet, turnip, and sweet potato, then place the vegetables in a large bowl, add the olive oil, and toss. 3. Spray the cook & crisp basket with cooking spray, then place the vegetables in the basket. Close crisping lid. Select Air Crisp and set time to 8 minutes, shaking halfway through. 4. While the chips cook, make the herb salt in a small bowl by combining the kosher salt and parsley. 5. Remove the chips and place on a serving plate, then sprinkle the herb salt on top and allow to cool for 2 to 3 minutes before serving.

Eggplant Fries

Prep time: 10 minutes | Cook time: 7 to 8 minutes | Serves 4

1 medium eggplant
1 teaspoon ground coriander
1 teaspoon cumin
1 teaspoon garlic powder
½ teaspoon salt

1 cup crushed panko bread crumbs
1 large egg
2 tablespoons water
Oil for misting or cooking spray

1. Peel and cut the eggplant into fat fries, ⅜- to ½-inch thick. 2. Preheat the pressure cooker to 390°F (199°C). 3. In a small cup, mix together the coriander, cumin, garlic, and salt. 4. Combine 1 teaspoon of the seasoning mix and panko crumbs in a shallow dish. 5. Place eggplant fries in a large bowl, sprinkle with remaining seasoning, and stir well to combine. 6. Beat eggs and water together and pour over eggplant fries. Stir to coat. 7. Remove eggplant from egg wash, shaking off excess, and roll in panko crumbs. 8. Spray with oil. 9. Place half of the fries in cook & crisp basket. You should have only a single layer, but it's fine if they overlap a little. 10. Close crisping lid. Select Air Crisp and set time to 5 minutes. Shake basket, mist lightly with oil, and cook 2 to 3 minutes longer, until browned and crispy.

Mushroom Tarts

Prep time: 15 minutes | Cook time: 38 minutes | Makes 15 tarts

2 tablespoons extra-virgin olive oil, divided
1 small white onion, sliced
8 ounces (227 g) shiitake mushrooms, sliced
¼ teaspoon sea salt
¼ teaspoon freshly ground black pepper

¼ cup dry white wine
1 sheet frozen puff pastry, thawed
1 cup shredded Gruyère cheese
Cooking oil spray
1 tablespoon thinly sliced fresh chives

1. Preheat the pressure cooker to 300°F (149°C). 2. In a heatproof bowl that fits into the basket, stir together 1 tablespoon of olive oil, the onion, and the mushrooms. 3. Place the bowl into the cooking pot. 4. Close crisping lid. Select Bake and set time to 7 minutes. 5. After about 2½ minutes, stir the vegetables. Resume cooking. After another 2½ minutes, the vegetables should be browned and tender. Season with the salt and pepper and add the wine. Resume cooking until the liquid evaporates, about 2 minutes. 6. When the cooking is complete, place the bowl on a heatproof surface. 7. Unfold the puff pastry and cut it into 15 (3-by-3-inch) squares. Using a fork, pierce the dough and brush both sides with the remaining 1 tablespoon of olive oil. 8. Evenly distribute half the cheese among the puff pastry squares, leaving a ½-inch border around the edges. Divide the mushroom-onion mixture among the pastry squares and top with the remaining cheese. 9. Spray the cooking pot with cooking oil. Working in batches, place 5 tarts into the pot; do not stack or overlap. 10. Bake at 390°F (199°C) for 8 minutes. 11. After 6 minutes, check the tarts; if not yet golden brown, resume cooking for about 2 minutes more. 12. When the cooking is complete, remove the tarts and transfer to a wire rack to cool. Repeat with the remaining tarts. 13. Serve garnished with the chives.

Garlic-Parmesan Croutons

Prep time: 3 minutes | Cook time: 12 minutes | Serves 4

Oil, for spraying
4 cups cubed French bread
1 tablespoon grated Parmesan cheese

3 tablespoons olive oil
1 tablespoon granulated garlic
½ teaspoon unsalted salt

1. Line cook & crisp basket with parchment and spray lightly with oil. 2. In a large bowl, mix together the bread, Parmesan cheese, olive oil, garlic, and salt, tossing with your hands to evenly distribute the seasonings. Transfer the coated bread cubes to the prepared basket. 3. Close crisping lid. Select Air Crisp and set time to 350°F (177°C) for 10 to 12 minutes, stirring once after 5 minutes, or until crisp and golden brown.

Jalapeño Poppers

Prep time: 10 minutes | Cook time: 20 minutes | Serves 4

Oil, for spraying
8 ounces (227 g) cream cheese
¾ cup gluten-free bread crumbs, divided
2 tablespoons chopped fresh

parsley
½ teaspoon granulated garlic
½ teaspoon salt
10 jalapeño peppers, halved and seeded

1. Preheat the pressure cooker to 370°F (188°C). Spray cooking pot lightly with oil. 2. In a medium bowl, mix together the cream cheese, half of the bread crumbs, the parsley, garlic, and salt. 3. Spoon the mixture into the jalapeño halves. Gently press the stuffed jalapeños in the remaining bread crumbs. 4. Place the stuffed jalapeños in the cooking pot. 5. Close crisping lid. Select Roast and set time to 20 minutes, or until the cheese is melted and the bread crumbs are crisp and golden brown.

Dark Chocolate and Cranberry Granola Bars

Prep time: 5 minutes | Cook time: 15 minutes | Serves 6

2 cups certified gluten-free quick oats
2 tablespoons sugar-free dark chocolate chunks
2 tablespoons unsweetened dried cranberries

3 tablespoons unsweetened shredded coconut
½ cup raw honey
1 teaspoon ground cinnamon
⅛ teaspoon salt
2 tablespoons olive oil

1. Preheat the pressure cooker to 360°F(182°C). Line cooking pot with parchment paper that comes up the side so you can lift it out after cooking. 2. In a large bowl, mix together all of the ingredients until well combined. 3. Press the oat mixture into the pan in an even layer. 4. Close crisping lid. Select Bake and set time to 15 minutes. 5. Lift the granola cake out of the pot using the edges of the parchment paper. 6. Allow to cool for 5 minutes before slicing into 6 equal bars. 7. Serve immediately, or wrap in plastic wrap and store at room temperature for up to 1 week.

Skinny Fries

Prep time: 10 minutes | Cook time: 15 minutes per batch | Serves 2

2 to 3 russet potatoes, peeled and cut into ¼-inch sticks
2 to 3 teaspoons olive or

vegetable oil
Salt, to taste

1. Cut the potatoes into ¼-inch strips. Rinse the potatoes with cold water several times and let them soak in cold water for at least 10 minutes or as long as overnight. 2. Preheat the pressure cooker to 380°F (193°C). 3. Drain and dry the potato sticks really well, using a clean kitchen towel. Toss the fries with the oil in a bowl and then transfer to the cook & crisp basket. Close crisping lid. Select Air Crisp and set time to 15 minutes, shaking a couple of times. 4. As soon as the fries are done, season them with salt and transfer to a plate or basket. Serve them warm with ketchup or your favorite dip.

Spiralized Potato Nest with Tomato Ketchup

Prep time: 10 minutes | Cook time: 15 minutes | Serves 2

1 large russet potato (about 12 ounces / 340 g)
2 tablespoons vegetable oil
1 tablespoon hot smoked paprika
½ teaspoon garlic powder
Kosher salt and freshly ground black pepper, to taste

½ cup canned crushed tomatoes
2 tablespoons apple cider vinegar
1 tablespoon dark brown sugar
1 tablespoon Worcestershire sauce
1 teaspoon mild hot sauce

1. Preheat the pressure cooker to 400°F (204°C). Using a spiralizer, spiralize the potato, then place in a large colander. Rinse the potatoes under cold running water until the water runs clear. Spread the potatoes out on a double-thick layer of paper towels and pat completely dry. 2. In a large bowl, combine the potatoes, oil, paprika, and garlic powder. Season with salt and pepper and toss to combine. Transfer the potatoes to the cooking pot and Close crisping lid. Select Air Roast and set time to 15 minutes, shaking halfway through. 3. Meanwhile, in a small blender, purée the tomatoes, vinegar, brown sugar, Worcestershire, and hot sauce until smooth. Pour into a small saucepan or skillet and simmer over medium heat until reduced by half, 3 to 5 minutes. Pour the homemade ketchup into a bowl and let cool. 4. Remove the spiralized potato nest from the pot and serve hot with the ketchup.

Turkey Burger Sliders

Prep time: 10 minutes | Cook time: 5 to 7 minutes | Makes 8 sliders

1 pound (454 g) ground turkey
¼ teaspoon curry powder
1 teaspoon Hoisin sauce
½ teaspoon salt
8 slider buns

½ cup slivered red onions
½ cup slivered green or red bell pepper
½ cup fresh chopped pineapple
Light cream cheese, softened

1. Preheat the pressure cooker to 360°F (182°C). Combine turkey,

curry powder, Hoisin sauce, and salt and mix together well. 2. Shape turkey mixture into 8 small patties. 3. Place patties in cooking pot and Close crisping lid. Select Bake and set time to 5 to 7 minutes, until patties are well done and juices run clear. 4. Place each patty on the bottom half of a slider bun and top with onions, peppers, and pineapple. Spread the remaining bun halves with cream cheese to taste, place on top, and serve.

Lebanese Muhammara

Prep time: 15 minutes | Cook time: 15 minutes | Serves 6

2 large red bell peppers
¼ cup plus 2 tablespoons extra-virgin olive oil
1 cup walnut halves
1 tablespoon agave nectar or honey
1 teaspoon fresh lemon juice

1 teaspoon ground cumin
1 teaspoon kosher salt
1 teaspoon red pepper flakes
Raw vegetables (such as cucumber, carrots, zucchini slices, or cauliflower) or toasted pita chips, for serving

1. Preheat the pressure cooker to 400°F (204°C). Drizzle the peppers with 2 tablespoons of the olive oil and place in cooking pot. Close crisping lid. Select Roast and set time to 10 minutes. 2. Add the walnuts to the pot, arranging them around the peppers. Roast for 5 minutes. 3. Remove the peppers, seal in a resealable plastic bag, and let rest for 5 to 10 minutes. Transfer the walnuts to a plate and set aside to cool. 4. Place the softened peppers, walnuts, agave, lemon juice, cumin, salt, and ½ teaspoon of the pepper flakes in a food processor and purée until smooth. 5. Transfer the dip to a serving bowl and make an indentation in the middle. Pour the remaining ¼ cup olive oil into the indentation. Garnish the dip with the remaining ½ teaspoon pepper flakes. 6. Serve with vegetables or toasted pita chips.

Egg Roll Pizza Sticks

Prep time: 10 minutes | Cook time: 5 minutes | Serves 4

Olive oil
8 pieces reduced-fat string cheese
8 egg roll wrappers

24 slices turkey pepperoni
Marinara sauce, for dipping (optional)

1. Preheat the pressure cooker to 375°F (191°C). Spray the cook & crisp basket lightly with olive oil. Fill a small bowl with water. 2. Place each egg roll wrapper diagonally on a work surface. It should look like a diamond. 3. Place 3 slices of turkey pepperoni in a vertical line down the center of the wrapper. 4. Place 1 Mozzarella cheese stick on top of the turkey pepperoni. 5. Fold the top and bottom corners of the egg roll wrapper over the cheese stick. 6. Fold the left corner over the cheese stick and roll the cheese stick up to resemble a spring roll. Dip a finger in the water and seal the edge of the roll 7. Repeat with the rest of the pizza sticks. 8. Place them in the basket in a single layer, making sure to leave a little space between each one. Lightly spray the pizza sticks with oil. 9. Close crisping lid. Select Air Crisp and set time to 5 minutes. 10. These are best served hot while the cheese is melted. Accompany with a small bowl of marinara sauce, if desired.

String Bean Fries

Prep time: 15 minutes | Cook time: 5 to 6 minutes | Serves 4

½ pound (227 g) fresh string beans
2 eggs
4 teaspoons water
½ cup white flour
½ cup bread crumbs
¼ teaspoon salt
¼ teaspoon ground black pepper
¼ teaspoon dry mustard (optional)
Oil for misting or cooking spray

1. Preheat the pressure cooker to 360ºF (182ºC). 2. Trim stem ends from string beans, wash, and pat dry. 3. In a shallow dish, beat eggs and water together until well blended. 4. Place flour in a second shallow dish. 5. In a third shallow dish, stir together the bread crumbs, salt, pepper, and dry mustard if using. 6. Dip each string bean in egg mixture, flour, egg mixture again, then bread crumbs. 7. When you finish coating all the string beans, place them in cook & crisp basket. 8. Close crisping lid. Select Air Crisp and set time to 5 to 6 minutes, misting with oil or cooking spray halfway through.

Kale Chips with Tex-Mex Dip

Prep time: 10 minutes | Cook time: 5 to 6 minutes | Serves 8

1 cup Greek yogurt
1 tablespoon chili powder
⅓ cup low-sodium salsa, well drained
1 bunch curly kale
1 teaspoon olive oil
¼ teaspoon coarse sea salt

1. Preheat the pressure cooker to 390ºF (199ºC). In a small bowl, combine the yogurt, chili powder, and drained salsa; refrigerate. 2. Rinse the kale thoroughly, and pat dry. Remove the stems and ribs from the kale, using a sharp knife. Cut or tear the leaves into 3-inch pieces. 3. Toss the kale with the olive oil in a large bowl. Arrange kale in the cook & crisp basket. 4. Close crisping lid. Select Air Crisp and set time to 5 to 6 minutes, shaking once. 5. As you remove the kale chips, sprinkle them with a bit of the sea salt. 6. When all of the kale chips are done, serve with the dip.

Polenta Fries with Chili-Lime Mayo

Prep time: 10 minutes | Cook time: 28 minutes | Serves 4

Polenta Fries:
2 teaspoons vegetable or olive oil
¼ teaspoon paprika
1 pound (454 g) prepared polenta, cut into 3-inch × ½-inch strips
Chili-Lime Mayo:
½ cup mayonnaise
1 teaspoon chili powder
1 teaspoon chopped fresh cilantro
¼ teaspoon ground cumin
Juice of ½ lime
Salt and freshly ground black pepper, to taste

1. Preheat the pressure cooker to 400ºF (204ºC). 2. Mix the oil and paprika in a bowl. Add the polenta strips and toss until evenly coated. 3. Transfer the polenta strips to the cook & crisp basket. Close crisping lid. Select Air Crisp and set time to 28 minutes until the fries are golden brown, shaking once during cooking. Season as desired with salt and pepper. 4. Meanwhile, whisk together all the ingredients for the chili-lime mayo in a small bowl. 5. Transfer the polenta fries to a plate and serve alongside the chili-lime mayo as a dipping sauce.

Taco-Spiced Chickpeas

Prep time: 5 minutes | Cook time: 17 minutes | Serves 3

Oil, for spraying
1 (15½-ounce / 439-g) can chickpeas, drained
1 teaspoon chili powder
½ teaspoon ground cumin
½ teaspoon salt
½ teaspoon granulated garlic
2 teaspoons lime juice

1. Preheat the pressure cooker to 390ºF (199ºC). Spray cooking pot lightly with oil. Place the chickpeas in the cooking pot. 2. Close crisping lid. Select Roast and set time to 17 minutes, shaking and spraying lightly with oil every 5 to 7 minutes. 3. In a small bowl, mix together the chili powder, cumin, salt, and garlic. 4. When 2 to 3 minutes of cooking time remain, sprinkle half of the seasoning mix over the chickpeas. 5. Transfer the chickpeas to a medium bowl and toss with the remaining seasoning mix and the lime juice. Serve immediately.

Zucchini Feta Roulades

Prep time: 10 minutes | Cook time: 10 minutes | Serves 6

½ cup feta
1 garlic clove, minced
2 tablespoons fresh basil, minced
1 tablespoon capers, minced
⅛ teaspoon salt
⅛ teaspoon red pepper flakes
1 tablespoon lemon juice
2 medium zucchini
12 toothpicks

1. Preheat the pressure cooker to 360ºF (182ºC). 2. In a small bowl, combine the feta, garlic, basil, capers, salt, red pepper flakes, and lemon juice. 3. Slice the zucchini into ⅛-inch strips lengthwise. (Each zucchini should yield around 6 strips.) 4. Spread 1 tablespoon of the cheese filling onto each slice of zucchini, then roll it up and secure it with a toothpick through the middle. 5. Place the zucchini roulades into the cooking pot in a single layer, making sure that they don't touch each other. 6. Close crisping lid. Select Bake and set time to 10 minutes. 7. Gently remove the toothpicks before serving.

Appendix 1 Measurement Conversion Chart

MEASUREMENT CONVERSION CHART

VOLUME EQUIVALENTS(DRY)

US STANDARD	METRIC (APPROXIMATE)
1/8 teaspoon	0.5 mL
1/4 teaspoon	1 mL
1/2 teaspoon	2 mL
3/4 teaspoon	4 mL
1 teaspoon	5 mL
1 tablespoon	15 mL
1/4 cup	59 mL
1/2 cup	118 mL
3/4 cup	177 mL
1 cup	235 mL
2 cups	475 mL
3 cups	700 mL
4 cups	1 L

VOLUME EQUIVALENTS(LIQUID)

US STANDARD	US STANDARD (OUNCES)	METRIC (APPROXIMATE)
2 tablespoons	1 fl.oz.	30 mL
1/4 cup	2 fl.oz.	60 mL
1/2 cup	4 fl.oz.	120 mL
1 cup	8 fl.oz.	240 mL
1 1/2 cup	12 fl.oz.	355 mL
2 cups or 1 pint	16 fl.oz.	475 mL
4 cups or 1 quart	32 fl.oz.	1 L
1 gallon	128 fl.oz.	4 L

TEMPERATURES EQUIVALENTS

FAHRENHEIT(F)	CELSIUS(C) (APPROXIMATE)
225 °F	107 °C
250 °F	120 °C
275 °F	135 °C
300 °F	150 °C
325 °F	160 °C
350 °F	180 °C
375 °F	190 °C
400 °F	205 °C
425 °F	220 °C
450 °F	235 °C
475 °F	245 °C
500 °F	260 °C

WEIGHT EQUIVALENTS

US STANDARD	METRIC (APPROXIMATE)
1 ounce	28 g
2 ounces	57 g
5 ounces	142 g
10 ounces	284 g
15 ounces	425 g
16 ounces (1 pound)	455 g
1.5 pounds	680 g
2 pounds	907 g

Printed in Great Britain
by Amazon